YOU STARTED IT

YOU STARTED IT

Rock 'n' Roll's Most Notorious and Bitter Feuds

Ken McNab

Backbeat
Books

Essex, Connecticut

Backbeat Books

An imprint of Globe Pequot, the trade division of
The Rowman & Littlefield Publishing Group, Inc.
4501 Forbes Blvd., Ste. 200
Lanham, MD 20706
www.rowman.com

Distributed by NATIONAL BOOK NETWORK

British Library Cataloguing in Publication Information Available

Library of Congress Cataloging-in-Publication Data

Names: McNab, Ken, author.
Title: You started it : rock 'n' roll's most notorious and bitter feuds /
   Ken McNab.
Description: Lanham : Backbeat, 2022. | Summary: "Ken McNab provides fresh
   takes on the human stories behind the in-fighting that saw a stairway to
   heaven become a highway to hell for the biggest bands of this or any
   other time."— Provided by publisher.
Identifiers: LCCN 2022013959 (print) | LCCN 2022013960 (ebook) | ISBN
   9781493067800 (paperback) | ISBN 9781493067831 (epub)
Subjects: LCSH: Rock musicians. | Interpersonal conflict—Case studies. |
   Vendetta—Case studies.
Classification: LCC ML3534 .M4708 2022 (print) | LCC ML3534 (ebook) | DDC
   782.42166092/2—dc23/eng/20220412
LC record available at https://lccn.loc.gov/2022013959
LC ebook record available at https://lccn.loc.gov/2022013960

♾️™ The paper used in this publication meets the minimum requirements of
American National Standard for Information Sciences—Permanence of Paper
for Printed Library Materials, ANSI/NISO Z39.48-1992.

CONTENTS

ACKNOWLEDGMENTS

This book is dedicated to Norah "Bebe" McDonald (She started it).

I would like to pass on my gratitude to all those who, unlike myself, actually have a life but who have all helped me to complete this book. My biggest thanks and all my love go to my beautiful wife Susanna and my children Jennifer and Christopher, who are used to seeing their old man chipping away at the rock face of truth. And sincere shout-outs to all the extended family that include Caroline and Alan Cullen, Linda and Kieran Sharkey, Jacqueline and Ronnie Brown, Terrance and Anne-Marie Porter, Drew and Maureen Porter, and Ian and Margaret McNab. Thanks also to my three lifelong compadres—Stephen Jack, Martin McCartney, and Graham McCurrach, who continue to be baffled by my harmless obsession for all things Beatles, Tolkien, and Star Trek. And finally . . . give it up for the bands. They really started it.

INTRODUCTION

The music business is a cruel and shallow money trench, a long plastic hallway where thieves and pimps run free, and good men die like dogs. There's also a negative side. —Hunter S. Thompson

Paul Simon felt simmering resentment toward Art Garfunkel in his heart and in his bones. Paul McCartney was forced to read the runes when John Lennon split the Beatles at an otherwise routine business meeting. Stevie Nicks's animus toward Lindsey Buckingham sparked all sorts of rumors. Jagger and Richards went off-script in a Stones video and almost traded real punches. Dave Gilmour weaponized a pair of pig's testicles in his forty-year war with Pink Floyd bandmate Roger Waters. And the Everlys swapped their celestial singing for diatribes and discord.

It's an ineluctable truth: rock and roll wouldn't be so fascinating were it not for the appetite for dysfunction it has brought out in so many great bands. Musical feuds are like car crashes—they're a grim business and you hope that no one gets hurt, but it's hard to look away from the wreckage.

Instead of kissing and making up, many bands take the easy escape, with middle fingers raised in the air and knives plunged into backs. Angry silences sour the once joyous and creative atmosphere; musicians who seemed to be closer than brothers can no longer bear to be in the same room with each other and communicate via terse letters drawn up by expensive lawyers.

They may have been able to make beautiful music while together on the stage, but what began as a stairway to heaven quickly turns into a highway to hell when the slow-burning fuse finally detonates internecine strife.

Of course, that's not how it all starts out. Initially, they are the closest of friends, roped together for the climb. Some, like the Everlys, of course, and the Kinks, are helix-linked by brotherly DNA. Others, such as the Supremes, were childhood friends, bound by the kind of tribal closeness that can only emerge from adolescent hardship. And then we have those whose meeting is, like for example the Eagles, simply an amalgam of fate and circumstance.

Few of those who carry the male gene go through their lives without dreaming the dream about becoming leonine, testosterone-fueled rock gods, imperiously strutting the stage and holding an audience of thousands—even millions—in the palms of our hands. It's a rite of passage.

And for the gentler sex, the sight of Nicks floating around the stage twirling a diaphanous scarf, or Debbie Harry staring seductively into the camera, was mostly aspiration wrapped inside a fantasy.

Since the big bang of rock 'n' roll in the fifties, pop stars have become the Biblical apostles of our age. Theirs was a new religion, one that embraced acolytes and neophytes. Some of them—Presley, with his libidinous hip shaking, and the Beatles—attracted an almost messianic following. And still do.

By the sixties, a handful of them, like the screaming rockets of novelist Thomas Pynchon's "Gravity's Rainbow," had reached *brennschluss*—the point of altitude at which the thrust fails, leaving behind nothing but dying momentum.

But the vapor trails they left behind remained all-too-visible on music's cloudless skies for the generations that followed, mesmerized. As Bruce Springsteen put it, "Until I realised that rock music was my connection to the rest of the human race, I felt like I was dying, for some reason, and I didn't know why."

Arguably, the sixties was the decade that gave free artistic reign to musical expression: ten years that spawned some of the world's greatest groups and trickled down unstoppably into the seventies, eighties, nineties, and even the new millennium. From the outside, being in a band just looked like a turbo-charged ride: an entrée into a heady world of rebellious liberation, one that circumscribed glamour, danger, and—let's not forget the ultimate elixir of rock 'n' roll—unlimited sex.

Down through the ages, we all had our heroes—Zeppelin, Floyd, the New York Dolls, David Bowie, Creedence, Nirvana, U2, the Clash, REM,

Queen, the Grateful Dead, CSNY, and Fleetwood Mac. This is not to dilute the sugary allure of pop's sweeter confections—Abba, New Kids on the Block, the Four Seasons, the Carpenters, the Bee Gees—hell, I'll even throw in the Bay City Rollers.

Being a rock star really is the symbol of ultimate cool. But all things do pass. Especially when age takes hold and the initial bloom of stardom fades. Those early dreams that provided the accelerant for musicians to reach for the stars often came crashing back to earth when the sweet turned to sour. Rarely was there a common denominator at the core.

Generally, bands break up for a myriad of reasons. The songs dry up. The hits wither on the vine. The band is fleeced by greedy managers. The front man suffers from lead-vocal syndrome and starts to believe his or her own legend. Touring burnout sears the band to a crisp. The drugs fry their brains. And then there's that age-old excuse: musical differences.

Underlying issues swiftly bubble up. The swaggering upswing of success is often swallowed up by the hubristic downside of fame. Eventually, you reach that nexus where the finger-pointing starts and the band splinters—and that is when you go from showtime to showdown.

Band splits are often financially messy. When it dawns on the singer that his beach house in the French Riviera isn't as grand as that of the lead guitarist, the accountant can expect a call.

When the band sees the accountant driving a Ferrari while they're tooling about town in a Hyundai, take cover. And there's no point in arguing that your guitar riff is the reason why certain songs are now anthems and automatically merits a 20 percent songwriting royalty check.

Very few groups go down without fighting. Lennon and McCartney famously took their beef public through the poison-tipped lyrics of their own songs. In case anyone missed the point, the rear cover of McCartney's first solo album included a picture of two beetles copulating.

Stevie Nicks drove a stiletto into the heart of Buckingham, her former lover, in her classic song "Dreams." (The line "Players only love you when they're playing," was directed at him.) Buckingham fired back on the same album with "Go Your Own Way," the title itself a self-explanatory essay on character assassination.

When Keith Richards sang a song called "You Don't Move Me" on his first solo album, no one was in any doubt about who his target was. More recently, Taylor Swift has made a career out of getting even with former lovers and rivals through her scabrous lyrics.

As fans, though, it's hard for us to sit on the sidelines and watch our heroes descend into the kind of mudslinging that sometimes forces us to take sides.

Of course, the flipside of the coin is this: in many cases that tension was always there. That music that formed the soundtracks to our lives was often powered by the force majeure of internal strife that was critical in shaping the creative process.

Yet, as music lovers, we can't help but be strangely captivated by the internecine warfare that is part of their shared ubiquity—along with the timeless music those heroes of all our adolescences left behind.

Who started it? The truth is often buried beneath the sediment of time and history. For me, though, the excavation process entailed in the pages that follow yielded stories of guilt, recrimination, sadness, forgiveness, bitterness, embarrassment, and a steadfast refusal to admit that, perhaps, you were wrong. For some, any hoped-for reconciliation comes too late: death overtakes détente, as in the cases of Lennon and McCartney, Diana Ross and Florence Ballard, and Tupac and Biggie Smalls. For others, though, the smell of filthy lucre is perhaps the most powerful stimulant of them all—we're looking at you, Axl and Slash. Money doesn't talk, it swears when millions of dollars are on the table, and you're happy to overlook youthful disagreements and decide to become a heritage act in the pursuit of a rock star pension.

I've enjoyed sifting through the debris of these relationships to bring new stories to life by talking to those friends and allies who witnessed the mushroom-shaped fallouts among the greatest artistes of our time.

Set aside all you've read about sex, drugs, and rock 'n' roll. When it comes to vendettas, grievances, and sheer human drama, nobody does the dance better than music's biggest legends.

And if all else fails, remember this enduring maxim: Blame Yoko.

The Beach Boys: From left, Carl Wilson, Dennis Wilson, Mike Love, Al Jardine, and Brian Wilson
Capitol Records/Photofest © Capitol Records

1

THE BEACH BOYS

A Melbourne hotel provided an appropriate setting for a kangaroo court. Staring defiantly from the makeshift dock was Beach Boy Carl Wilson, accused of scoring heroin from a tour flunky for his mentally fragile and drug-addicted brother Brian. Sitting alongside him was his other older brother Dennis, himself no stranger to narcotic excess.

Meantime, pressing the case for the prosecution while acting as judge, jury, and executioner were three men: Mike Love, the group's lead singer and cousin to the Wilson brothers, his own brother Stan Love and Rocky Pamplin, two men whose primary job was to be Brian's minders, a role that primarily involved ring-fencing him from every conceivable opiate temptation during the band's 1978 tour of Australia.

An interested third party was David Frost, the urbane British TV broadcaster best known for his forensic post-Watergate interviews with Richard Nixon, whose promotion of the tour was in serious danger of unspooling that very moment amid fears of multimillion lawsuits.

Earlier that day, and hours from a nighttime show, Brian had slipped the shackles of his two gatekeepers. They later found him retching violently in his room, the repercussions of him being unable to handle the smack churning through his body. Amazingly, Brian still made it onstage that night at the Myer Music Bowl. But press accounts noted all three Wilson brothers were clearly stoned and barely functioning. The *Melbourne Herald* reported Brian, Carl, and Dennis disappeared so often "it was like Exodus gone wrong."

Now, hours later, they had arrived at the formal inquest, a Beach Boys' post-mortem into the night the group, famed for their surfing songs, struck a critical reef. Pamplin and Stan Love had carried out their own investigations and concluded that Carl had indeed acquired and fed the drugs to Brian, an accusation he emphatically denied. The highly charged atmosphere quickly turned venomous until Carl could bite back on his temper no more.

"Fuck you," he shouted at Pamplin, a former college football player who was built like a linebacker. In an instant, Pamplin, tall, lean, and muscular, had delivered a brutal uppercut that laid out the youngest Beach Boy flat on the deck. "He doesn't tell me to get fucked," said Pamplin.

Summary justice had been dispensed. Stunned though they undoubtedly were, neither Brian nor Dennis, himself an extremely volatile individual, raised a word in protest. It was unquestionably a shocking new low in the life of a band that once epitomized the American Dream, resonating the very best in apple pie wholesomeness. But it would not be the last time that Stan Love and his heavy-handed accomplice would dole out arbitrary, vigilante-style sanctions to a Wilson brother/cousin.

It was also the moment the truth finally dawned on Mike Love over the untold depths that had now been plumbed. Mortified by what he saw, he recalled in his autobiography, *Good Vibrations, My Life as a Beach Boy,*

> I don't know what motivated Carl, and to a degree Dennis, to give heroin to Brian. They both idolized him. Maybe they thought he would enjoy it or maybe their judgment was clouded by their own drug use.
>
> Stan believed that Carl, frustrated by Brian's endless struggles, wanted him off the stage and even out of the band and figured the heroin would do it. Whatever their motives, the spectacle for me was a reminder of how vulnerable Brian was in trusting those around him, even his own brothers, to his detriment . . . that was not a great thing for the Beach Boys to be involved with. I think our music and our way of life and what we always promoted was positivity and harmony and stuff. It didn't fit.

The story of the Beach Boys is a tale of two Californian families ultimately mired in a black hole of dynastic envy, violent parental abuse, drug degradation, explosive egos, court cases, and inter-band sexual liaisons bordering on incest. Occasionally lost in this swirling nexus was the unforgettable magic of the spellbinding music they created, of the days they surfed the new wave of JFK's sun-dappled presidency, and for a while, left even the Beatles in their creative wake.

And at the core sat Brian Wilson, the gifted young Icarus who touched the sky with his enchanting lyric-visions, then crashed to earth, a burned-out, paranoid, drug-addled husk. Riding shotgun was Mike Love, whose longtime stewardship of the Beach Boys' performing legacy has polarized the band's fans and seen him demonized down through the decades.

"For those who believe that Brian walks on water, I will always be the Antichrist," is Love's prosaic summary of the contempt in which his critics hold him. Inside the Beach Boys' bivouac, Brian was indeed lionized as a musical messiah by the other members of the band, Mike, Carl, Dennis, Al Jardine, Bruce Johnston, and, occasionally, David Marks.

His intuitive ability to knit their voices onto a tapestry of perfect pop songs ensured the Beach Boys left indelible motifs upon the cultural landscape from the first hits in 1962 through to their groundbreaking album *Pet Sounds*. That record was released in May 1966—thirteen months before the Beatles' *Sergeant Pepper's Lonely Hearts Club Band*—and was instantly hailed as a milestone in pop music, one that cemented Brian's reputation as a songwriting genius.

Between 1963 and 1966, he wrote and produced eleven Beach Boys albums and sixteen singles in an incredible outpouring of creativity. *Pet Sounds*, though, would be the high watermark of the Beach Boys' career and the last time the band was properly in harmony with each other and the world. By the time of *Pet Sounds*, Brian's descent into a form of mental purgatory had been ongoing for twelve months.

Unknown to almost everyone, he had been shoring up his fragile psyche with a growing cocktail of drugs. But it was only when he began dosing himself with LSD—almost two years before the Beatles took the same, precarious trip—that he found himself trapped in a frightening and never-ending vortex of auditory hallucinations and inner voices telling him he was going to be killed. It was the fork in the road that changed Brian's life forever, sauteed his brain, and paved the way for decades of soap-opera feuding between almost every band member, but most notably with Love, as the Beach Boys were caught in the undercurrents of their own riptide.

Overnight, he quit touring—opening the door for Bruce Johnston to join the band—and shuttered himself inside the studio for months while slowly becoming a recluse at home. "It was like losing our quarter-back," said Love.

But the seeds of Brian's estrangement from reality were undoubtedly sewn during a troubled childhood and most notably the abusive relationship each Wilson sibling had with their father. Murry Wilson was a failed songwriter who saw in the Beach Boys' growing musical talents a conniving opportunity to escape his humdrum life as a salesman in the Californian town of Hawthorne.

More so since he coveted the affluent lifestyle enjoyed by his sister Emily, who had married Edward Love, a successful businessman whose children—including their first-born Mike—wanted for nothing growing up. At the outset of their career, Murry took on the role of the Beach Boys' manager, each member having no reservations about placing the band's finances and music publishing rights in the trusting hands of a family member.

Relying on a salesman's persuasive instincts—and armed with several promising demos—he was ideally placed to pitch the Beach Boys as "The Next Big Thing." Concealed inside the Wilson family cupboard, however, were several dark skeletons. Murry, who had lost an eye in an industrial accident, was a bullying, sadistic father who rarely thought twice about dishing out severe beatings to his sons if they broke the family's strict code of discipline.

"My dad was violent. He was cruel. He drank too much and became a monster—and he didn't know how to deal with his sons' fears," confessed Brian years later in his own memoir, *I Am Brian Wilson: The Genius Behind the Beach Boys*, acknowledging the layers of neurosis his father was guilty of applying.

> Whenever I got afraid, he would yell at me or slap me or call me a pussy. When he didn't put his hands on us, he tried to scare us in other ways. He would take out his glass eye and make us look into the space where the eye used to be.
>
> Sometimes I provoked my dad. Once I took a shit on a plate and brought it to my dad. "Here's your lunch," I said. He was sitting down with his pipe in his mouth. "Get in the bathroom," he said. Then he came in and whipped the hell out of me. I was bringing the plate to him because of the times I didn't deserve. There were hundreds of those times.

Less submissive was Dennis, a brawny teenager who already had resistance tattooed on his rebel heart. And he was prepared to answer fist with fist.

"My dad was a tyrant. He used to physically beat the crap out of us," declared Dennis, who watched his dad turn their family home into a bully pulpit. "He just had a very unique way of expressing himself physically with his kids. I don't know kids who got it like we did."

Ad hoc Beach Boy David Marks, whose family lived across the street, witnessed one particularly, no-holds-barred fight between Dennis and his dad. "I did see them having it out in the garage. We heard a scuffle, and it was Dennis and his dad pushing each other around. My father was a big, strong man and he tore them apart like dogs and broke the fight up."

Later, Brian summoned up the courage to bullet his dad as the band's manager, though he was left in charge of the Beach Boys' song catalog, Sea of Tunes, a decision that would have dire financial consequences down the line. For three years from 1963, the Beach Boys rode the crest of the new wave sweeping across America, the happy, vibrant mood music interrupted only by the assassination of JFK.

But by 1966, even before the release of *Pet Sounds*, Brian's behavior was sending up red flags inside and outside the band. The planned follow-up album to *Pet Sounds* would be called *SMiLE* and, according to Brian, was a "teenage symphony to God" and would take the band down a more experimental path and away from songs about surfing, California girls, and hot rods. But rehearsals and studio sessions quickly unraveled as it became clear to everyone that Brian, the Beach Boys' chief auteur and rainbow colorist, was in the grip of a deepening drug-fueled psychosis. Until then, no one had been prepared to take Brian on, but Mike Love now found himself at a career crossroads. And during one band discussion to thrash a way out of the impasse, he finally gave vent to his feelings: "Don't fuck with the formula," he bawled at Brian. To shovel salt into an open wound, he allegedly added for good measure, "Who's gonna hear this shit? The ears of a dog?"

They are, of course, perhaps the most disputed quotes in rock history. Love has always denied making them specifically but doesn't shirk from the overall sentiment. He had cowritten many of the band's classic hits, including "I Get Around," "Little Deuce Coupe," "Surfer Girl," "California Girls," and "Good Vibrations," and he had serious doubts about ripping up a script that had served the band so well and rewarded them with undreamed of wealth. And he had nothing but contempt for the "self-indulgent" lyrics on some of the new tracks written by Brian and his new writing collaborator Van Dyke Parks.

Accusing them of abandoning pop music for pretentious high art, he later let rip in *Rolling Stone*:

> I never said anything bad about any of the tracks. I admit to wanting to make a commercially successful pop record, so I might have complained about some of the lyrics on *SMiLE*, calling them acid alliteration, which even the guy who wrote them, Van Dyke Parks, couldn't explain. But I wasn't resistant to. . . I mean, crazy stupid sounds, like animals, farmyard sounds, I did all that shit, laying in the bottom of an empty pool, singing up at the mic. I did all that stuff. My contribution was positive lyrics. Why the fuck should I be the scapegoat and the fall guy for that other stuff?

The band was now split firmly into two distinct camps; the Wilsons, each of whom was in thrall to drugs such as LSD and pot, and the sidelined Love, who preferred to get his highs from booze and broads and, later, Eastern spiritualism. Inevitably, *SMiLE* was shelved, most likely by the man who could no longer bring to sonic bloom the sounds he heard in his head.

It became an unfinished and unloved album around which a legend grew. Hailed as a lost masterpiece, it took on a mythic quality that rivaled the Ark of the Covenant. The truth was more mundane. *SMiLE* was a patchwork quilt of unfinished songs, half-baked ideas, and druggy pretentiousness which, had it been released, would have held the Beach Boys up to ridicule in the face of *Sergeant Pepper*.

Beach Boys chronicler Mike Eder told me in an email, "*SMiLE* isn't easy to sum up, but I think Brian lost the plot somewhere along the way. I feel he didn't have the confidence to finish it. Whether this was because of some of the Beach Boys doubts, or because of his own problems I don't think we will ever fully know. I think Brian was the leader at the time, so it was likely his decision to not put it out. The others simply didn't have enough power at the time to force Brian to abandon it. Even if he had had their full support, Brian may not have finished it."

Ranged against him was a 4–1 majority and a refusal from Carl, Al, and Mike especially for the plug to be pulled. Delivering the last rites, Carl recalled, "To get that album out, someone would have needed willingness and perseverance to corral all of us. Everybody was so loaded on pot and hash all of the time that it's no wonder the project didn't get done."

Love added his own valediction by saying, "Brian just didn't have the will or the ability to finish it. A lot of the Brian bullshit rests around that album and it's nothing." Only Dennis stood fully behind his older brother's new, avant-garde, direction, saying, "Brian Wilson is the Beach Boys. He is the band. We're his fucking messengers. He is all of it. Period. We're nothing. He's everything."

Under pressure from Capitol to bring new product to market, a quick salvage operation was mounted. The result was *Smiley Smile*, an album that contained fragments of songs initially earmarked for *SMiLE*, but which now bore no resemblance to Brian's nascent visions.

Smiley Smile, an album rubbished by Jardine as a "poor facsimile," was the line in the sand from which the Beach Boys' critical and commercial appeal never fully recovered. It also lit the blue touch paper on the never-ending feud between Brian Wilson and Mike Love for the soul of the Beach Boys. By the end of the sixties, they were a band on ventilators. Brian, while still a de facto member of the band, abdicated his role as creator-in-chief to Carl while Mike, who by now had embraced the teachings of Transcendental Meditation, remained an energetic powerhouse for their live shows. Love was committed to touring while Brian, psychotic and addicted, stayed in bed for literally years, chain-smoking, drinking heavily, letting his weight balloon, and seemingly having bought a one-way ticket to Palookaville.

The downward turn in the band's fortunes was naturally reflected in the bottom line. By 1969, bankruptcy was a serious possibility for the Beach Boys, as their record sales plummeted, and they were forced to play casinos and smaller venues just to turn a much-needed dime. Yet, at the same time, some of these records contained arguably some of their best post-SMiLE material.

Their 1970 album *Sunflower* and the subsequent follow-up *Holland* in 1973 were both hailed as critical returns to form. But they were largely unable to shake off their sun 'n' surf shadow.

Meanwhile, another serious family fault line had erupted with volcanic force. Convinced that the Beach Boys were all washed up, Murry Wilson secretly sold Sea of Tunes, their lucrative song publishing company, for $700,000 to Irving Almo Music in 1969.

Years later, Love said he and Brian were forced to sanction the deal in the face of financial duress. It was, nevertheless, a shocking family betrayal, made worse when it was discovered that the exchange was part of an elaborate plan orchestrated over two years by Abe Somer, the Beach Boys' lawyer.

Somer concealed the fact that he was also Irving Music's lawyer, keeping hidden a clear conflict of interest. Over the years, the catalog would generate more than $100 million in publishing royalties, little of which the band members ever received. Love had good reason to be especially outraged—he was shamefully never credited on many of the songs he had cowritten with Brian and accused the Wilsons of cheating him out of a fortune in royalties and publishing money. And now here he was being screwed over by his uncle and his cousin.

"I kept asking Brian about the credits and he just said his dad had fucked up," said Love. "That was his standard reply. The whole affair deepened my contempt for Uncle Murry. I knew he wanted to keep the Beach Boys a family band but in his eyes, I was never part of the family. When I told my dad what had happened, he said he wasn't surprised.

He said he was always a crook but that he really had it in for him. Murry wasn't going to let the entitled son of his rich brother-in-law receive the credit he was due. My uncle wanted the glory for his sons and through his duplicity he got it."

The issue became another open sore between Mike and Brian, one that was batted back and forth through the decades and was inevitably doomed to end up in court. In the early 1990s, Brian sued to reclaim the band's catalog, claiming the deal was a massive fraud, one carried out while he was in the throes of mental illness.

He even alleged his dad had forged his signature on the takeover documents and insisted the whole deal had been clouded in "malpractice, misrepresentations, suppression of facts, breach of contract and conflicts of interest."

"No one could believe it," said Brian. "He had taken away the only thing we knew would last—our songs—and sold it off like he was running a garage sale. I was scared of my dad lots of times, but that was one of the only times that I was just disappointed. He made the wrong business decision for the wrong reasons, and he created a bad situation that would last for years."

Eventually, Brian was awarded $25 million in damages and Mike Love saw his chance to pounce for a slice of the cake. He took Brian to court himself and accepted an out-of-court settlement for $5 million. He told *Mojo*, "I didn't want to sue Brian at all because I knew he had been sick and I've been very understanding because of that. The facts are I wrote the words to seventy-nine songs for which I didn't receive a credit let alone royalties. It's always been Brian Wilson this, Brian Wilson that."

Love's lingering sense of betrayal and anger over historical revisionism is as pointed today as it has ever been. In one interview, he declared,

> There was always the perception that Brian did the writing as well as the producing. That was not true. I was the coauthor of so many of the big hits. It is just an unfortunate thing that happens, a terrible thing. Because you have your uncle and your cousin.
>
> I don't think I cheated people but there are plenty of people out there who do—and my uncle was one of them.

It would not, however, be the last time the two bandmates would square off in court. Love sued Wilson for defamation over remarks in his autobiography. Amazingly, Carl Wilson and Al Jardine also sought massive damages against Brian over the book. Mike also resorted to legal action over loss of earnings when Brian secretly sanctioned a *Beach Boys Greatest Hits* album giveaway in the *Daily Mail*, which Love claimed cost him millions.

"Brian's book told lies about me," Love said. "And when it came to the first deposition in court, he admitted it was made up. Phoney. He couldn't remember what happened to him back then and he was using other people's distorted version of events and calling it his own."

Brian was not the only Wilson brother Love was constantly at odds with. A perennial state of war existed between himself and Dennis. A self-destructive thrill seeker and the only member of the band who actually surfed, Dennis was the Beach Boy who went overboard when fame delivered its calling card. Sex, drugs, and rock 'n' roll was a motto that could have been invented for the band's drummer, who possessed little of the musical flair of Brian and his younger brother Carl.

"Dennis Wilson was the essence, the spirit of the Beach Boys," recalled Fred Vail, a longtime business associate of the band's. "We used to think of him as the Steve McQueen or James Dean of the group."

In the late 1960s, as his life spiraled out of control, he had drifted into the orbit of Charles Manson, whose "family" carried out a blood-thirsty orgy of murder in Los Angeles. Dennis's hair-trigger temper often brought him into conflict with Love and Mike's younger brothers Stan and Stephen, who, by the 1970s, were both on the band's payroll. Indeed, Stephen would in time assume the role as the group's business manager before eventually being convicted of embezzling almost $1 million from the Beach Boys.

During one scuffle, Mike came off worst but saw an opportunity when Wilson stood above him with his legs wide apart. "Hit me again and you'll never have children," he warned. In 1977, the two again clashed violently on an airport tarmac. And at one LA concert in 1979, simmering offstage tensions finally exploded in front of thousands of fans.

Love recalled Dennis being high on drugs or booze or both: "I was trying to get him to focus on his drums and he stood on the riser, glared at me, kicked the set over and jumped me." Security staff rushed to pry them apart as other band members dragged them to the wings. "We all returned to the stage, though I stayed away from Dennis as far as possible."

It was an extraordinary moment. Weeks later, Love incredibly took out a restraining order against Dennis, a legal necessity that also hastened Wilson's temporary dismissal from the Beach Boys until he dried out. This all followed the remarkable standoff in Melbourne between the Wilsons and the Loves as they re-created their own version of a bun-fight at the cookie corral.

But the wounds continued to fester, especially with Stan Love and Rocky Pamplin, the bodyguard who had knocked Carl Wilson out cold for allegedly becoming Brian's family heroin fixer. In January 1981, despite no longer being part of the Beach Boys' entourage, word reached both men that Dennis had supplied Brian, still battling his own mental demons, with a huge score of cocaine.

It was, they reckoned, another act of brotherly treachery. Fired up with umbrage, they headed over to Dennis's house in Venice, Louisiana, and proceeded to mete out their own brutal punishment. The beating left Dennis with a broken nose, severe bruising, and a concussion.

Dennis pressed charges, and in March 1981, both Love and Pamplin agreed to a mutual restraining order in a Santa Monica Supreme Court. Love was fined $750 and Pamplin was fined $250 for the assault. Both were placed on six months' probation. Stan Love said, "Rocky had to pull me off because he didn't want me to kill him by accident."

But just when it seemed as if relations between Dennis and the Loves had hit rock bottom, Dennis found a basement and the opportunity for wicked revenge. Months after the incident, Dennis, one of rock's most notorious lotharios, who by then had been married and divorced four times—twice to the same woman—had moved in with his teenage daughter after a three-year relationship with Fleetwood Mac's Christine McVie ended.

One day she brought home a striking friend who looked distantly familiar. The girl told Dennis her name was Shawn . . . Shawn Love. She insisted she was Mike's illegitimate daughter, whose paternity he had always questioned. Soon, the pair, who were also second cousins, were lovers, the young girl seduced by the famous rock star suddenly lavishing attention on her.

Within two years they were married after she gave birth to a son called Gage—allegedly Mike Love's first grandchild. When they first met, Dennis was thirty-six and Shawn was seventeen, not that age was ever an impediment to Dennis's rampant libido. It took what was already a complicated and combustible relationship between Dennis and Mike to DEFCON 1.

"Some people believe he slept with Shawn as revenge against me, a final act of sexual conquest with a tinge of incest for good measure," wrote Mike in *Good Vibrations*. "Perhaps he saw it as an act of defiance against all three Love Brothers. Or maybe it was just Dennis being Dennis. He met an attractive teenage girl and he couldn't help himself."

One of Dennis's former wives, Karen Lamm, was less circumspect. She said, "He did it to fuck Mike Love, pure and simple." The entire sexual psychodrama turned the Beach Boys into rock's equivalent of the Borgias, with rival factions plotting to undermine the other. Largely cocooned from all the subplots, however, was Brian Wilson, whose precarious grip on reality continued to veer from recovery to relapse.

In 1973, his father died at the age of just fifty-five from a heart attack. And Beach Boys historian Mike Eder is convinced his father's premature passing was the trigger that sent Brian even further down the rabbit hole to drug-addled hell.

Brian had some very bad periods, but I feel they mainly happened later on than *SMiLE*. He was very active in the years following, and periodically active until his father passed away. I think Murry's death had a lot to do with his mental illness getting worse, but as early as 1963 Brian was trying to get off the road. I think the pressures of fame didn't suit him from the start. It just took a while before mental illness took over his life completely.

The reason I feel Murry's death was the sad turning point for Brian is that they had many unresolved issues. I think he also was working too hard from 1961–68. Brian was pushing himself to the point where it got unhealthy. I think Brian did do somewhat better in the late Sixties than was reported because the band was getting along during that period. Once the band began to fight more—mid to late seventies—Brian lacked that support that his family once gave him. They all suffered for the fighting in the band.

Throughout the seventies, eighties, and nineties, he occasionally reunited with the Beach Boys both onstage and on record. In the mid-seventies, his return to writing and performing was hyped with the misguided public relations campaign "Brian's Back." During this time, Brian had been placed under the medical supervision of a controversial therapist called Eugene Landy at the request of the band and, especially, his own family who feared he was on a drug-fueled suicide mission.

One interviewer was dumbfounded when Brian actually asked him if he had any drugs. At first, Landy was credited with saving Brian's life, but he later embarked on a self-serving quest to destroy it by taking control of all aspects of Brian Wilson PLC, including sharing lucrative songwriting credits and, on one occasion, even appearing onstage with the rest of the band. There were sinister parallels between Landy's Svengali-like influence and the autocratic whip once wielded by Brian's father.

At one point he even insisted on receiving part of the Beach Boys' income as payment for trying to restore his patient's mental equilibrium. Mike Love remained steadfast in his suspicion that Landy was fleecing Brian dry—and jeopardizing any faint hope he had of resurrecting their musical collaboration.

The final legal split came in December 1991 when a court ordered Landy to stay away from his longtime client, while Brian was forced to submit his finances to a conservator. The lawsuit, filed by Carl, Mike, and Stan Love, portrayed Landy as an opportunist who had brainwashed Brian and used him as a multimillion-dollar cash cow.

Melinda Ledbetter, a former model-turned car saleswoman who had been romantically involved with Brian for several years, laid much of the groundwork for the case. She doggedly resisted Landy's threats to stay away and produced documentary evidence that formed the basis of the lawsuit. Melinda and Brian were eventually married in 1995 and remain together.

Freed from Landy's predatory grasp, Brian suddenly underwent a creative rebirth. Over the next fifteen years, he released several solo albums to commercial and critical acclaim and even resurrected the aborted *SMiLE* project for its fortieth anniversary, for which he toured in the United States and Europe.

Curiously, while the hits had long ago dried up, the Beach Boys remained a huge concert attraction, largely thanks to Mike Love's relentless dedication to keeping the band's flame alive onstage. Nostalgia for their music had never waned, as they took their audience with them into middle age and then the autumn of their years. Inevitably, there were casualties along the way.

Dennis Wilson died in 1983 at the age of thirty-nine in a drowning accident. He was a hopeless alcoholic who, at the time of his death, was homeless and virtually bankrupt. Carl Wilson's lifelong addiction to nicotine finally caught up with him when he died in 1998 at fifty-one from lung cancer, fifteen years after his older brother had passed through the pearly gates. That left Brian, Mike, and Al Jardine as the last men standing of the original lineup. Soon, however, another legal front opened up, this time bizarrely involving Love and Jardine. Both men took to the road with their own versions of the Beach Boys. And it wasn't long before they sued each other after Love insisted he had sole licensing rights to use the band's name in concert. It all helped to fan the popular narrative that Love was a career villain who fed off the talent of others. Multimillion writs flew back and forth for several years before eventually being settled out of court. It didn't augur well for those fans who hoped that a sense of harmony could yet prevail for the band's fiftieth anniversary in 2012. But against all odds, a delicate truce was put in place for a fifty-date world tour to celebrate the landmark anniversary that would climax with triumphant sellout shows at London's Royal Albert Hall and Wembley Arena.

Back in the fold was Brian alongside Love, Jardine, and Bruce Johnston, the first time this iteration of the Beach Boys had appeared onstage since 1965. In a further attempt to prove that old animosities had been laid to rest, they even recorded a new album—*That's Why God Made the Radio*—which climbed to #3 on the *Billboard* charts, paving the way for an unexpectedly happy onstage reunion.

The tour was a massive financial and critical success—but détente was not long in crumbling. Barely had the last notes of the final show faded into the night than Love promptly delivered a bombshell announcement in the *LA Times*. The Beach Boys' show would go on—but without Brian, Jardine, and David Marks, who had also received his call-up papers.

In public relations terms, it was a disaster. Love stood accused of another massive power grab on the band's name, which he insisted was legally his to do with what he wanted. Though he asserted he was still open to recording more music under the auspices of the band's classic lineup and even held out a songwriting olive branch to Brian.

Blindsided by Love's actions, and furious at the prospect of missing out on a multimillion-dollar fortune, all three turned their guns on Mike, who also faced a furious worldwide backlash. Already a divisive figure among millions of fans, this latest move exposed him to accusations of monumental greed and only served to further ostracize the band's long-term front man.

The *Daily Telegraph*'s music critic Neil McCormick, who witnessed for himself the band's shaky alliance in a preshow interview, was among those who rued the twilight of the sixties gods. He wrote, "Their earliest incarnation was a pure expression of the heady, escapist joys of youth, but by the end of the sixties, with Wilson's deteriorating health, their songs had already turned to a kind of perpetual mourning for the loss of innocence. Perhaps more than any other band, they represent pop's complicated relationship with ageing."

Group historian Eder was among many lifelong fans who could only watch through the cracks in his fingers as old, dry scabs were once again picked over to reveal unhealed, septic wounds. He is, however, reluctant to paint Love as the rapscallion so beloved by history.

Mike Love deserves a lot of credit for the hard work he did both in the studio and on stage. However, after *Endless Summer* hit, he made a lot of poor artistic choices, and also some poor personal choices as far as how he treated the other Beach Boys. In their 1961–73 prime, I think he was a major asset, after that more of an ass. Still, he put in the time and worked hard in early years.

I think he and Brian could get along at times, such as when they were writing together. Brian and Mike are simply very different people. Mike was outspoken and, although he was in awe of Brian's talents, I think they eventually grew apart because Mike was so opinionated. Mike Love may not have been the easiest to work with, but his lyrics and his voice were essential to the group. In my opinion, he made a positive difference most of the time. Later, they all made some questionable choices by becoming an oldies band; Mike is the most guilty of this, but during their prime Love was important.

Defending the controversial move to axe the classic lineup, Love was adamant the plan was always to part ways after fifty shows, despite promoters clamoring to extend the tour. "Let me get right to it: I did not fire Brian Wilson from the Beach Boys," he wrote.

> I cannot fire Brian Wilson from the Beach Boys. I am not his employer. I do not have such authority. And even if I did, I would never fire Brian Wilson from the Beach Boys. I love Brian Wilson. We are partners. He's my cousin by birth and my brother in music. But you've got to be careful not to get overexposed.

But Brian laid bare his own contempt for Love in a right of reply to the same newspaper.

> I'm disappointed and can't understand why he doesn't want to tour with Al, David, and me. We are out here having so much fun. After all, we are the real Beach Boys. As far as I know I can't be fired—that wouldn't be cool.
> The negativity surrounding all the comments bummed me out. What's confusing is that by Mike not wanting or letting Al, David and me tour with the band, it sort of feels like we're being fired. What's a bummer to Al and me is that we have numerous offers to continue, so why wouldn't we want to? We all poured our hearts and souls into that album and the fans rewarded us by giving us a No. 3 debut on the *Billboard* charts, and selling out our shows.
> We were all blown away by the response. It's Al's and my opinion that all of us together makes for a great representation of the Beach Boys. While I appreciate the nice cool things Mike said about me in his letter, and I do and always will love him as my cousin and bandmate, at the same time I'm still left wondering why he doesn't want to continue this great trip we're on. Al and I want to keep going because we believe we owe it to the music. That's it in a nutshell, all these conversations need to be between the shareholders, and I welcome Mike to call me. [He didn't.]

Jardine went as far as to petition his Facebook followers for signatures beneath an open and barbed letter to Love that read as follows:

> In order to preserve the validity of "the Beach Boys" as a whole, and not as a "money-saving, stripped-down version" that only contains one original member, and one member that joined in 1965, we ask you to reinstate the three other members to the touring group for your final years performing. It's the right thing to do, and it's what the fans want!

This time, though, there would be no going back and there was no love lost. But just when it seemed the Beach Boys story was finally over for good, they found a way to reunite once more, albeit for a nonmusical purpose. For the first time since 2012, the surviving classic members reconvened in 2019 for a Q&A session for *SiriusXM* radio. Brian Wilson, Mike Love, Al Jardine, Bruce Johnston, and David Marks sat side-by-side in Studio A at the landmark Capitol Records building in Hollywood, the same room where they made some of their earliest songs five decades earlier for an hour of reminiscing over tortuous and toxic years gone by.

Eder is just one of millions who remains enthralled by the music they made together while acknowledging the pain it often took to create. He offered this: "I think history should and will remember the music over their personal lives. The music they made in their prime will hold up forever, and their personal issues get less and less relevant because so much time has passed. Of course, people will always want to know the story of the band, but at the end of the day albums like *Pet Sounds*, *Sunflower*, *Today*, those will be what matters. But it's understandable that people will be perplexed about all the infighting and puzzled really."

So what really happened to the Beach Boys, America's band and their answer to the Beatles? Apart from Brian Wilson and Mike Love, God only knows.

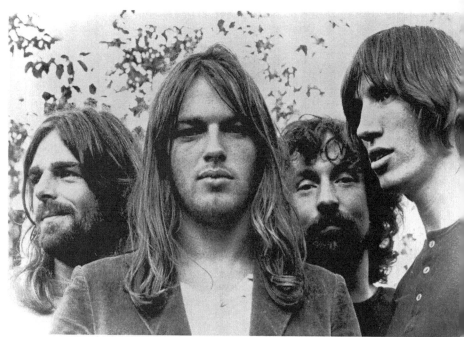

Pink Floyd: Rick Wright, Dave Gilmour, Nick Mason, and Roger Waters
Harvest/Photofest © Harvest

2

PINK FLOYD

Which one's Pink? It was the ultimate color-coded conundrum wrapped inside a rock 'n' roll riddle. Roger Waters, the cofounder of the legendary British band, whose visionary lyrical prowess had largely shaped the optics through which the world viewed the band? Or Dave Gilmour, the virtuoso guitarist whose musical flair had always created the arcane "sound" of Pink Floyd?

In the mideighties, the question took on a more serious cadence and divided the band's audience into distinct binary camps. Waters quit after recording *The Final Cut*, their twelfth studio album and the follow-up to 1979's dystopian concept *The Wall*. The album was wholly conceived and executed by Waters, whose dictatorial impulses could no longer be held in check by Gilmour or the band's two other primary members, drummer Nick Mason and Richard Wright, whose lush keyboard textures had always added another distinctive layer to the band's songs. Indeed, Waters had already fired Wright, like him a cofounder of the band in the midsixties, during the fractious sessions for *The Wall*.

By the time *The Final Cut* was in the can—Gilmour said the album should have been called *The Final Straw* and belittled it as "meandering rubbish"—Waters was heading over the horizon into a different future, having exchanged his lead role in a cage for a walk-on part in a coming war. Nestling in his pocket, he vigorously believed, was his steadfast and legal right to retain ownership of the name Pink Floyd. This minor difference of opinion only emerged when, months later, Gilmour, Mason, and Wright regrouped as Pink Floyd to begin recording *A Momentary Lapse of Reason* and, simultaneously, map out a world tour.

On hearing this, Waters promptly cranked up all the legal military hardware at his disposal and trained the guns on his former compadres, insisting that if anyone were going to call themselves Pink Floyd it would be Roger Waters and not some second-class imitation. And so the fuse was officially lit on arguably the most pernicious vendetta in rock music, a descent into madness that wrecked personal friendships, band camaraderie, and a musical unity first forged two decades earlier. Overnight, aggravation and hostility became the new normal.

In an interview with *Rolling Stone*, Gilmour recalled, "I remember meetings in which he said, 'You'll never fucking do it.' That's precisely what was said. Exactly that term . . . except slightly harder."

Over the next several years the band's alpha males turned the music press into their personal combat zones, happy to dish out spite and hate in equal measure. And each interview only served to ratchet up further the malign hostility between the two leading protagonists.

Gilmour admitted to *Rolling Stone* that *The Final Cut* was more like a Waters solo record than a group effort—and he was never fully on board with the project.

> We'd been having these meetings in which Roger said, "I'm not working with you guys again," recalled Gilmour. He'd say to me, "Are you going to carry on?" And I'd say quite honestly, "I don't know. But when we're good and ready, I'll tell everyone what the plan is. And we'll get on with it."

The story of Pink Floyd is punctuated by egotistical themes that tore at the band for almost four decades. It's a diorama of madness, alienation, hubris, and eventually, defenestration. And right in the middle stand the polarizing figures of Roger Waters and Dave Gilmour, two men who slowly and steadily chipped away at the pillars of their own legacy within Pink Floyd. Gilmour admitted the seeds of discontent had been sewn as far back as 1974's album *Wish You Were Here*. By the time of *The Wall*, relations between Waters and the other three were being strangled by the weeds of their own Arcadia.

When work began on the album, a follow-up to 1977's *Animals*, it quickly became clear that Waters's megalomania was rampant. Guilty as charged would have been the standard response to claims of an ego out of control. Waters insisted on total creative control over a project that would become the Floyd's magnum opus. Reduced to supporting actors, the other three gently shuffled to the side of the stage, although Gilmour disputes long-held assertions that the rot between him and Waters set in during the making of *The Wall*.

"There's a lot of misconceptions about the start of major hostilities between myself and Roger," he said. "We had a highly productive working relationship that operated pretty well through *The Wall*. There were some major arguments, but they were artistic disagreements. The intention behind *The Wall* was to make the best record we could."

Common ground, though, was often hard to find. Even the album's standout track, "Comfortably Numb," saw Gilmour and Waters on different pages, although these creative differences can often improve the end product in any band. Gilmour said as much when he described the song as "the last embers of mine and Roger's ability to work collaboratively together."

Democracy, however, quickly flickered and then just as rapidly died in the grim solitude of the studio. Arguments raged over the direction of the album, with its themes of loneliness, war, loveless marriages, and overbearing mothers. Isolated and wounded by what he saw as a lack of inter-band support, Waters sacked Wright, ostensibly for still claiming an equal share of production royalties while musically contributing zilch.

Mason, his self-confidence drained through repeated confrontations with the bass guitarist, was occasionally replaced by freelance drummers. Gilmour survived as an untouchable, his peerless guitar playing the essential ingredient to the Pink Floyd "mystique." But he only had four writing credits out of twenty-six tracks on *The Wall*—one for "Comfortably Numb"—lending further credence to Waters's claim that he alone was the driving force behind the album. "I was no longer interested in working in committee with anybody," he declared.

Dressed in combat fatigues amid the Floyd flare-ups was Bob Ezrin, the fabled American producer brought on board to help raise *The Wall* to new sonic heights. More often, though, he found himself cast as a referee in the ongoing conflict between the chief Floyds, even though hostilities never required Marquis of Queensberry rules. He recalled, "It was all done under that English smiling, left-handed adversarial stance they take, with the smiles on their faces and soft voices. But basically they were saying, 'I hate you and I'm going to kill you.' The war that existed between those two guys was unbelievable."

In the frosty hiatus that followed the release of *The Final Cut*, Gilmour and Waters released solo albums, both of which largely failed to find much traction even with Floyd audiences. Their subsequent world tours also saw a shedload of money disappearing into two financial black holes. In 1985 Waters finally acted on his impulses and handed in his resignation to the band's record companies Columbia and EMI. Naturally, litigation followed on both sides, with Waters eventually suing his old band to prevent them using the name Pink Floyd.

In his High Court deposition, he claimed,

> Pink Floyd has become a spent force creatively and this should be recognised in order to maintain the integrity and reputation of the group name. It is only realistic and honest to admit that the group in practical terms has disbanded and should be allowed to retire gracefully from the music scene.

Waters was convinced that, without him, the band was dead, though he nursed a secret dread that Gilmour and Mason could yet pull off a Lazarus-like resurrection. "I am not going to be hung out to dry in court for years and years while you guys are calling yourselves Pink Floyd," said Waters during one meeting. He later added, "I still think it's completely wrong. I don't think they should be called Pink Floyd."

The resulting legal imbroglio was played out over the best part of the next eighteen months in London's High Court. Several lawyers were able to fund their children's private education on the back of the vast riches their clients spent hunkering down in their respective bunkers. Bristling with indignation, Waters complained,

> In the best of all possible worlds my public, the Pink Floyd public, will turn round and say, "No, this is not the Pink Floyd, it meant more than this. No, it shouldn't just be a kind of franchise." When does a band stop being a band? They [Gilmour and company] presumably have the same sort of definition as the people going round calling themselves The Drifters.

Gilmour naturally parried Water's verbal punches with jabs of his own. "I had an awful lot of time invested in the group," he declared. "It was an intolerable situation, but I was damned if I was going to be forced out. I am an extremely stubborn person, and I will not be forced out of something I consider to be partly mine."

Mark Blake, author of the acclaimed book about the band, *Pigs Might Fly*, has sympathy with Gilmour's stance as he stared into the crystal ball of an uncertain future. He told me in an email,

> I don't believe Gilmour kept the band going out of petty jealousy. I think he kept it going because he had invested a lot in Pink Floyd for the previous six or seven years and felt it was his right to do so.

Also, as he has said on previous occasions, he did not want to start over as a solo act, especially as his recent solo album, *About Face*, and the tour had been only moderately successful.

Ultimately, as with all legal standoffs, a compromise was reached—at least in court. Waters and Gilmour laid down their gloves long enough to broker the outlines of a truce during a summit on Gilmour's houseboat by the Thames, which also doubled now as the band's studio. On December 23, 1987, it was announced that Waters had officially accepted an out-of-court settlement from Gilmour's legal team to rip up their partnership. Under the terms of this accord, Waters agreed that Gilmour and Mason had the rights to the Pink Floyd name in perpetuity. In return, he was allowed to cut the ties with the band's management company. As befitting the spirit of Christmas, the band also undertook to cede to Waters full rights to the concept of *The Wall*, giving him some small measure of satisfaction. Somehow, though, it felt like a hollow victory.

"My QC told me that the kind of justice I was after I could only get from the public," he admitted later. "The law is not interested in the moral issue bit in the name as a piece of property." Buried amid the legal verbiage, however, was one clause that perhaps summed up the craziness of the fighting Floyds. Throughout the whole process, Waters was adamant that one item of Floyd's legacy was nonnegotiable—the giant inflatable pink pig that had first adorned the cover of *Animals* and which was now rightly regarded as perhaps the most famous visual symbol of Pink Floyd as rock theater.

Laughable as it sounds now, the battle over Algie—yes, the pig even had a name—dominated several fraught meetings between the rival camps. Waters insisted he held the "creative rights" to Algie, which was always a sow. In the back and forth, it emerged that the bass guitarist had indeed commissioned the floating hog—giving him the rights to use the giant prop at his concerts. He had no problem with Pink Floyd also using the pig—provided they pay him $800 per show for the privilege. Meanwhile, the Floyds resumed their respective musical paths; Gilmour and Mason rehired Wright on a weekly wage of £11,000—a figure juicily dropped into the public domain by Waters—to circumvent legalities and carried on recording *A Momentary Lapse of Reason*, the title of which may have been a veiled jibe at Waters.

Blake pointed out that the band's former bassist heaped scorn on the music even before it had been released. "There was a lot of sniping in the music press, mostly instigated by Waters," he said. "He gave a very inflammatory interview to *Billboard* in which he poured piss on *A Momentary Lapse* and claimed someone from Floyd's U.S. record label had heard early work on the album and was unimpressed. Gilmour always strenuously denied this."

Gilmour, meanwhile, took on the arduous task of living up to Waters's lyrical legacy, often drafting in cowriters to help him punch ahead into foreign territory. Chastened by the court decision, Waters, nevertheless, finished recording his second solo album, *Radio K.A.O.S.* Both albums, not surprisingly given the air of internecine rivalry enveloping each party, were released in 1987 within months of each other. Waters was first out of the traps to condemn his rival's offering as nothing less than a shameless counterfeit of everything Pink Floyd stood for, a lightweight confection of songs that were lyrically appalling.

> *A Momentary Lapse of Reason* had a couple of really nice tunes on it that, had I still been in the band, those chord sequences and melodies would have made it onto a record that I was involved in. But conceptually and lyrically, it's just rubbish, partly because it's not true. It's like, "Let's try and write songs that sound as if they're Pink Floyd and make records that sound like Pink Floyd records."

Fighting talk like this peppered every interview, often forcing fans to take sides: Which one's Pink indeed? In terms of album sales for *A Momentary Lapse of Reason*, the Gilmour-led Floyd were the no-contest winners, offering them some feeling of validation. Indeed, its more mellifluous songs attracted a whole new audience who were largely oblivious to Waters's existence. Waters responded by taking the fight to the court of public opinion and deliberately timed his own tours to coincide with those of his old band.

During the autumn of 1989, the two bands crisscrossed North America, offering up rival musical visions of Pink Floyd. The closest they came to each other was in Toronto where Roger's band was playing only miles from a rehearsal studio for Gilmour's Floyd. It proved to be a momentary lapse of judgment that hit Waters in his wallet. Waters's tour found him performing in modest-sized theaters, many barely half full.

Acknowledging the irony, he admitted, "I'm out on the road in competition with myself—and I'm losing. I'm sure I would be much happier if I could murder them professionally as Pink Floyd."

In contrast, Gilmour, Mason, and Wright played 200 high-profile arenas before an estimated 5.5 million fans. The sound of £100 million trundling into the band's bank account was augmented by the noise of Waters grinding his teeth. The Floyd shows were a resounding success, with Waters already being left in his old band's slipstream, his current musical output looking like a lumbering relic from a bygone age. Even though his own shows still featured a Floyd-heavy set list that included revamped versions of "Welcome to the Machine," "Money," "Wish You Were Here," and several songs from *The Wall*.

However, many younger commentators, unaware of Waters's enormous input into the Floyd, were beginning to see Gilmour as the real driving power behind the band's past, present, and future. The guitarist used the variations in audience sizes to make his point.

"Roger hasn't helped his own cause by trying to time his records and tours to coincide with ours," said Gilmour. "He thinks it's going to do us some damage, whereas all it's doing is damaging him. If he spent half as much time and energy making his records and getting his tours right, he could have a better career than he currently has."

In another interview with *Q* magazine, however, he acknowledged the huge risk element of traipsing a full-blown Roger Waters–less Pink Floyd show round the globe while querying why any Floyd fan would settle for the sloppy seconds being served up by Waters.

> There were people in the audience who would make their feelings heard about Roger not being there, just by shouting very loudly during moments when the audience was being respectfully quiet. I just can't understand why the fuck they bothered to pay for the tickets. If they don't like us, go see Roger instead.
>
> There was one guy wearing one of Roger's tour T-shirts, which had the name Roger Waters in green fluorescent lettering across the top, so I only had to glance into the audience and his name would be beaming at me. This guy started off by shouting at us. By the end of the second half, he took the T-shirt off, tore it up into little bits, put it on the floor and stamped on it.

Adopting the position of a man impugned, Waters then had to watch as his former bandmates twisted the knife even further. On the world tour to promote *A Momentary Lapse of Reason*, a giant pig floated above audiences to resounding cheers. At first, this looked like a flagrant breach of the 1987 court agreement, which gave Waters sole copyright of the famous inflatable porker, which had always, always, been female. Until you looked at what lay beneath. Dangling below the giant hog was a pair of massive testicles. It was the ultimate fuck-you-Roger moment in the feud of the Floyds. Gilmour said, "A pig's a pig, for Christ's sake, but adding the testicles was amusing for us."

Never mind the bollocks, though. Waters was soon handed a gilt-edged opportunity to prove once and for all who had the bragging rights to Pink

Floyd's true legacy. He had over the preceding years since splitting with the band snubbed lucrative offers to stage his own version of *The Wall* in its entirety, saying he would only do it if the real Berlin Wall came crashing down.

In 1989, fate called his bluff. The dismantling of that grim symbol of the Cold War came exactly a decade after Waters had presented his own apocalyptic vision of the barriers that divide ordinary people trapped in a geopolitical web. Mike Worwood, one of the promoters behind Live Aid, contacted Waters on behalf of seventy-two-year-old British war-hero-turned-activist Leonard Cheshire. In September 1989, Cheshire had created the Memorial Fund for Disaster Relief, a program designed to hold £500 million in trust, the interest from which would go to help the victims of war. Cheshire was looking for a concert event on a grand scale to promote his cause.

Waters, whose serviceman father was killed in action in Italy during World War II, was impressed with Cheshire, and agreed to stage *The Wall* sometime in the future. When the Berlin Wall came down just a few weeks later, the venue seemed to suggest itself. Waters would present an all-star performance of Pink Floyd's 1979 tour de force at Berlin, Germany's Potzdamer Platz and the Brandenburg Gate, the site that had straddled the frontier between east and west for twenty-eight years.

He persuaded an all-star cast of the biggest names in music to help him reconstruct *The Wall* in his own image, among them Van Morrison, Joni Mitchell, Cyndi Lauper, Bryan Adams, and three members of The Band, Rick Danko, Levon Helm, and Garth Hudson, themselves no strangers to being in a dysfunctional group. He even tossed out an olive branch to Gilmour, though no one seriously expected him to pick it up. Especially after he snippily declared, "I suspect that the motivation for putting *The Wall* show on in Berlin is not charitable."

The "greatest gig in the world" took place on July 21, exactly three weeks after the Floyd had headlined before a crowd of 200,000 at Knebworth in England. Waters's show, though, was a spectacular triumph, attracting 350,000 people, at that time a record for a paid concert. But the media buildup had inevitably been largely overshadowed by the ongoing grudge between him and team Gilmour. Discord between music legends—witness Lennon and McCartney—always made great copy. The September 1990 edition of *Q* set Waters and Rogers up to roast each other, and they duly obliged. The cover headline memorably screamed "Don't Mention the Wall"—which perfectly captured the polarizing theme of Us and Them.

Waters told the magazine,

They would like to believe, for whatever reasons, that the making of *The Wall* was a group collaboration. Well, ok, they collaborated in it, but they were not collaborators. This was not a co-operative. It was in no sense a democratic process. If somebody had a good idea, I would accept it and maybe use it, in the same sense that if someone writes and directs a movie, he will often listen to what the actors have to say.

It sounds to me a bit like *Animal Farm*, the pig fight about who was more equal than others. Since the breakup they've been at great pains to point out how it wasn't really my work at all and we all did it together. Well, that's bollocks. It's just not true, as anyone who's listened to what they've done since can see—the fact that they don't actually do it, they get other people to do it. It's so clear.

Rick didn't have any input at all, apart from playing the odd keyboard part, and Nick played the drums, with a little help from his friends. And Dave, yeah, Dave played the guitar and wrote the music for a couple of songs, but he didn't have any input into anything else really.

He even kept a straight face by insisting that his old band had betrayed all the overriding principles that *The Wall* embodied by playing it in huge arenas. "I wrote *The Wall* as an attack on stadium rock and there's Pink Floyd making money out of it in stadiums! That's for them to live with. They have to bear the cross of that betrayal."

Over the next few years, Gilmour and Waters mostly played nice but the differences that had always existed between them often spilled out between the lines of various interviews.

They continued to snipe from the tramlines, an obligatory side effect of trying to maintain successful group and solo careers. In 1994, Pink Floyd released *The Division Bell*, their first album since *A Momentary Lapse of Reason*. The album artwork, designed by Storm Thorgerson, depicted two opposing Easter-Island type faces and was reportedly intended to represent the absences of Syd Barrett and Waters from the band. The tour that followed, which eventually included playing *Dark Side of the Moon* in its glorious entirety, was the last one they ever did.

Waters, meanwhile, took a twelve-year break from the music industry, returning in 1999 with a tour that was carefully paced over the next three years, and which was hailed as a bravura return to form and an unqualified commercial and financial success.

Admirably, both Waters and Gilmour continued to resist the mountain of dollars promoters waved under their noses to reform Pink Floyd. But then, in 2005, altruism suddenly proved to be the force that broke the impasse. Bob Geldof, a man whose persuasive profanities had helped raise millions to help combat famine in Africa by turning the world into a global jukebox for Live Aid in 1985, was hoping to repeat the trick with Live 8, a similar clarion call for multimillionaire rock stars to do their bit to raise awareness of poverty, debt, and the AIDS crisis in developing nations.

Top of his wish list of performers was a reunited Pink Floyd, whose last show together had been on June 17, 1981, at London's Earls Court, the final gig of *The Wall* tour. The lineup already looked impressive—Paul McCartney, U2, Elton John, Madonna, George Michael, Sting, and REM shared the billing with the next wave of artists such as Travis, Robbie Williams, Snow Patrol, Pete Doherty, and the emerging Killers. Geldof's record in convincing battling bands to lay down their arms for a worthy cause was impressive; Live Aid's running order had included Led Zeppelin, the Who, Black Sabbath, and Crosby, Stills, Nash and Young, groups noted as much for their internecine power struggles as their music.

Reuniting Pink Floyd, however, looked like mission impossible even for music's very own Kofi Annan. Especially since they had snubbed his entreaties to play at the original concert at Wembley all these years ago. But he did have a crucial connection with all the warring parties; three years earlier he had played the part of Pink in a low-budget film adaptation of *The Wall*. Geldof's first call was to Gilmour, and he immediately ran into a brick wall, so to speak.

The guitarist recalled,

> He didn't mention Roger, he just said, "Will you put Pink Floyd back together to do fuckin' Live 8?" I said, "No. I'm in the middle of my solo album." He said, "I'll come down and see yer," and jumped on a train. I thought, "No, no, no." When I rang him on his mobile he was at East Croydon. I said, "Bob, there's no point, get off the train." He said, "I'm coming down anyway."

The narrative, as outlined in *Q*, then went along the following lines:

Geldof: I went down to his farm, tried to take him through it.

Gilmour: He arrived and explained the whole thing to me in detail, which made me feel a bit guiltier, but I was hanging on to my selfishness. I said, "You've got enough great people, you don't need us." But he wanted us.

Geldof: I could see he felt awful for saying, "No." But he was gonna say, "No." And he said, "I don't know, man, I . . ." I said, "Don't say, 'No'. . . Drive me

to the station, think about it." He said, "But you know I'm going to say, 'No.'"
And I said, "Don't say, 'No' before you think about it, and promise me you'll
think about it."

Geldof next rang Nick Mason, who then called Waters.

Nick Mason: He [Geldof] was looking for a real novelty act, to reconstitute
this particular lineup of this particular band. I thought it was a great idea. He
started with David and gradually worked his way round. I think he was probably as surprised as we were.

Waters: I was the one who immediately promised to play on Live 8. Dave had
first said "No" to Bob Geldof.

Geldof: Then Waters called me, and he wanted to know what happened with
the Gilmour conversation. I told him and he said, "Can I have David's number?" I said, "OK. Why don't you have it? . . . here it is."

Gilmour: He [Geldof] managed to connive with Nick to get Roger and he got
Roger to ring me. My mobile rang and it was "Hi, this is Roger, how about it?"

And so it came to pass. Waters was prepared to trade in his usual intransigence for a cause that transcended pettiness and simply touched his
politically conscious heart. On July 2, 2005, four decades after Waters,
Mason, Wright, along with the legend that was Syd Barrett, first performed
as the Pink Floyd Sound, the three men found themselves back onstage
with Gilmour, who, of course, had joined three years later. Perhaps pigs do
indeed fly after all.

Musically, it sounded joyous. Onstage at least there were no residual
traces of acrimony. They played "Time/Breathe," "Money," "Wish You
Were Here," and a blistering sixteen-minute version of "Comfortably
Numb." Waters, especially, appeared to be caught up in the glow of the
reunion, cranking his bass guitar up and down and mouthing the lyrics to
the songs he rightly always considered part of his Floyd endowment. The
crowd also caught the mood of reconciliation, although, strictly speaking,
this was not a Pink Floyd audience.

As the first acoustic guitar chords to "Wish You Were Here" floated over
the darkness, Waters stepped up to the microphone. Arms outstretched and
glancing toward Gilmour, he said, "It's actually quite emotional standing up
here with these three guys after all these years, standing to be counted with
the rest of you. Anyway, we're doing this for everybody who's not here . . .
particularly, of course, for Syd."

The twenty-five-minute set was a gloriously uplifting triumph, causing
fans to wonder about what might have been. Among those watching at

home on TV was Pink Floyd author Mark Blake, who was as surprised as anyone by the onstage warmth that seemed to exist. He told me,

> I didn't expect it. I think they were won over by Geldof's persuasion and the fact it was for "a good cause." My understanding is there were quite a few problems in the early rehearsals—disagreements between Waters and Gilmour over what songs to play and how to present the material. Gilmour won out. I thought the final performance was great, but I don't think the process of getting there was a particularly pleasant experience.

These comments were indeed borne out by Gilmour who admitted the difficulties in ironing out some wrinkles. "The first meeting was pretty cagey. The songs that Roger wanted to do were not the same ones that I thought we should do," he said. Inevitably, it instantly stoked unfounded speculation of a new Floyd album, with all four once again writing and singing under the same flag of truce.

Unfortunately, the armistice didn't hold. It was, of course, like being asked to reheat a soufflé. Again, they were offered jaw-dropping sums for a world tour. Gilmour, however, was simply unfazed. "I've been offered the same amount of money to tour Pink Floyd with or without Roger." Both factions again went their separate ways, Gilmour and Waters maintaining twin track solo careers that, nevertheless, continued to lean heavily toward Pink Floyd's back catalog.

In 2008 Rick Wright died, his passing, like that of John Lennon, guaranteeing there would never again be a reunion of a legendary band. Mason, the band's gentleman drummer, reckoned Live 8 was, however, the perfect way for Floyd to finally shuffle off the stage.

> I think in some ways it was one of the best gigs we ever did. Just because everyone knew there was a war going on [between Waters and Gilmour]. Yet everyone was able to say, "You know what . . . this is more important than differences of opinion, the band, the music." I think it was a lovely example of being grown up.

Over the years, there was the occasional moratorium between Gilmour and Waters, most notably in 2012 when Gilmour coaxed his old sparring partner to join him onstage at a gig to raise money for the children of Palestinian refugees. The request came as Waters was hauling his own, revamped, production of *The Wall*—it was the third highest grossing tour of the year—across the continents. Waters was hesitant, fearing he would be upstaged by Gilmour's superior singing skills, so a deal was hatched. If

Waters agreed to appear, Gilmour would guest at one of his Wall shows. "You could have knocked me down with a feather," said Waters. "I was blown away. How could I refuse such an offer? I couldn't. There was no way. Generosity trumped fear. And so explaining that I would probably be shite, but if he didn't mind, I didn't, I agreed."

To further remove any pent-up expectations, Gilmour suggested they do their own gender-altering spin on the fifties doo-wop classic by the Teddy Bears, "To Know Her Is to Love Her." Who says he didn't have a sense of humor? Gilmour's subsequent appearance atop the wall at Waters's London O2 show literally brought the house down and caused the wall to fall.

But not, unfortunately, the one that still continued to divide him and Waters long after the dry ice had melted away. Earlier, Gilmour was quick to tamp down any fan expectations. His official blog noted, "Tonight is most definitely a one-off. David is not repeating his special guest performance at a later occasion. I'm sorry to disappoint those of you with fingers crossed and tickets for later shows."

Neither man, it seemed, could escape the shackles of their embittered past, despite a grudging admission by Waters that his decision to sue the band back in the eighties had been a mistake. Appearing on the BBC *HARDtalk* program, he said, "I was wrong! Of course I was. Who cares?" It was a rare moment of contrition, but Waters still seemed unable to find a release valve for all that pent-up rage. Psychiatrists could have had a field day.

In a 2017 interview with the *Daily Telegraph*'s Neil McCormick, he finally admitted what the whole world already knew: "Dave and I are not mates, we never were and I doubt we ever will be." In the same publication, he continued to seek some kind of validation for his own vaunted legacy, doubts over Pink Floyd's storied history chipping away at his psyche.

> The music is hugely important to me. It may sound daft to say, but over the years I maybe haven't taken quite enough credit for it. I think the idea that Rick and David particularly tried to sell me in the band, when I was a young man, was that I was a bit of a headmaster but I shouldn't bother myself with music because I wasn't musical. It's absolute crap. I'm twice the musician either of those guys ever were. I just am. I've got it in me.

In 2019, the band's phlegmatic drummer who often doubled as a mediator during the Borgias-like realpolitik between Gilmour and Waters, decided, at the age of seventy-five, to launch his first solo tour. Nick Mason's *Saucerful of Secrets* was in many ways a tribute to the Floyd before his two bandmates surrendered to the dark side of musical differences.

The tour, oriented wholly on psychedelic-era Floyd with a set list that included "Interstellar Overdrive," "Astronomy Domine," and "Atom Heart Mother," was an unexpected revelation. Waters was a surprise guest during a show at New York's Beacon Theatre and sang on "Set the Controls for the Heart of the Sun." He told the stunned and cheering audience, "We're very, very close and old friends." Then he turned to Mason and added, "My considered opinion is that you sounded a lot better than we did back in the day."

Gilmour, however, remained in the shadows, having zero interest in reliving that trippy part of his past. His final rebuff came when Waters offered a surprising truce in the summer of 2019.

> We had a big meeting where I came up with a big peace plan that has come to nothing, sadly. [Pink Floyd fans] all hoped that we could kiss and make up and everything would be wonderful in a cozy, wonderful world. Well, it wouldn't be all that cozy or wonderful for me, because I left Pink Floyd in 1985 for a reason. The reason being that I wanted to get on with my work. Well, thank goodness I've been able to get on with my work. Work is its own reward.

Months later, during the 2020 coronavirus lockdown, Waters's inner beast again broke free when he claimed he had been "banned" from Pink Floyd's website and social media channels. This latest war of words flared after he had recorded a new version of *The Wall* track "Mother" to raise money for the NHS. During a five-minute video rant, he asked why the video for the track had not been made available on Pink Floyd's official website.

> The answer to that is because nothing from me is on the website. I am banned by David Gilmour from the website. About a year ago, I convened a sort of Camp David for the surviving members of Pink Floyd at a hotel at the airport in London, where I proposed all kinds of measures to get past this awful impasse that we have and predicament that we find ourselves in. It bore no fruit, I'm sorry to say. I suggested that because whoever the 30 million of you are who subscribe to the web page, that you do that because of the body of work that the five of us created. That's Syd [Barrett], me, Rick [Wright], Nick and David, over a number of years. And in consequence, it seems to me that it would be fair and correct if we should have equal access to you all and share our projects.

Directing his strongest criticism at Gilmour, Waters said, "David thinks he owns it. I think he thinks that, because I left the band in 1985, he owns Pink Floyd, that he is Pink Floyd, that I'm irrelevant and I should just keep my mouth shut. We're all welcome to our opinions."

The verbal escalations often left Mason dismayed and bewildered when he was put on the spot about the grudge that refuses to retreat into old age. He told one interviewer,

> It's a really odd thing in my opinion, but I think the problem is Roger doesn't really respect David. He feels that writing is everything, and that guitar playing and the singing are something that, I won't say anyone can do, but that everything should be judged on the writing rather than the playing.

He went on to add that Waters, in particular, struggles to see beyond the band's acrimonious past.

> I think it rankles with Roger that he made a sort of error in a way that he left the band, assuming that without him it would fold. It's a constant irritation, really, that he's still going back to it. I'm hesitant to get too stuck into this one, just because it's between the two of them rather than me. I actually get along with both of them, and I think it's really disappointing that these rather elderly gentlemen are still at loggerheads.

At the time of writing, relations between Dave Gilmour and Roger Waters, both of them now grizzled and gnarled by time itself, remained comfortably numb.

Fleetwood Mac: Mick Fleetwood, Stevie Nicks, John McVie, Christine McVie, and Lindsey Buckingham

3

FLEETWOOD MAC

In Lindsey Buckingham's mind, it was supposed to be a graceful moment of healing. A straightforward acceptance from him signaling that the forty-three-year cold war with ex-lover and Fleetwood Mac bandmate Stevie Nicks was at last over. A bitter and, occasionally intemperate, bloodletting that resembled Dante's *Inferno* set to spellbinding music.

Two kites trapped in a never-ending "I-love-you-I-hate-you" emotional vortex. Time, perhaps, to hit the reset button on their tempestuous relationship. Leaning into the microphone at a musical benefit, and with Nicks standing a few meters behind, Buckingham attempted to shine a syncopated torch on Fleetwood Mac's conflicted past, present, and future.

He told the audience at the *MusiCares* show in January 2018,

> Fleetwood Mac is well known for being a dysfunctional family and it's certainly a true thing. [It provided] much of the fuel for our material. It was also the subtext of heroism that led us to be able to follow our destiny, despite all the emotional and social difficulties we were having.
>
> And I think the reason for that is that not very far below that level of dysfunction was what really exists and what we are feeling right now more than at any other time in our career is . . . love.

Standing on the stage behind him, Mick Fleetwood, John McVie, the two members on whom the band's name was predicated, McVie's former wife

Christine, and Nicks stared blankly into the blackness of Los Angeles' Radio City Music Hall. Then it was Nicks's turn to take the stand.

Her speech to a crowd that included uber fans Bill and Hillary Clinton, and which also paid warm tribute to the recently deceased Tom Petty, lasted six minutes. Behind her, Christine McVie mockingly looked at her watch to demonstrate the amount of airtime the band's hippy chick was consuming before indulging in a pretend waltz with Fleetwood. John McVie, an Arsenal scarf draped over his shoulders, remained implacably taciturn, his features an impenetrable mask.

But the same could not be said for Buckingham, whose occasional smug glances and whispered asides to McVie telescoped his impatience at yet another marathon Stevie talkathon. He had already been ticked off when they walked out to the sound of "Rhiannon," one of Nicks's most famous Fleetwood Mac songs. Eventually, Nicks wrapped it up, a cue for the stage to be cleared and the band to play a truncated five-song closing set that consisted of "The Chain," "Little Lies," "Tusk," and "Gold Dust Woman" before bowing out with "Go Your Own Way," rock 'n' roll's most contemptuous breakup song and a notorious reminder of the tumultuous Buckingham-Nicks disconnect.

They then left the stage, arms entwined, seemingly in perfect unison. Unknown to each of them, however, it was the moment when the last grain of sand finally fell from the fractured hourglass encasing Fleetwood Mac's classic cast. And Buckingham, in particular, was guilty of failing to read the room—and the runes.

Two nights later, he was at home watching the Grammys when he received a call from Irving Azoff, the band's manager and one of music's most powerful figures. And it quickly became clear that Fleetwood Mac's own nuclear clock had suddenly struck midnight. The gist of the call, Buckingham says, quoting Azoff was this: "Stevie never wants to be on a stage with you again."

It was a bombshell moment that, nevertheless, was still cloaked in ambiguity. Azoff had a rap sheet of grievances that, as Buckingham puts it, "Stevie took issue with" during that particular evening, including the guitarist's outburst just before the band's set over the intro music—the studio recording of "Rhiannon"—and the way he "smirked" during Nicks's thank-you speech.

In an interview with *Rolling Stone*, Buckingham conceded the first point. "It wasn't about it being 'Rhiannon,'" he insisted. "It just undermined the impact of our entrance. That's me being very specific about the right and wrong way to do something." As for smirking, "The irony is that we have this standing joke that Stevie, when she talks, goes on a long time," Buckingham said. "I may or may not have smirked. But I look over and Christine and Mick are doing the waltz behind her as a joke."

His explanation appeared flimsy at best and smacked of misjudgment and sanctimony. Amazingly, he still hadn't heard the sound of Azoff firing a gun. At the end of that call, Buckingham somehow assumed Nicks was quitting Fleetwood Mac. He wrote an e-mail to Fleetwood assuring the drummer that the group could continue. There was no reply.

A couple of days later, the scales began to fall from his eyes. Buckingham said, "I called Irving and said, 'This feels funny. Is Stevie leaving the band or am I getting kicked out?'" Azoff then for a second time verbally discharged the chamber of a Colt 45, the bullets for which had been loaded years earlier by a woman long scorned. He told the guitarist he was "getting ousted" and that Nicks gave the rest of the band an ultimatum: "Either he goes or I go."

In that time-frozen moment, Buckingham became an outlier. Written more than four decades ago as a requiem for his own romance with Nicks, "Go You Own Way"—the last song the classic lineup would ever perform together—had now mutated into an unexpected funeral hymn for his days with Fleetwood Mac. And Nicks had unequivocally hammered home the final nail in the coffin in a brutal takedown.

Even as this book was taking shape, there was no sign of the permafrost thawing. Asked by the *Guardian* in 2020 if she had spoken to Buckingham since he left, she replied, "No." Do you really think you'll never appear on stage with him again? "Probably never." Really? "Uh-uh," she said slamming the door shut in her ex-lover's face.

Fleetwood stood in solidarity with Nicks's position, while refusing to admit Buckingham had been fired. "The truth is, call it what you want, a parting of company took place, and it had to take place, and it was supported by the remaining band members around something that for sure was a major problem to two people—Lindsey and Stevie," he explained.

Support for the decision also came from Christine McVie, perhaps the band member who was, at that time, closest to Buckingham.

It was the only route we could take, because there was too much animosity between certain members of the band at that point, there was just no way it could've gone on as a five-piece, a group with Lindsey in the band. So it was either just completely break up the band or make the best of it.

In later interviews, Buckingham called his incendiary dismissal a coup. It was an extraordinary twist in the tale of a band that, in the 1970s, epitomized rock 'n' roll hedonism by diving full length into a crazy world of inter-band sexual entanglements, tempestuous breakups, back-stabbing, reckless spending, and a never-ending pipeline of the sweetest cocaine.

And one which neither Buckingham nor Nicks could ever have imagined when they abandoned a stagnant solo career to join a British blues band that in 1974 was patrolling the zone between life and death. Fleetwood Mac had been at the forefront of the blossoming British blues boom, which had taken root in 1967. But by the midseventies, having survived several personnel changes—including the departure of founder member and key songwriter Peter Green—the band was largely musically moribund and creatively bankrupt. Record company debts were piling up, a direct result of album sales drying up. And the first signs of the emotional turbulence that became synonymous with the group were already in play.

The McVie's six-year marriage was in a downward spiral, wrecked by John's heavy drinking and Christine's barely concealed affair with a member of the group's touring crew. Fleetwood had also just fired Bob Weston, his lead guitarist, after he discovered he had been mattress surfing with his wife Jenny Boyd, sister-in-law of ex-Beatle George Harrison.

"The affair I had with Bob, I felt so guilty about it," she told the *Guardian*. "It took me many years to get over it, because it was so against my nature. I'm a naturally monogamous person."

Arriving as innocents into this maelstrom were aspiring singer/songwriters Buckingham and his girlfriend Nicks. She was a part-time waitress in a Beverly Hills singles bar earning $1.50 an hour and he was a full-time dreamer with an audacious talent for playing guitar and writing songs.

"I believed that Lindsey shouldn't have to work, that he should just lay on the floor and practise his guitar and become more brilliant every day," explained Nicks. "And as I watched him become more brilliant every day, I felt very gratified. I was totally devoted to making it happen for him. And when you really feel that way about somebody, it's very easy to take your own personality and quiet it way down."

Even then, Nicks was a hostage to Buckingham's controlling temperament and pot-fueled mores. Posing together for the cover of their self-titled debut album in 1973—just a year before that fateful fork in the road—the photographer told Nicks to remove her blouse. When she refused, Buckingham reportedly flew into a foul-mouthed rage. "Don't be a fucking child, this is art."

By late 1974, Fleetwood, searching for a replacement for Weston and the band's other guitarist Bob Welch, saw Buckingham-Nicks play a local downtown gig and was immediately impressed by the Afro-haired Buckingham's musical muscle. But when asked by the rangy drummer to join Fleetwood Mac, Buckingham loyally and stubbornly insisted he and Nicks came as a package.

After all five went out to dinner at a Mexican restaurant, the casting vote over whether to have another woman in the band went to Christine McVie. Having quickly bonded with the "hippy chick" who was the very antithesis of her own fragrant Englishness, the deal was sealed.

None of them, however, could have known they had just inked a deal with Mephistopheles or that Buckingham and Nicks would provide the match to the powder keg already taking hold inside the band. "Lindsey and I were in total chaos a year before we met Fleetwood Mac," Nicks told *UNCUT* almost thirty years on.

"I had already moved out of our apartment a couple of times and then had to move back in because I couldn't afford it. But if we'd broken up within the first six months of Fleetwood Mac, there would have been no record and we would have been in big trouble, so when we joined the band we took the decision to hang in there."

The impact on the band's musical identity and live shows was both immediate and profound. Almost overnight, the two Americans transformed Fleetwood Mac from a jaded English blues group to a transatlantic rock phenomenon. Between 1974 and 1979, the band recorded three brilliant albums—the eponymous *Fleetwood Mac*, *Rumours*, and *Tusk*. Proof, if any were needed, that Buckingham and Nicks's gamble had paid off. "If we hadn't joined Fleetwood Mac, would Lindsey and I have carried on and made it?" she asks today. "I was really tired of having no money and being a waitress. It's very possible that I would have gone back to school and Lindsey would have gone back to San Francisco."

Rumours, of course, was the record that propelled them into the troposphere occupied by stadium-filling contemporaries such as Led Zeppelin, the Stones, Pink Floyd, the Eagles, and Santana. It was also the album that did much to plow the furrow of scandal that ran on parallel lines to the group's musical brilliance. Buckingham and Nicks were, by the time Fleetwood Mac came to start the long *Rumours* sessions in Sly Stone's studio in downtown San Francisco, already enmeshed in their own volatile and predictable disintegration.

The first Fleetwood Mac album featuring the new lineup had become an unexpected success thanks in no small part to "Rhiannon," a dreamy and bewitching Nicks's song, becoming a major stand-alone radio hit. And that only ramped up the internal pressure on them to produce an even better album to further cash in on their growing reputation as a band that had risen phoenix-like from the ashes of a former life.

Ultimately, though, *Rumours* became the soundtrack of two warring couples mired in strife trying to plant their feet in the middle of a landslide, looking for strength amid all the emotional carnage.

At its beating heart lay the kinetic war between Buckingham and Nicks who traded sparks in the only way they knew how—through the songs that now sounded more like a conduit for a couple's breakup therapy. The Buckingham-penned "Second Hand News" and "The Chain" wielded lyrical stilettos that foreshadowed all the portents of the drama still to come. But the rawest nerve was touched by Buckingham's "Go Your Own Way," which painted Nicks as a sly Jezebel with a vampish attitude toward men. She was horrified when she first heard the lyrics and demanded that her former lover remove the barbs. He point-blank refused. Revenge came in the form of "Dreams," Nicks's timeless counterblow.

"'Dreams' was my kind of airy-fairy, spirituality saying 'when the rain washes you clean, you'll know.' In other words, we are all going to come out of this and we'll be friends and it will be ok. But Lindsey's 'Dreams,' which was 'Go Your Own Way,' was angry and nasty and in my opinion extremely disrespectful."

In another interview with *Rolling Stone*, she vented further over the song's lyrics.

> I very much resented him telling the world that "packing up, shacking up" with different men was all I wanted to do. He knew it wasn't true. It was just an angry thing that he said.
>
> Every time those words would come onstage, I wanted to go over and kill him. He knew it, so he really pushed my buttons through that. It was like I'll make you suffer for leaving me. And I did.

Punishment then followed in the shape of "Silver Springs," an extraordinarily beautiful Nicks track left off *Rumours* but when resurrected almost twenty years later took on a life of its own as a live favorite. Onstage, Nicks often fixed Buckingham with her steeliest stare when singing the words that reminded him that she would forever haunt his every footstep.

Buckingham admitted "Go Your Own Way" was a revenge track for being dumped. "I was completely devastated when she took off," he remarked.

> And yet I had to make hits for her. I had to do a lot of things for her that I really didn't want to do. And yet I did them. So on one level I was a complete professional in rising above that, but there was a lot of pent-up frustration and anger towards Stevie in me for many years.

As the only noninstrumentalist in the band, Nicks was forced into the margins for long spells at the studio. Often she decamped to a backroom with her crochet and her journals. At the same time, she had emerged as a principal songwriter. But, as had happened so often in the past, it was Lindsey who sculpted her potter's clay into a thing of beauty.

"Lindsey had an amazing way of taking my songs and making them wonderful," said Nicks. Except in the here and now those old rules no longer applied. Tensions already inflamed would erupt further as Nicks, running counter to her own instincts, occasionally accused Buckingham of sabotaging her songs.

Before long, they would literally be at each other's throats. Buckingham confessed he was finding it harder to be part of the creative process with his by now former lover. "I just knew exactly what to do with her songs—and that never went away. It just became a little more bittersweet in terms of wanting to do it. There were times when I had an urge not to want to help her and that's a weird thing to admit."

Anger and jealousy inside Fleetwood Mac's own heartbreak hotel was not confined to the Buckingham-Nicks's axis. By the time *Rumours* was being recorded, the McVies had officially parted, with Christine now officially entwined with the group's lighting director Curry Grant (I kid you not).

In song, she never played the blame game with her estranged husband or dunked on him in verse. Instead, she embraced life with her new partner by proclaiming "he made loving fun," which was, of course, a knife of a different blade. Inside the frat house that doubled as the studio, an arctic chill enveloped both of them as the relationship completely degraded.

"We literally didn't talk, other than to say, 'What key is this song in?'" Christine recalled.

> We were as cold as ice to each other because John found it easier that way. We all split into smaller groups. I got on with everybody except John. Stevie got on well with everyone except Lindsey and Lindsey got on with everybody except Stevie. But if you got the wrong people in the same room, that could be difficult.

The room temperature plummeted further when Christine openly flirted with her new beau in front of John. He, in turn, would relish the chance to flaunt his rebound girlfriend. A tipping point was inevitable, and it was witnessed by the album's producer Ken Caillat, who had a ringside seat at the day-to-day dramas.

> John would come into the studio and see Christine after she'd already left him for someone else. And every time John would see her, it would just kill him. He still wanted her, but she didn't want him because of his drinking. There was constant drama.
>
> I remember John had already moved on to a new girlfriend, Sandra, a beautiful British girl, and John had her up there while we were recording *Rumours*. The Record Plant feels like you're locked into first class on a plane. You all get to know each other very well and very fast.

Christine said, "Hey, John, Valentine's Day is coming up and I want to have my boyfriend, Curry, come up." And John said, "No way! I don't want to see that bastard anywhere around here." He said that as Sandra was sitting right next to him. Christine said, "It's not fair. You have Sandra right here." And John said, "She means nothing to me." Sandra and Christine both threw a glass of champagne at John and stormed out. And John was like, "What did I say?"

Nicks was also dragged into the McVies' domestic morass after she and Christine moved into a condo together on the outskirts of Sausalito. Nights were often interrupted by the sound of John, high on drink and low on self-esteem, wailing for Christine to take him back. "Chris saw me at my worst one time too many," he later reflected.

I drink too much and when I've drunk too much, a personality comes out. It's not very pleasant to be around. And, bless her heart, Chris said, "I don't want to be around this person." It was awful. You're told by someone you adore and love that they don't want you in their life any more.

McVie's double standards underpinned rock 'n' roll's worst hypocrisy—the Dionysian male who romps his way round the world is hailed as a sex god, the women, by comparison, are castigated for using their gender as a weapon. "We almost always had boyfriends," said Nicks of herself and McVie.

But they weren't on the road because they'd just get stomped on. For me to have a guy out on the road with us, and have Lindsey glaring at him the whole time? Or for Christine to have a guy out and John just walk past and flip him off? No, we both learned very early on that we would never bring boyfriends on the road because it created arguments.

And yet, as with ABBA on the other side of the Atlantic, they were taking inspiration from their personal lives and pouring it into their best songs, even if bitterness and recrimination lay just below the surface.

Caillat had hoped the success of the previous album would act like a balm to the scars that were appearing every day during the sessions for *Rumours*. The opposite was true.

What I didn't realize is, the lyrics still existed. So, every time we'd be working on a song, like working on a vocal harmony or an organ part, the lyrics would piss somebody off again. For this album, they wrote all the songs in the studio. So everything they wrote and put on tape was doused with gasoline and tears, and every lyric was hurtful. All these songs were painful reminders of what was going on. That pain was completely painted into the layers of sound we worked so hard to create.

Rumours hit the shelves in February 1977 to the kind of widespread critical acclaim that had greeted the Beatles' *Sergeant Pepper* a decade earlier. The album's rich pastel shading gave it a shimmering and emotional appeal that saw it shift 20 million units worldwide—a staggering return from what was ostensibly only their second album together.

Adding to the frisson of music industry excitement, however, were the songs that clearly laid bare the level of personal hostility inside the band. Even the album's name—an in-house joke suggested by John McVie to depict the current state of affairs (no pun intended)—added to the gossipy soap-opera allure and a sense of true-life confessions. Served up was a cornucopia of delectation. *Rolling Stone* magazine was among those who quickly sussed out that scandal sells with a front cover that showed all five band members cavorting under a bed sheet.

The frisky fresco showed a semi-naked Mick Fleetwood grinning lasciviously with his arms wrapped around Stevie Nicks, sexily alluring in a satin slip. It was, accidentally, a flirtatious harbinger of salacious events still to unfold.

Later that year, they embarked on a massive tour to promote *Rumours*, one that established Nicks as the undoubted star of the show. Onstage, she was a mesmerizing figure, a gossamer butterfly in chiffon twirling her silk scarves and shaking her embroidered tambourine. Buckingham, wrestling with the demons of their breakup, understandably found it hard to deal with, as did John McVie, forced night after night to stand just meters apart from his estranged partner.

Thrown together onstage, old wounds duly appeared between the warring couples only to be cauterized the next day before the whole cycle started again. It felt as if they were the victims of a Tantalus-tinged vicious circle. "What we were doing was so powerful and focused that no one, not even in a whole heap of emotional pain, was going to walk away from," Fleetwood said in a 2016 Fox News interview. "All five of us were going through the same thing. I was just spared that my partner wasn't singing into a microphone six inches away."

But, by the time the tour reached Australia, Fleetwood and Nicks were inexplicably sharing a bed for real. The band's cofounder was still a married father of two young children but separated from their mum Jenny Boyd and Nicks was intimately involved with Don Henley of the Eagles. The lovers went to desperate measures to keep their affair secret—trysts in hotels, meetings in safe houses, including one in Maui, Hawaii. But they were fooling no one but themselves.

Devastated by this betrayal—and fearful for the impact on their children—was Jenny. And she confronted Nicks on at least two occasions, one of them at the reception for John McVie's second wedding.

Fleetwood, meanwhile, was compelled to more or less seek permission from Buckingham to go the full nine yards with his former lover, like a prospective son-in-law asking a father for permission to marry his daughter. It came as no surprise to the guitarist, who eighteen months earlier had predicted it to Fleetwood's face during a night of serious pot-taking.

"I thought it was terrible that he thought that way about me and her even for a minute," declared the drummer. "At the time I'd not even given it a thought. Of course I found Stevie attractive, what man wouldn't? But she was Lindsey's girlfriend." Nicks's emotions, meanwhile, veered from unfettered retribution directed at Buckingham to nail-biting guilt. She and Christine McVie had always regarded Fleetwood as the Big Daddy of the band.

Now here she was indulging in a dangerous liaison that brought with it almost a whiff of incest. Factor in copious levels of chemical indulgence and all the ingredients were there to construct a narrative of Shakespearian proportions. Before matters turned intimate, Fleetwood and Nicks had always enjoyed a warm connection.

One night he even suggested to his estranged wife that he and Stevie had known each other in a former life—a notion that rightly sent alarm bells ringing through her mind. She had good reason to be worried, separated though they were. When news of the affair inevitably leaked out, it poured more oil on already troubled waters inside the band hive.

Buckingham naturally struggled to shut out the carnal images swirling through his mind's eye. "I am sorry that we didn't think about Lindsey enough," said Fleetwood, who called it a "classic intergalactic mess." "We just thought he was OK, but he needed to be acknowledged."

Years later, they both blamed the ill-judged affair on a combination of cocaine and pent-up passions. "Mick and I never would have had an affair had we not had a party and all been completely drunk, messed up and coked out," declared Nicks. "[We] ended up being the last two people at the party. So guess what? It's not hard to figure out what happened—and what happened *wasn't* a good thing. It was doomed. It was a doomed thing, caused a lot of pain for everybody, led to nothing."

Fleetwood, however, saw it in more baroque terms.

I was in love with her and she loved me and it was not something passing in the night. In terms of intensity, it was a proper Hollywood affair on a par with Richard Burton and Elizabeth Taylor. We still have the same connection to this day; we just love each other in the true sense of the word, which transcends passion.

I will take my love for her as a person to the grave, because Stevie is the kind of person who inspires that devotion. I have no regrets and neither does she.

It was manna from heaven for the tabloids on both sides of the Atlantic, who suddenly saw the band as the epitome of rock 'n' roll voyeurism. Even more so since it now placed the band's seductive star front and center of a Fleetwood Mac ménage-a-trois. The end, when it came, was messy and, in many ways more angst-driven and personal than Nicks's split from Buckingham. Both she and Mick had agreed not to cramp each other's romantic style when they were apart—in other words there were no strings attached. But all bets were off when Fleetwood admitted he was also sleeping with Nicks's best friend, Sara Recor, whose husband worked with the band's touring crew.

It left Mick still trying to salvage his marriage while at the same time having an on-off affair with his bandmate then betraying her with her best friend. The optics, as Fleetwood candidly admitted, were not good.

"This was pretty out there behavior and I'm not proud of it. What I stirred by seeing Sara was a maelstrom," wrote Fleetwood, who eventually married Sara in 1988 before they later divorced, in his autobiography *Play On*. "Stevie wouldn't talk to me, and my other bandmates expressed their disapproval. Sara's friends completely cut her off and sided with her husband. So she was stuck with my circle, one of whom was the best friend she had betrayed."

Nicks, reeling from a double-edged sword to her heart, naturally poured all her feelings out in a song called, with all the subtlety of a sledgehammer, "Sara," which was one of the standout tracks on *Tusk*, the hugely anticipated follow-up to *Rumours*.

> Sara was banished by the band but not by me. So Mick is living with Sara and coming into the studio every day very stressed out and I'm not speaking to him or looking him in the face.
>
> Even Lindsey, who was horrified that I was having a relationship with Mick, was even more horrified that he had fallen in love with my friend and broken my heart.

The song, however, also spoke to another secret heartache. Unknown to only a few close friends was the fact that Nicks terminated the baby she was due to have with Don Henley—and the girl, she said, would have been called Sara.

There was another constant, but more pernicious, reminder for Nicks over the end of her affair with Fleetwood. Tusk was the cocksure drummer's narcissistic pet name for his own penis. Bizarrely, he had tusks adorning the studio walls and even the console so they were literally in Nicks's face every time she set foot in the studio. "There was nothing beautiful or elegant about the word tusk," she later said. "I don't recall it being Mick's joke about a . . ." she trailed off in one interview, as if she couldn't even bring herself to say it. "That went right over my little prudish head. I wasn't even told that until after the record was done, and then I liked the title even less."

Phallic references aside, a bigger battle was raging for the musical soul of Fleetwood Mac. Buckingham, his ears closely attuned to the aftershock of punk rock's earthquakes and the sounds of the Clash and New York Dolls, was keen to tear up the band's musical playbook with *Tusk*, which was mapped out as a monumental double album. The idea of filling four sides with radio-friendly hits like "Dreams" was anathema to him; the last thing he wanted to make was *Rumours Mark Two*.

He cut back his hair, took to wearing thick gothic eyeliner, traded his rock star jeans for sharp suits and started prowling the stage like a man possessed, often overshadowing Nicks's own performances, much to her irritation. Only Keith Richards looked more elegantly wasted.

"He was not the Lindsey I knew," observed Nicks. In the studio, he insisted on total control, often overdubbing McVie's bass parts and even playing Fleetwood's drums on some tracks. Channeling punk's anarchic rhythms on the song "Tusk" itself and "The Ledge," Buckingham deliberately steered Fleetwood Mac away from the safe harbor of *Rumours* and even the songs like "Landslide" that had made the Fleetwood Mac album so successful.

He started hearing beauty in dissonance, like the way recording on a boom box could give music a stark, compressed sound, or the tone you got from playing percussion not on a drum kit but an empty box of tissues. Old tensions, however, quickly resurfaced, especially with Nicks, an artist as far removed from music's new wave as you could get.

Sex and rock 'n' roll had, of course, been part of the band's narrative for years. But the eye-watering success of *Rumours* had brought in the third part of the unholy trinity. Suddenly there was a money-is-no-object attitude toward drugs, particularly cocaine. That, combined with Buckingham's increasingly controlling tendencies and his refusal to work the graveyard shift with the rest of the band, often produced angry standoffs with the other four.

Ken Caillat recalled,

> We had to have duplicate tapes made in case someone working at four in the morning erased what Lindsey had done earlier. It was unbelievable. *Rumours* was not much of a party in my opinion, there wasn't a lot of drugs or drink.

But the third album, with Lindsey's antagonizing position, was more tedious. People started to drink a little more and then when they had too much to drink, they would counteract it with some kind of stimulant.

Unlikely as it sounds, Fleetwood later claimed he had snorted the equivalent of seven miles of cocaine when the band was at its drug-fueled zenith; Nicks eventually needed surgery to repair the hole in her septum from years of taking coke. As usual, drugs only served to prize apart further the fault lines that were already visible between Buckingham and Nicks.

Asked whether drugs were indeed the fossil fuels driving the band's creative energies, Nicks replied, "It did not make us nice people, it did not make us have the relationships we might have had. It stole a lot from us. We were all very, very addicted." Watching from the sidelines was Carol Ann Harris, Buckingham's new girlfriend who witnessed the reactor level-four meltdowns with Nicks over songs. "There was a lot of screaming between Lindsey and Stevie and a lot of tears. People were always storming out." Control was not something Buckingham was prepared to let go, especially when it came to his vision for the most polarizing Fleetwood Mac album of them all. It sometimes teetered toward physical violence—later it passed that tipping point when Buckingham allegedly assaulted Nicks over the trunk of his car while Fleetwood tried to pull them apart.

"There definitely was a certain amount of paranoia," agreed Nicks. "What do you mean you don't like this song? So I have to do more drugs to make me feel better for the fact you don't like this song?"

The completion of *Tusk* in 1979, with its bass-heavy groove and punky percussion, sent horrified executives at their record company Warners searching for tin helmets. Critics denounced the band's twelfth LP as more like a white elephant and lambasted Buckingham's unchecked arrogance. But the album, at that point the costliest LP in history, contained a set of songs that replaced the burnished AM glow of *Rumours* with a sonic landscape that was broader and more colorful—yet in part more arid, and studded with sharper angles.

Debonair and demented, it still sold 4 million copies in the United States alone, spawned six hit singles, and was the climax of this band's golden run. Never again, would they reach such creative heights. *Tusk* drew a line under the first act of this iteration of Fleetwood Mac and its beautiful absurdities and contradictions. The song, however, would in many ways, remain largely the same for Buckingham and Nicks over the next four decades, their turbulent push and pull symbolizing the heartbeat of a relationship that defied any easy decipherment. Until that fateful appearances at the MusicCares awards in 2018 when Nicks, at the age of seventy, finally decided to permanently cut the ties that had bound her to Lindsey Buckingham for most of her life.

More recently, new tensions had come to the boil over conflicting touring schedules between the band and Lindsey—and they finally spilled over in the aftermath of that fateful night. Among the witnesses to the dying embers of Fleetwood Mac's classic lineup was veteran keyboard player Brett Tuggle, who had been a mainstay of the band's touring ensemble for more than two decades.

He told *Rolling Stone* how the house finally burned down:

> Tensions had been building a lot over the past year regarding this tour that was going to happen with Lindsey still involved. There were some key things that had caused tension between Lindsey and Stevie regarding this thing at *MusiCares*. There had been some meetings that didn't go well and people would walk out.
>
> There were some pretty upset people at other people. A lot of this was coming from Stevie and Lindsey's differences about how they viewed this next tour. We were all on board for this tour. Everyone had signed on for it. They were booking it. Everything was going fine. And what Lindsey originally wanted to do was have three or four months to do some solo touring and get that out of the way because he had a new record he wanted to put out, and then do the Mac.
>
> They framed it in the press that he didn't want to tour. That isn't true. He wanted to tour. But there were a couple of bad exchanges in meetings and other things that led to some high drama with Stevie. When Stevie came out and did her speech and talked about Tom [Petty], I felt that she did a wonderful job. But they were there to celebrate the legacy of Fleetwood Mac.
>
> I think Stevie felt that Lindsey was rolling his eyes behind her and not being respectful. And he had a little outburst over the house music they played before we went on. He was a little short with some people. That's the only thing I saw happen. It wasn't worth someone getting a life sentence and getting fired for it.

Fleetwood, while agreeing with the decision which kept the band alive even though they were now all in their seventies, called Buckingham's exit "traumatic." But rather than fold up the band totally, he rebooted Fleetwood Mac once again, recruiting longtime Nicks ally Mike Campbell from the Heartbreakers and Crowded House's Neil Finn to plug the huge gap left by Buckingham's departure. And this, he reckoned, was the only way forward for Fleetwood Mac to continue on their own way.

Hardly surprisingly, Buckingham, for so long the band's sonic scientist, took it badly. Within weeks, he signaled his intention to sue. Staring down the barrel at decades of dirty laundry being aired inside a courtroom, the band agreed to a multimillion dollar settlement to keep reputations intact and to prevent another knock-down, drag-out rerun of the Buckingham-Nicks's backstory being played out for a new generation. This time, the chain really was broken, although the musical links forged by the legacy all five of them remain.

And this, according to Mick Fleetwood, should properly be their lasting monument. Speaking in 2019, he reflected on the turbulence of those excess-all-areas times:

> For a while within Fleetwood Mac there were romances and that lifestyle . . . and the other stuff got forgotten—and we really asked for that trouble. We were too open about who we were and what we were doing—probably very naive. All anyone ever asked about was "Who is sleeping with whom?" or "Who is angry with who?"
>
> And you start to feel it's a shame. Now they intelligently talk about what we did musically. That's important to us. We never wanted to make fools of ourselves too many times. I don't think there will be a point where the band's former members all end up back in a good place together. If you'd asked me that years ago, I would have said so, being the old dreamer that I tend to be. But now I just accept things how they are, and try to be civil and open. All of these lovely people have put their hearts and souls into Fleetwood Mac. The music comes back to haunt everyone afterwards anyway—and usually that wins out in the end.

Without control of the board, Buckingham had no choice but to accept checkmate, a king deposed by his own subjects. He told *Rolling Stone*,

> The one thing that does bother me and breaks my heart is we spent forty-three years always finding a way to rise above our personal differences and our difficulties to pursue and articulate a higher truth. That is our legacy. That is what the songs are about. This is not the way you end something like this.

The Supremes: Florence Ballard, Mary Wilson, and Diana Ross
Photofest

4

THE SUPREMES

The black limo, the kind of celebrity vehicle only A-listers use, inched its way toward Detroit's New Bethel Baptist Church. Rising up from the crowded sidewalk was an almost imperceptible hum—a murmur that was a mixture of awkward anticipation and breathless excitement. A phalanx of police officers cleared a path for the car, ushering away all the people craning their necks for a glimpse of its famous passenger through the tinted windows.

When the car trundled to a halt in front of the church, a dinner-jacketed chauffeur leaped out. Two more men dressed in menacing black emerged from the back and assumed their default positions, eyes darting nervously toward the sea of faces. Seconds later the object of their vigilance emerged into the early morning daylight, a small, almost frail-looking woman dressed in a black coat trimmed with sable at the collar and cuffs and wearing a matching knit cloche-style hat.

Flanked by four stony-faced bodyguards, Diana Ross picked her way gently through the throng and the battery of news reporters, TV cameramen, and photographers jostling for space. She kept her eyes fixed on the ground but could not have failed to notice the shift in the crowd's mood. Slowly, a few catcalls became the cue for other stronger shouts of derision. Up ahead in the long line waiting to be seated stood Mary Wilson, and Diana's mother, Ernestine, whose pained expression mirrored what everyone else knew was an inconvenient truth.

Diana Ross was an unwelcome mourner at the funeral of Florence Ballard, her former teenage friend who, with Mary, had emerged from the
ghettos of Detroit to become the Supremes, thoroughbreds in the gilded
stable of the emerging Motown music label. Three black ingénues who, for
a while in the 1960s, were part of music's elite, the most famous girl group
on the planet. Three gender-assertive girls who rode the elevator of fame
right to the top before it crashed back to earth without a safety override.

The Supremes blended sassiness and sequined dresses with sex appeal
and sizzling honeyed vocals. But the sweetness had long ago turned to
sour in a tragi-tale of dreams, sex, success, and heartbreaking betrayal.
And Florence Ballard, who had founded the group as an escape from the
slum-ridden projects of Detroit, was the principal patsy, a hapless victim
churned up inside the grinder of Motown politics and spewed out like
a piece of garbage. Kicked out of the band at the height of their fame,
bloated, burned out, and spiraling headlong into a life of alcoholism, marital abuse, and abject poverty.

Raped at the age of fifteen, she naturally carried the scars throughout
a life that once shone like a comet only to burn out like a meteor on its
reentry into a world shorn of showbiz artifice. But when the blame game
was later played out over Florence's professional and personal downfall, the
chips always fell at the feet of Diana Ross. The bandmate whose cutthroat
ambition and unflinching determination to be out front was said to have
ultimately forced Florence out of the Supremes. A shattered sisterhood that
lit the fuse on years of bitchy bickering and finger-pointing recriminations.

And now here they were, in February 1976, Mary and Diana awkwardly
reunited in grief, Florence lying in a silver open casket, a Cinderella life
turned to dust at the age of just thirty-two. And Diana having to fight off
angry accusations from fans of rank hypocrisy, while shedding "crocodile
tears" over the fate of tragic Flo. Appalled by this "self-serving sanctimony"
was Mark Bego, a friend of Flo's who insists Diana's presence at the funeral
smacked of a public relations sham. And, despite the passing of time, the
events of that day still leave a bitter aftertaste. He recalled,

> All of a sudden, in one grand and dramatic motion, Miss Ross catapulted her-
> self into the church, flanked by two burly male bodyguards. She quickly shot
> through the open doorway, and down the center aisle. She simultaneously ap-
> peared and let out a sobbing scream. She then appeared to swoon to the point
> of being seconds away from collapsing mid-aisle. The two male bodyguards
> swept her up by the arms and whisked her to the front of the church.
>
> I had never seen such a choreographed display of drama in my life. It ap-
> peared to be the worst act of mock mourning that I had ever seen. It was

Florence's funeral, and Miss Ross acted like she was out to steal the show, in much the same way—I feel—she stole the Supremes away from Ballard, and turned the group into Diana Ross and the Supremes. In my opinion, Diana didn't even allow Florence to be the star of her own funeral.

Stardom, of course, was once the dream for Flo, Diana, and Mary. Liberation from the cul-de-sac of a dead-end future in a downtown typing pool or a factory production line. Raised in a Baptist tradition, Florence quickly discovered the joy of singing in church, a talent she nurtured through her teens. And music was the bond that tied her to Mary Wilson, a fellow pupil at Northeastern High School who lived in the same projects. Detroit's nascent music scene was already catching fire.

A number of groups were fast emerging from the giant melting pot of Motor City. Among the most promising was the Primes, a black doo-wop group whose ranks included Eddie Kendricks and Paul Williams, who years down the line would be the key components of the Temptations. The Primes were managed by local talent hustler Milton Jenkins, who was then scouring the streets of Detroit to create a female counterpart called the Primettes.

A talent show was held, and Flo saw her opportunity to trade mundane for the main chance. Jenkins was struck by the doe-eyed girl whose soulful vocal delivery conjured up echoes of Etta James and Aretha Franklin. Impressed, he even agreed to Flo's cheeky suggestion that her friend Mary be allowed to join the fledgling group. Mary, in turn, recommended her neighbor, Diane Ross, as a third member—the name-change to Diana was a social affectation that came later.

The lineup was completed by Betty McGowan, who was dating Paul Williams. This gave both groups the kind of interconnection that suited Jenkins perfectly. Word quickly spread about the hottest music tickets in Detroit. Promoters saw dollar signs and fell over themselves to book both bands at local sock hops. In 1960, the Primettes auditioned for Motown Records, the pioneering Detroit record label started just a couple years earlier by Berry Gordy. Motown, a contraction of Motor City, had turned Gordy into the city's starmaker supreme, but he turned them down, tossing them back into the school pool and telling them to come back when they had honed their act into something worthy of his time.

Undaunted, a year later—minus Betty—they were back in his office and this time a swish of Gordy's pen put them on the company payroll. There was, though, one nonnegotiable condition; they had to change their name. Thinking Ballard held most sway over group decisions, Gordy gave her a list of names to choose from that included suggestions such as "the Darleens," "the Sweet Ps" "the Melodees," "the Royaltones," and "the Jewelettes." Ballard chose "the Supremes," a name that Ross initially disliked as she felt it too masculine.

Nevertheless, on January 15, 1961, the group signed with Motown as the Supremes, and they became Gordy's special project. Over the next few years, the Supremes toiled away at Hitsville, Motown's equivalent of New York's Brill Building. They recorded several songs, none of which even dented the outer rim of the *Billboard* 100. But Gordy was convinced they had chart-topping potential. Most observers singled out Ballard and Wilson as the group's strongest vocalists. But even in those incipient days, Ross—all pipe cleaner limbs and bright, bulging eyes—projected a quintessential combination of charisma, desire, and sex appeal. And her talent for self-promotion was evident to anyone who had eyes.

Despite still being in her late teens, Diana had already traded innocent coquettishness for sexual control. The corridors at Motown already buzzed with rumors of affairs with the likes of Smokey Robinson, then second in command to Gordy. But power, to Diana Ross, was the real aphrodisiac, and her femininity was the quid pro quo that established dominion—over Florence and Mary, over the future of the Supremes, over her own destiny, and, ultimately, over Berry Gordy, even though he was fifteen years her senior.

To a red-blooded man like Gordy, the pheromones were irresistible, even though it would be a few years before he eventually acted on his libido. Mentored by Gordy, encouraged by Smokey Robinson, and tapping into the hitmaking Motown pipeline of Holland-Lamont-Dozier, the Supremes eventually hit paydirt with "Where Did Our Love Go"—a song, incidentally, they all disliked—which in 1964 topped the charts on both sides of the Atlantic.

It was the start of an unbroken seven-year golden run of hit singles that ensured Diana Ross, Mary Wilson, and Flo Ballard reigned supreme as the decade's most successful all-female group. Fame and fortune naturally followed—as did the forces of enmity that can tear asunder even the closest of friendships.

Scottish broadcaster Stuart Cosgrove, a former commissioning editor for *Channel4* and the author of a highly acclaimed trilogy of books chronicling the growth of soul music in America, is convinced the seeds of their future rifts were first planted in the earliest days of their teenage years growing up in the Brewster projects. Even in poverty, there were social distinctions.

He told me,

> The Supremes met on the Brewster-Douglass Housing Projects in Detroit, an area of the city that has been built for the city's "working poor" but poverty had so many meanings—poverty of opportunity, poverty of racial discrimination and poverty in the purer sociological sense. Mary Wilson told me that whilst the girls grew up as neighbors, they came from quite different social experiences.
>
> Diana Ross's house was immaculate, fastidiously domesticated and well provided for. Her mother Ernestine (a chaperone at Motown) was a stickler for table manners and decorum, whilst Flo Ballard's household was chaotic, troubled and mired by alcoholism. Although they were both black, their upbringings could not have been more different.

During these early years at Motown they worked tirelessly in the studio to find their breakthrough moment, while accepting the grind of touring. Cosgrove offered this observation:

> In 1965 The Supremes worked harder than any group before or since, travelling daily, never turning down television and working through illnesses to make the break. No one grafted the way they did. It was common for them to be in concert in the Midwest at night but to fly to-and-from New York to record TV shows. Their itinerary of live shows is exhausting just to read. They are the personification of the adage that perspiration is more important than inspiration.

In those aspirational days, all three members took turns singing lead: Wilson favored soft ballads, Ballard preferred soulful, hard-driven songs, and Ross was a fan of mainstream pop songs. Florence was a feisty woman, who often spoke her mind without a filter.

Unlike the sylph-like Diana, Florence was all curves and refused to conform to, especially, Gordy's template of what he envisioned a pop star goddess should look like. The two often clashed over songs, over her appearance, and, eventually, over everything.

"He would say, 'Flo, you don't know how to be a star,'" said Ballard of Gordy.

> And maybe I didn't because as far as I was concerned, I was a person and I had to be a person. I couldn't be anything else. It's frightening to go all the way to the top, and somebody says to you that you have to be a star, that you can't mingle with certain people.

I was supposed to carry myself like a star. I knew I was a big entertainer. I knew I was rich. I knew I was making lots of money; I knew this. I had beautiful clothes, diamonds, everything at my feet; but to me a star is something in the sky, and to me I was a human being.

Away from the carefully choreographed stage moves and photo sessions, tensions inevitably crept in. Especially since, by 1965, Gordy's interest in Diana Ross had officially shifted from the boardroom to the bedroom. And Mary and Flo would soon become the casualties of this lust-filled obsession.

Diana was the embodiment of everything Gordy believed a star should be: sexy, sassy, sensual, suggestive—those come-to-bed eyes—and single-minded. Sleeping with the boss only empowered Diana even more, knowing that she was virtually untouchable when it came to internal band politics. More and more, she decided on the songs and the sequins, often opting on a last-minute costume change to ensure she stood out more to a live audience.

Slowly, Diana took center stage and sang lead on more songs, especially the singles. In the public's mind, the Supremes were fast morphing into Diana Ross and two backing singers. Away from the stage, she insisted on being called Miss Ross by Motown flunkies. And any time she didn't get her own way, she was quickly on the hotline to the man in the big chair.

Wilson said, "Diana was obsessed not with being a star, but *the* star. Flo and I were still hopeful that we might be singing more leads or more solo spots in live shows. Little did we know that our fates were sealed."

Still understandably traumatized by having been raped as a teenager, Flo was a young woman riddled with insecurity while, at the same time, riding the train to fame. Mark Ribowsky, author of the book *The Supremes: A Saga of Motown Dreams, Success, and Betrayal*, said, "Once she was replaced by Diana as the lead vocalist, it blended along with all her other demons. It ate away at her like battery acid and she would do anything to cross Gordy. It was almost like she was seeing what she could get away with. But it was a game of chicken she could not possibly win."

Ballard, though, refused to be cowed or forced into the margins of a group she had founded. She recalled, "We had a routine when performing 'Stop! In the Name of Love' where, at the end of the tune, we'd throw both arms up in the air. Well, people used to ask me: 'Why did Diana always get in front of Mary, right in front of her when she threw her arms up?' blocking Wilson completely from view."

"Mary," said Flo,

would always tell me, "Whatever she says to you, don't say anything back to her, because you know what they want you to do—they want you to keep arguing back and forth so they can get you out of the group." This was the first I'd heard of that. I told Mary that if Diana said something mean to me, I would tell her to go to hell—and a lot of other things.

Watching the drama unfold, Mary couldn't avoid the carefully stage-managed pincer movement between Gordy and Diana to oust Flo from the group. When Gordy stripped Flo of her one moment in the solo spotlight, singing "People" from the musical *Funny Girl*, handing the song to Diana, the game was up. Mary recalled in her own memoir *Dreamgirl: My Life as a Supreme*,

> Diana's blatant scene-stealing could not be ignored and my two best friends were starting to act as if they hated each other. . . . I could sense that our friendship had changed. It was no longer the three of us—it was Diana and Berry on one side and me and Florence on the other. With all this success, we were falling apart internally. It came to light in early 1967 that plans were underway to change our name to Diana Ross and the Supremes.
>
> This was not just a crisis for Flo, it was a turning point for the Supremes. Whenever we had drama before, I had always been in the middle. I usually remain calm amid chaos, but I knew I couldn't fix this situation. Flo had never dealt with being abused as a teenager and now fear and depression were taking over her life. She could no longer hide her pain.
>
> While Diana and I loved the constant touring, Flo did not. She racked up hundreds of dollars in telephone bills calling her family. There were missed gigs, excessive drinking and an increased amount of resentment toward Diana and Berry. My life became consumed by trying to keep the peace and watching over Flo.

Mary wasn't alone in fearing for Flo's existential future as a Supreme. Rumors of Gordy's determination to move the needle and drive a wedge between Diana and the others were rife among those in the Motown family. The Temptations' Otis Williams, with whom Ballard had a brief affair, was among those who warned her about the forces of darkness shadowing her. He told her in the frankest terms: "Berry wants you out so Diana can be the star." There would be no letup in the personal onslaught. Nothing was off the table, including fat shaming a young woman riddled with self-doubt.

"Berry knew how to get to me. He wanted to control me and if he couldn't control me he didn't want me around," declared Flo. "He treated me like a puppet who should dance to his tune. Well, I ain't anyone's puppet and I don't dance to anyone's tune. He would say to me: 'Florence you're too fat.' I'm a size twelve and maybe next to Diana I was fat, but I knew I was pretty well put together. I had a nice body."

Of course, Gordy held all the cards, insisting it was nothing personal, just business. Wilson said, "Unlike Berry, Flo could not separate the personal from the professional. You were either her friend all the way in everything or you were her enemy. There was no in between." Resentful and depressed at having been pushed out of the spotlight, Ballard relied heavily on alcohol as a balm for her frustration. She began to miss studio sessions and gigs, forcing the promoters to find a last-minute replacement from another group.

She gained more weight, her stomach occasionally seen protruding beneath her top in a further act of rebellion. Truthfully, she provided all the bullets for Gordy to fire. With a jet-set life had come a jet-set lifestyle for each Supreme. Feted wherever they went, they each acquired a taste for fine champagnes and wines. Mary and Diana could hold their booze, but Flo was a notorious lightweight when it came to the corrosive effects of alcohol.

There would also be no pause from the carousel of appearances, studio sessions, and TV shows, a relentless pace that only helped to pour oil on troubled waters within the group. The end finally came in May 1967 at New York's Copacabana Club when Berry fired her for allegedly being drunk onstage. "I had had me a few drinks and that is not unusual," she confessed.

> All of us had drinks before we went on stage. But Berry knew how to get to me. He wanted to control me and if he couldn't control me, he didn't want me around. And they kept calling me fat so much until I went on stage, and I poked my stomach out as far as I could, giving Gordy the excuse he'd been looking for. He called me up the next morning and he said, "You're fired." And I said, "I'm what?" And he said, "You're fired." I said, "I'm not." And he said, "Well, you're not going on stage tonight." I said, "Yes, I am; who's going to stop me?" He said, "I will. I'll have you thrown off if you go on."

And so it went on and on. It was the end of the sister act for Ballard, who was quickly replaced by Cindy Birdsong, an identikit singer who had, in fact, been secretly primed as her replacement for more than a year. Amazingly, Birdsong looked so like Flo that from a distance some fans never noticed the difference. Even though the move had long been telescoped, other Motown acts were furious.

Few of them, especially the likes of Martha Reeves and the members of the Marvelettes, had any time for Diana's get-out-of-my-way ambition. "I saw them get to the point where they disagreed big time," recalled Reeves. "I think it was mainly at the point when they put Diana Ross's name out front."

The Temptations scolded Wilson for failing to defend Ballard when she was ousted from the group. They were "so pissed off" at Flo's sacking that they fired off a telegram to [her], which read, "Mary, stick with Flo, you might be next—the Tempts." Flo's expulsion was immediately followed by the official renaming of the group.

Overnight, they became "Diana Ross and the Supremes," the meaning and the symbolism crystal clear. With her major rival for lead singer finally out of the way, Diana could take over. It was the first serious step toward Gordy's ultimate goal of eventually easing Diana out of the group and into the stratosphere of solo stardom. Under the terms of a hastily agreed settlement, Flo was given $140,000. But, in a twisted act of petulance, Gordy shockingly forbid her to even mention that she had been in the Supremes— or that she had, in fact, picked the group's name. A ploy that was clearly a nonstarter, no matter how much money was involved. His goal was to all but airbrush Flo out of the group's history.

Abandoned by Gordy, abandoned by her soul sisters, abandoned by the system—until that day eight years later when she took her final curtain call not just as a Supreme but also as a member of the human race. Mark Ribowsky remains outraged over the way Gordy—and by association, Motown—treated Flo. He said, "What happened to Flo was the shame of Motown. If Flo were alive today, it would be scarifying for her to look back on those years. She was actually due about $1.6 million . . . that's how much the Supremes had earned. Imagine being due $1.6 million and having to settle for $140,000."

In these intervening years, Diana Ross had quit the group to follow the route that had long been mapped out for her by Gordy, her mentor, her lover, and clandestinely, the father of her first child. But, equally importantly, it was a path she had always mapped out for herself. She was seen as the ultimate Motown star, one that was always going to break free from the group's suffocating prison to soar onto even greater heights. Her final appearance with the Supremes came in January 1970.

The band's last single with her name emblazoned in neon was the ironically titled "Some Day We'll Be Together." Neither Mary nor Cindy Birdsong sang on the record, one final, symbolic stiletto to the heart. As a solo star, and under Gordy's guidance, Diana's career shone brighter than it ever had under the flag of her former group. Her eponymous solo album included the #1 hit "Ain't No Mountain High Enough," a song that could have doubled as her own personal mantra.

Throughout the seventies and beyond, her records continued to sell in spectacular numbers. She was Oscar nominated for her stellar performance as Billie Holiday in the 1972 movie *Lady Sings the Blues*; *Billboard* magazine feted her as "The Female Entertainer of the Century," and in 1993 the *Guinness Book of World Records* declared her the most successful female pop artist of all time for her work with the Supremes and as a solo artist. In 2007, she was garlanded with Kennedy Center Honors and ten years later was presented with the Presidential Medal of Freedom by Barack Obama, a blue-ribboned salute to a lifetime of greatness from one black icon to another.

Hailing her as an inspiration for so many women of color—such as Beyonce, Whitney Houston, and Alicia Keys—Obama said, "She has exuded glamour and grace and filled stages that helped to shape the sound of Motown." It was yet more vindication of the drive and ruthless aspiration—not forgetting the luminous and genuine talent—that had propelled her from the Detroit projects some six decades earlier. Yet, for many, the perception remained of egotistical vanity, a stop-at-nothing diva, who would trample over anyone to get her own way.

Florence Ballard's shocking and premature death and Diana's eyebrow-raising behavior at the funeral only served to underline that widely held viewpoint. A few months before her death, Mary Wilson had thrown Flo a lifeline by inviting her onstage for her first live show in five years to sing as a Supreme one last time at a benefit in their home city of Detroit.

"It was so obvious that the public loved her," said Mary, who had remained in close contact in the eight years since she had left the group. "Yet that just wasn't enough." Her sudden death from a coronary thrombosis caused an outpouring of grief among those around her, if far too little reaction from the wider world. Diana, for all their frostiness, spoke with commendable honesty in the immediate aftermath of Ballard's passing to *Sounds*.

"She was a good mother, she was talented, she had a lot of class, she carried herself very well," she said before releasing an arrow from her quiver, "but there was something inside of her that was just pulling, that she wasn't able to handle." Florence's death, however, gave Diana's critics further ammunition to lob verbal bullets over her own part in Florence's fall from grace. "When she lived with me, she tore up about ten telephones of mine, throwing them against the wall," said Flo's sister Maxine. "She would drink, she would smash things out of the anger that she felt. She felt betrayed by Motown and Berry Gordy and she felt betrayed by [Ross and Wilson] because she felt they should have stood up for her."

That simmering resentment was on full display the day she was laid to rest by the Rev. C. L. Franklin, father of Aretha. Then came the stage-managed drama. Inside, seated with Flo's family, Ross grabbed Ballard's youngest daughter, Lisa, and placed the child on her lap. Photographers snapped away, and the picture of Ross and little Lisa was published around the world—the only image, as it turned out, that most people ever saw of Florence Ballard's funeral.

Halfway through the ceremony, as flashbulbs lit up the packed church, Diana unexpectedly walked toward the altar and took the microphone. Then she told the congregation, "Mary and I would like to have a silent prayer." As she beckoned Mary toward her, her formed bandmate was left completely bewildered. "At first I was stunned," she recalled in *Dreamgirl*:

> Diana and I hadn't spoken to each other in months. I was furious that I was being dragged into this. My grief was private and personal. I didn't want to get up, but I was so taken aback by Diana's words that I felt I had no choice. Declining would have made a bad situation worse. There were things I wanted to say, but to Flo, by myself. But I got up and stood beside Diana, who said, "I believe nothing disappears and Flo will always be with us." Then she handed me the mic. "I loved her very much" was all I could say.

The scenes at the funeral did nothing to defrost the layers of ice that now separated the two women. After Diana's exit from the Supremes, Mary had tried to keep the group's flame alive. But without Miss Ross's megawatt star power, it was always going to be a losing battle. The last iteration of the band eventually died in 1977, leaving Mary to join the likes of Martha Reed and other acts in Motown revue packages. But, like Diana, there was no real escape from her ever-present past. Almost every interview would rake over old coals. Deep-rooted resentment was inevitably brought out of cold storage, even though Mary would often preface any criticism of her former school friend and bandmate with the words "I love Diana but. . . ."

As music historians began to peel back the veils of the group's tangled history, a picture emerged of Diana that contrasted completely with the familiar Motown image of the doe-eyed fawn who was the picture of innocence as the lead singer of the Supremes. She was, in fact, portrayed as a predator who weaponized sex to achieve her career ambitions—an accusation normally leveled at men. But Stuart Cosgrove insists that kind of stereotypical observation is wide of the mark.

He told me,

I have much more respect for Diana Ross than her many distractors. She was an extremely ambitious teenager, supposedly the first black girl to be hired as an assistant in Hudson's department store and she attended Cass Technical College studying fashion, which was not taught at mainstream schools.

She had an intolerant streak, but it was mostly intolerant of unprofessionalism or of slacking. She wanted to be a solo star and drove that aspiration, but she had something else—she made the Supremes international with a pop culture aura that stretched out beyond the soul groups of the American ghetto. However, it is measured, she had star quality.

Over the years, plans for a Supremes reunion between Diana, Mary, and Cindy Birdsong would intermittently surface only to just as quickly become yesterday's news. Their one appearance together—at a star-studded 1983 concert to celebrate Motown's 25th anniversary—turned into an awkward collision of egos and Diana's unquenchable need to be center stage.

"Someday We'll Be Together" had been earmarked as a showstopping finale, one that could signal closure and bring an end to old hostilities. Instead, it swiftly turned into a shambles when Mary started singing the second verse. Unknown to her, a host of Motown icons like Smokey Robinson and Stevie Wonder emerged from the wings to take part in the finale.

Mary blamed Diana for upstaging her and got her revenge by introducing Gordy from the stage—a tribute call that was supposed to be done by Diana. And then, according to Mary, Diana actually pushed her, drawing gasps from the audience.

"In a flash I saw something in her eyes that told me she had crossed the line," declared Mary.

The sad part about this is that we were kind of put together without really having any pre-idea of what we were going to do—that being Diana and myself. We had very little time to really get together and hug and kiss and all. Our rehearsal time was cut down to maybe fifteen minutes, and we hadn't seen each other in a long time. So, when we got on stage, what happened was that I didn't know that certain things had been planned to say.

I kind of said certain things, and I guess I wasn't supposed to say those because they had been planned to do it another way. And that disrupted the program. That's really kind of what happened. It not only spoiled my moment, but it kind of spoiled the Supremes' moment in terms of coming together. And we weren't able to finish our song.

Sparring from the sidelines continued over the years as both women fought to control the moral high ground over their past, present, and future. But in terms of success, there was only one real winner. Diana's career arc had long justified her decision to free herself from the group.

Cosgrove, for one, remains convinced Ross has no reason to adopt a guilt complex over the fortunes of others. He said, "No, she once talked of civil rights in very unusual ways saying, 'I have the right to be as famous as any white girl on the planet.' It was not what Dr. Martin Luther King had in mind, but it is a civil right which had been denied many African-American singers before her, so that deserves recognition and respect."

But, like so many others in the music industry, she found it impossible to completely cast off the shackles of her past. Calls for a Supremes' reunion became even more shrill as one millennium turned into another. So Diana's surprise announcement to reform the group in 2000 for a world tour, with Cindy Birdsong again stepping into old heels—thirty years after they had disbanded—was met with a combination of surprise and skepticism.

The simple question was why? She didn't need the money, and she certainly didn't need the hassle of reopening still-festering wounds with Mary. But the corona-watering figures being banded around by promoters SFX told their own story. The ultimate multimillion payday was at stake for all three woman, then all in their fifties. The kind of nest egg ordinary people could only dream of. But it quickly became the stuff of nightmares.

As in days of old, Diana legitimately saw herself as being first among equals. She was the star who deserved top billing and top remuneration. That meant a reported $20 million for her, $2 million for Mary, and $1 million for Cindy. To no one's surprise the wheels sheared off the reunion bandwagon almost instantly. Mary complained she had been frozen out of the financial negotiations and dismissed the offer as "degrading"; Diana, unconvincingly, blamed the promoters for the financial disparities. "Diana and I should have been there from the start to talk about it," said Mary, who, nevertheless, watched a shedload of money vanish into the mist. "She did not want to talk first, she wanted to do the business first."

Asked by one interviewer about a reported $12–$15 million dollar payday for Diana, she bristled:

How about $15–20 million? I was supposed to get $2 million, then maybe $3 million. That's not enough? What do you mean? I think fair would be the better word. Or deserving. I think it's about what my significance in the group is as a founding member. Some people say it shouldn't be about money, but I'm not stupid anymore; I'm not naive anymore. For once in my life, I'm going to think about me. How degrading.

Elsewhere, she got down to the nitty-gritty: "They didn't want to pay me. It was all about the money."

Horrified that age-old enmities were again being played out in public, Diana called in favors from prime-time American broadcasters in a rare public rebuttal of Mary's furious claims. She told Barbara Walters,

> I did not want to get into the numbers of the tour. I did not negotiate with her. I called her on the phone and said, "The fans really want a reunion tour. Are you interested?" The first thing she said was "What took you so long to call?" And I'm saying it nicer than she did. I thought she would have been happy about it.
>
> I spoke to the promoters, and they made me an offer, they made Cindy an offer and they made Mary an offer. But it was never enough. I think if we had offered her the moon, she would not have been happy. I doubled their offer so she could come and do this tour. She didn't have to pay for anything—not a hotel room, not a car, not a music arrangement, not a set. Nothing. All she needed to do was show up.

In terms of PR optics, it was a disaster; two former Supremes bitching about each other in the media, kicking into the long grass that old adage about time and wounds. Diana forged ahead with the tour, now awkwardly billed as "Diana Ross and the Supremes Tour: A Celebration of the Music."

Not surprisingly, it quickly unraveled and was denounced as a sham. Fans who had shelled out top-dollar prices in the expectation of re-creating their 1960's adolescence and seeing three Supremes back onstage in shimmering gowns put Diana in the dock over the debacle and quickly returned a guilty verdict by shunning the shows in droves. Half-empty auditoriums were a huge embarrassment, arguably the lowest point of Diana's touring career.

The lowest point of the tour came in Columbus, Ohio, when there were fewer than 3,000 people in a 22,000-capacity arena. Bob Grossweiner, a concert industry analyst, blamed the failure of the tour on Diana's standoff over money. "There has never been a tour brought by a national promoter that's done as bad as this one and had a clash over money like this one," he told the *New York Times*.

"This is one of the first times that from the first press conference, a tour had bad press. Mary Wilson went on national TV and blasted the tour. So you had all this negativity coming in and high ticket prices and an audience that was confused. Plus, it was essentially a Diana Ross show, because she didn't interact with the other women." Bridges still burning out of control could not be rebuilt. And then, suddenly, the issue of a reunion was laid to rest with a numbing finality.

Mary's unexpected death at the age of seventy-six in February 2021 left Diana Ross as the last surviving member of the original lineup. She and Berry Gordy issued statements that sounded more superficial than sympathetic. Perhaps they simply wanted to avoid the kind of accusations of hypocrisy that followed Florence Ballard's death and funeral.

Before her death, Mary and Diana had drawn a line under their shared, antagonistic past while perhaps wondering where their love really did go. Embedded in their storied history, however, is a musical legacy in the sixties of twelve #1 hits—a feat only bettered by the Beatles and Elvis Presley.

Their influence has trickled down through the decades, inspiring other all-female black groups like Destiny's Child, Sister Sledge, and the Pointer Sisters. The Ross-Wilson-Ballard lineup was inducted into the Rock & Roll Hall of Fame in 1988. *Rolling Stone* later placed the group at #97 on their list of 100 Greatest Artists of All Time. Stuart Cosgrove is among those content to filter out the noise surrounding the group politic to laud instead the Supremes' monumental contribution to soul music.

He said, "I see them as the biggest success story of Motown's popularization of soul music in that they registered so many hit singles in countries around the world singing evergreen songs that remain popular to this day. They had another major influence in that they were the most successful African-American girl group in a decade when girl groups were in their prime."

Phil Everly and Don Everly
Photofest

5

THE EVERLY BROTHERS

The sniper's mocking barb found its mark with unerring accuracy, as if propelled by a laser-like verbal precision. "Where's your brother?" Squinting out toward a sea of faces in the half-filled auditorium, Don Everly tried to pick out the heckler before quickly realizing the futility of the situation. Shifting uncomfortably on the stage, he tried instead to parry the taunt with an awkward stab at humor: "I don't know . . . have you seen him?" But the follow-up remark, delivered in all seriousness, laid bare years of pent-up hostility, rancor, and bad blood between Don and his younger sibling Phil: "The Everly Brothers died ten years ago."

And now here was Don, flying without his wingman, delivering the last rites to one of music's most influential groups. Two hours earlier the same man, loaded with booze, had staggered about drunk onstage at the John Wayne Theater at Knotts Berry Farm theme park in California, forgetting the words to classic Everly Brothers' songs such as "Cathy's Clown," "Walk Right Back," "Wake Up Little Susie," and "Til I Kissed You," each of them a homage to their shared adolescence.

Watching from his side of the single microphone they had always shared, Phil Everly was horrified and knew they had finally reached rock bottom. Quickest to react was Bill Hollingshead, the venue's entertainment manager, who rushed onstage and signaled for the curtain to immediately come crashing down on the show and, metaphorically, the Everly Brothers' career. Phil stormed into the wings, throwing his Gibson acoustic guitar to the floor, and left the building, swearing to Hollingshead that he would never share a stage with his brother again.

The date was July 14, 1973, and the venue illustrated perfectly how far the Everlys' star had fallen since those heady days in the late fifties and early sixties when, as the early architects of rock 'n' roll heartbreak, they sold out vast theaters and, between 1957 and 1962, shipped a reported $35 million worth of singles and albums across the globe. Now, they were a group out of time and out of road, reduced to playing cabaret shows in front of a chicken-in-a-basket audience at a theme park. Both men were already resigned to these shows drawing a line under the Everly Brothers as a band, and closing the book on their beautiful mystery.

Don later told *Rolling Stone*, "I was very emotional before the show. I was half in the bag that evening—the only time I've ever been drunk on stage in my life. I knew it was the last night, and on the way out I drank some Tequila, drank some champagne—started celebrating the demise. It was really a funeral."

Standing in the wings on this fateful night was Crystal Zevon, wife of Warren, a key member of the brothers' touring band. She recalled,

> Warren wanted me to be there for the Everly Brothers' last performance. We arrived and Don was drinking heavily. I'd seen Don perform with the flu and a temperature of 103 degrees. I'd never heard him hit a sour note or be anything short of professional in front of an audience. But, this night, he walked onstage dead drunk. He was stumbling and off key, and I remember Phil trying to restart songs several times.
>
> It was embarrassing. The fourth or fifth song they did was "Wake Up, Little Susie," and Don was forgetting people's names and insulting the audience and Phil. Finally, Phil stormed offstage. He smashed his guitar and said, "I quit." It was stunning.

Ron Coleman, the brothers' long-time guitarist, was equally shocked by the ferocity of Phil's outburst. He recalled, "Phil took his guitar and just popped it on the floor and it just exploded. I don't think there was a piece left that was more than six inches long." This latest outbreak of quibbling siblings had been a long time in arriving. For years, stories about bust-ups, walk-outs, and nose-to-nose atmospherics had run on parallel lines to the sheer genius of the vocal blend they had long patented, of the ethereal beauty found in the magical lockstep of their voices.

No one close to them, however, could fail to notice an inescapable truth—their partnership had irreversibly flatlined. Still, for long-time fans of the group, it was a publicly jaw-dropping episode, the biggest onstage breakup in music history. Esteemed British music broadcaster Bob Harris reckons it was simply the culmination of two people being forced together when, really, they required their own form of social distancing.

He told me,

> They had been standing there side by side strumming their guitars for the best part of twenty years. And here they were in 1973 still doing the same thing, still singing the same songs, going to different dressing rooms, not really talking. Yes, they did appear on stage, but their relationship was very argumentative. It's very difficult when you have got a lot of stuff going on in your head, and yet you are expected to be this person on stage and be in the spotlight. Sometimes that contradiction just gets too much.
>
> Don, I think, was just sick of it. And the more he was forced back on to that stage, the more he began to resent it. So there is an inevitable bubble-bursting moment and that night was it. Though, I really do know how it could get to that point. Obviously, there's the pride. When you've been up on those big stages, and played to those massive, adoring audiences, and then bit by bit you've watched everything fall away, it's very, very hard.

Just a few weeks earlier that same year there had been at least one well-telegraphed signal of the blow-up to come. In May, the brothers had been engaged to play alongside Nancy Sinatra at the famous Sands Hotel in Las Vegas. Sinatra, a scion of music royalty, was an old friend of both men and a huge fan, having herself grown up to the sounds of the Everly Brothers' breakthrough hits, much to her father Frank's disdain. But she, too, was dismayed by the ferocity of an argument at an afternoon rehearsal that saw both men rip up the terms of their engagement at the venue that was, of course, a favorite Rat Park haunt where the Chairman of the Board (Frank Sinatra) would famously hold court with everyone from Vegas mobsters to corrupt local politicians paying fealty.

"It was a very sad thing to see," recalled Sinatra. "It wasn't a secret that they didn't always get along, but to see it with your own eyes was pretty shocking really." It was just another sign that the end was nigh as they acted out their own version of sneer and loathing in Las Vegas.

After the curtain came down at Knotts Berry Farm, the two men's relationship would be placed in a ten-year deep freeze, an alienation that only thawed once—at their father Ike's funeral in 1975.

Phil said later,

> We needed to take a long vacation, to get off the merry-go-round. There were too many people making money off us, keeping us going. The tensions between Don and I . . . well, we're just a family that is like that. Everything that

was happening then was contributing to it. You're up there nose-to-nose at the microphone and pretty soon he starts breathing your air. But you could just as easily say that the tension between us was there from day one, from birth.

And that has to be the starting point for anyone peeling back the layers of the Everlys' tangled pathology. For all their voices seemed to blend telepathically, Don and Phil Everly were polar opposites when family DNA was stripped out. Don, who usually took the lead vocals, was an extrovert who loved the spotlight that fame brought—and the attentive rewards of being on the road for weeks at a time; Phil, two years his junior, preferred the homespun charms of their Kentuckian upbringing and could quite easily find contentment in his own company while passing himself off as a soft-spoken southern gentleman; politically, they were also in opposite corners—Don was a freewheeling liberal Democrat but Phil put his faith in the conservative Republican values so redolent of many Southern states.

Then, of course, there was the added spice of quite normal sibling rivalry sprinkled over what was already a combustible mix. Binding them together, however, was the unbridled joy their singing brought. They first began performing together while both were still in short trousers.

Ike Everly had discovered his gift for playing guitar and singing provided a welcome escape from the Kentucky coalmines—and soon he had roped his two boys into the act. Young Don and Phil were schooled in the Appalachian hillbilly songs handed down through generations.

Growing into teenagers, they often sang together on radio shows, showcasing a synthesis of local traditional and country music. Listening from a distance was Chet Atkins, then a key mover and shaker in the influential Nashville scene. Mentored by Atkins, the two boys, by now teenagers, were introduced to Wesley Rose who, as president of local music publishers Acuff-Rose, carried enormous clout. Sensing a financial jackpot amid the first shoots of rock 'n' roll, Rose promised the brothers a record deal if they would sign on with his company.

This led to the Everly Brothers' deal with Nashville-based Cadence Records and also saw them team up with husband-and-wife songwriting team Felice and Boudleaux Bryant. It was a match made in musical heaven. Despite already being in their late twenties and early thirties, the Bryants had an uncanny knack of being able to tap into youth culture.

And Don and Phil turned out to be the perfect beneficiaries of the Bryant hit-making machine. Between 1957 and 1960, they released several Bryant songs that established them as the cornerstones of the rock 'n' roll wave alongside Elvis Presley and Buddy Holly, with whom they shared an especially close musical kinship. The songs they penned for the Everlys included "Bye Bye Love," "All I Have to Do Is Dream," "Wake Up Little Susie," and "Love Hurts."

With their hair piled high and their gossamer-like doo-wop harmonies, they were the embodiment of homespun pop and a world away from the sexually charged gyrations of Elvis Presley, Chuck Berry's libidinous leer, or even the scandalous lust personified by Jerry Lee Lewis, who had married his thirteen-year-old cousin.

During this period, the singles, backed by equally beguiling B-sides, established them as members of the exclusive new club that also included Presley and Holly. "They had a teeny bop appeal," noted Harris. "But the ballads they were recording appealed to a much more mature audience as well that had perhaps grown up with Johnny Ray, Nat King Cole, and Frank Sinatra. 'All I Want To Do Is Dream' would have been bought by mums and dads as well as teenagers. And, of course, they did look so great. They were good looking boys."

In 1960, they transferred their allegiances to Warner Bros in an eye-watering ten-year $10 million deal, the richest ever struck for a pop act. Each brother would receive $500,000 a year for the next decade, and all they had to do was dream—and keep the WB coffers full of money from their pipeline of hits. No one could criticize two impressionable adolescents cozying up to corporate America. But there would a high price to pay, personally and professionally.

The move to Hollywood coincided with a bitter falling out between the Everlys and Wesley Rose, who, in an act of vengeance, insisted on keeping them tied to his songwriting stable. At the time, Acuff-Rose had a virtual monopoly on all the best songs and songwriters in the music business, especially for the type of music the Everly Brothers played.

The duo's access to the Acuff-Rose catalog, specifically the Bryants, is one of the reasons they were so commercially successful, and the rift with Rose meant the pathway to A-list song material was immediately closed off. In effect, they were blackballed by the man who had helped make them stars.

As a further revenge tactic, Rose flooded the market with old Everly Brothers' songs recorded while they were at Cadence, a move that ensured they were often in chart competition with their own back catalog.

Harris said, "There was an overload eventually. The charts were saturated with the Everly Brothers. And the other thing is that by now Cadence are going deeply into the vault and were releasing songs that were not necessarily of great value. So the quality of the older material was beginning to fall plus the new songs weren't as good as the best of the old songs. So that was running against them as well."

The hits started to dry up and nervous Warners Brothers suits overnight began to question the rash wisdom of their $10 million investment. This despite their first WB single, the self-penned "Cathy's Clown," selling 8 million copies—numbers that, when adjusted for inflation, are largely unparalleled in music today.

Running on twin tracks, however, were the first serious signs of the toll the centrifugal forces of stardom were exacting on Phil's and Don's lives. At the tail end of 1961, they were drafted into the Marine Corps Reserves for a six-month national service stint. Unknown to anyone at the time, Don was slowly falling apart.

He had become hooked on Ritalin and was in the grip of a life-threatening psychosis. It reached the point where he couldn't go onstage without injections and would go days without sleeping. Attempts to keep his condition "in-house" were blown when the brothers were due to begin a month-long UK tour in October 1962. Phil arrived in London on October 9; however, Don had missed his flight and he and his actress wife, Venetia—who was pregnant with their first child—arrived the next day.

According to the Everlys' bass player at the time, Joey Paige, Don had broken down during rehearsals in Los Angeles and had consequently missed the flight to London. However, after arriving, Don passed out during run-throughs before the first show and was rushed to a London hospital. He discharged himself after six hours and returned to his hotel with Venetia.

Once there, Venetia explained that she watched him "gradually slide into unconsciousness," and he was once again taken to the hospital. Venetia told reporters that he was suffering from food poisoning while a spokesman for the Everlys blamed his collapse on "severe physical and nervous exhaustion."

Years later, Don admitted his addiction turned into a life-or-death struggle before the days when drugs and music stars became inextricably linked. "I was so high I didn't know what I was doing," he admitted.

"We were beginning this long tour of England and they sent me over there with all these bottles and needles. It left a hole in my soul and nearly left me for dead. I'm lucky to be alive."

Soon it became obvious Don was in no condition to be onstage. He was quietly shipped back home, leaving Phil to complete the tour on his own. The younger Everly was, nevertheless, surprised at the ease with which he took to singing without his brother. He didn't miss the customary, angst-ridden post-gig post-mortem followed by the usual slamming of doors.

Phil said, "Toward the end of (that) tour I was quite at ease with myself as a solo performer but that doesn't mean I had any thoughts of breaking up the partnership." Not that he could anyway. Neither man could now afford to walk away without incurring career-ending court action from Warner Brothers.

More than ever, they were trapped inside a gilded cage, a claustrophobic situation that only served to ratchet up further their increasingly virulent feelings for each other. Their ongoing legal wrangles with Rose also added to the overall feeling of a tapestry that was badly unraveling.

They were back on the British boards in 1963, for a package tour that saw them top the bill alongside R&B pioneers Bo Diddley, Little Richard—and a new British band called the Rolling Stones, who were on their first national tour. It allowed Mick Jagger and Keith Richards, especially, to pay homage to two of the founding fathers of rock 'n' roll. But Richards was equally impressed by the Everlys, especially their guitar playing while, unknowingly, getting a glimpse of his own complicated future with Jagger.

He wrote in his biography *Life*, "The best rhythm guitar playing I ever heard was from Don Everly. Nobody ever thinks about that. But I knew even then that the Everlys were having problems and that they always did. I didn't know it then, but it was like a mirror image of me and Mick and the way it turned out."

Phil and Don's band were often caught in the crosshairs of their outbursts. Day after day, all the musicians were forced to turn a deaf ear or look wistfully into the distance as rehearsals frequently turned toxic.

Drummer Jim Gordon, who went on to become one of rock's most famous players, said, "They were weird to work with as they fought like crazy. They would play Password on the (tour) bus. Then they would get into fights, and they would stop the bus and have it out. They always kept this star/band relationship. There were only six of us travelling but we would have to sit at the back of the bus, and they sat at the front doing that showbiz thing."

But the wheels of the Everly bus were now coming off at a fast rate as a new phenomenon loomed large in their rearview mirror. At the same time as the tour wrapped, Britain's youth was rocking to the first strains of Beatlemania. Within a year, young America was reeling from the British Invasion and the Everlys were left navigating the downslope of their careers. Overnight, they were being forced to imitate their imitators.

Survival lay in touring and the hope they could still tap into a loyal fan base. The flipside, of course, was that this only added to the intensity of working cheek to jowl. Contracts now called for not only separate dressing

rooms but also separate stage entrances. It was a form of Sisyphus-like torture, two brothers bound together, unable to make their separate ways in the
world, dependent and resentful of each other every minute of the long days.

They couldn't even find common ground on what kind of venues to
play—in America, Phil preferred swanky nightclubs like the Latin Quarter
in New York or the Landmark in Vegas; Don insisted fulfillment lay in
counterculture haunts like the Big Apple's Bitter End and the Fillmore
West in Los Angeles.

"We were working seven, eight, nine months a year—and if you do that
for a period of twenty years you've got a big chunk of your life spent traveling, being a duet in the music business," remembered Don. "Especially
when you do it like Phil and I do—with close harmonies, nose-to-nose. That
puts a lot of strain on the relationship. We were strapped together like a
team of horses."

His younger brother also acknowledged how the rising tide of boardroom
pressures were equally lapping about their ankles as their careers were
caught in the new wave spearheaded by the Beatles. He said, "The real
pressure for us was the business—we had much more to worry about than
some sort of sibling rivalry continuing past adolescence all the way into
adulthood. That's a simplistic kind of viewpoint of what led to the ultimate
end of the Everly Brothers."

Throughout the 1960s, they continued to release albums in order to meet
the terms of their lucrative Warner Brothers contract. Commercially, the
records failed to catch fire, even though the material was still strong. In
1968 they released *Roots*, a deeply personal double album that looked back
on their childhood and brilliantly channeled the growing country rock scene
of the Flying Burrito Brothers, and Crosby, Stills, Nash and Young.

It was, nevertheless, the decade of diminishing returns for the Everlys
and Warner Brothers, who naturally cut their ties and their losses as the
page turned to the 1970s. Don said, "We were associated with the fifties, so
being the Everly Brothers in the sixties was a handicap."

Still, by 1970 they had their own prime-time TV show that nevertheless
only served to bring their bickering into the homes of millions of Americans. It occasionally became a bear pit with each brother trying to humiliate
the other in a jokey-blokey fashion.

Don loved nothing better than referring to his brother as "baby boy Phil"
and delighted in telling viewers how Phil played with his plastic duck in the
bath. It sounded like harmless brotherly banter, but family insiders knew
each word was coated with toxins. Bizarrely, by the early seventies, they
were also at the center of their own love triangle. In 1962, Phil had dated

Ann Marshall, the Bel-Air-raised socialite daughter of a Hollywood actor, amid rumors of an engagement before they parted acrimoniously. She later revealed Phil had dumped her on her twentieth birthday.

Proving that hell indeed hath no fury like a woman scorned, ten years later she turned up on Don's arm shortly after his divorce from Venetia, and they lived together for two years before calling it quits. While it lasted, however, it muddied the waters further inside the Everlys' goldfish bowl. Tellingly, Marshall later wrote to mama Everly to thank her for not having a third son.

The man charged with acting as a Henry Kissinger–type peacemaker between the warring Everlys during these fractious days and nights was their manager, Jack Rael, a veteran of the big band era, who had joined the payroll in 1961.

"They never agreed on too many things, but they didn't actually fight until years later when it got to be a pretty bad problem," he recalled.

> I'd get a call at home from the road manager that the Everly Brothers were arguing like all the time, just constant, It was like Cain and Abel.
>
> They just didn't get along and at times I did have to take the eight-o'clock-in-the-morning plane when they would be arguing about something and not talking. But they both respected me, and when it got down to the nitty-gritty, they did what I told them.

But, by the early seventies, the relationship had eroded to breaking point. The 1973 meltdown at Knotts Berry Farm should have been the cue for some serious circumspection, a time out to allow tempers to cool and for brotherly relationships to perhaps be rebooted. But neither man was prepared to be the first to blink, not even at their father's funeral, the only time they came face to face during a decade apart.

The family fault lines also extended to the family matriarch, their mother Margaret. Don's ties to his mum suffered a serious breach somewhere along the line while Phil remained close to her for the rest of his life.

"People looked at Don and I like we were twins, but we weren't alike," said Phil in a 1981 interview. "Musically, we were very well educated but we had different values. Everyone has the feeling that all you have to do is to achieve stardom and once you are there you can relax. It's just the opposite. Once you get there, that's when the war really starts."

Don added his own observations round about the same time: "Like anyone who has had a marriage go sour, it was a buildup of a lot of things. We literally had no life of our own. There was never a time when Don and Phil mattered more than the Everly Brothers."

Caught in the crossfire when the brothers took up arms were a number of musicians who found themselves with feet in both camps. Chief among them was Albert Lee, the acclaimed British guitarist whose ability to play anything from bluegrass to heavy rock made him the go-to guy for many artists. He had met the brothers as far back as 1962. Initially, he was a fully paid-up member of Phil's camp before slowly gravitating toward Don during their ten-year hiatus.

So he was ideally placed to be the honest broker when, in 1982, Don blinked first by putting a call into his estranged brother. The reason was simple—money. The Warners Brothers' pipeline had been choked off long ago. Both men were low on funds but the Everly Brothers' brand, even in the eighties, could still be a very bankable commodity in an era that leaned heavily toward fifties nostalgia.

Talks about a reunion concert quickly followed and the amiable Lee found himself press-ganged into the twin roles of part musical director and part peace envoy. But once the duo was up and running again, the guitarist, ever the diplomat, says he didn't spend much time in an intermediary role. "Oh, no, you daren't do that," he said. "They'd have words, but most of the time everything was fun. They'd get a little bee in their bonnet every now and again about one subject or another."

Two reunion concerts earmarked for London's Royal Albert Hall on September 22 and 23 sold out within hours, a sign that the torch so many fans, especially in the UK, still carried for the Everlys' was even now well lit. The shows were an unqualified success. An album was swiftly recorded followed by a new round of touring as Phil and Don declared the Everlys were back in sweet, sweet harmony.

Media interviews naturally accompanied the reunion, a tortuous process that forced them both to relive the frostiness of the previous decade: "So why did you split up?" Journalists deliberately baited them in the hope of provoking some kind of outburst or, even better, a walkout by one or the other. Controversy always made the best copy. Mostly, they interchanged a straight answer with a soft-shoe shuffle. But it often made for uncomfortable viewing on television studio sofas as they did the rounds of talk shows and breakfast slots.

Time apart, they insisted, had made them reassess what they brought to the table together. Sometimes, there seemed genuine regret that matters had got so out of hand. "I'd love to snip those years out of my life," said Don. "Re-edit my life, re-arrange it if I could, re-assemble my life like a film. I'd like to put those ten years on another planet." Sitting beside him, Phil was more pragmatic. "We needed the distance to grow, Don. That was a positive period when the seeds were replanted. We're reaping the harvest of it now."

It wasn't long, however, before this hopeful new crop withered on the vine. Fleet Street veteran Ray Connolly was brought on board to steer the good ship Everly through a documentary that would chart the rocky undulations of their careers. But Connolly found himself drowning amid age-old hostilities. Writing in the *Daily Mail*, he recalled, "My job was to interview them for a promotional documentary, which was being released with the album, the idea being they would talk about their careers. But they just refused to sit down together.

> I got some idea of how far back the enmity went when a mutual friend who was working with them overheard a row between the brothers—then in their 40s—which carried on into the early hours in their motel room. Between the shouting and sobbing, over and over again, she heard both referring to their deceased father, who had nurtured their early careers. While the Everlys were famous for their close harmony on record, off stage there was little concord in their relationship. "Daddy said this . . ." and "Daddy said that . . ." went the allegations and counter allegations. That, as adults, they weren't more able to enjoy the gift they shared is sad.

Joel Selvin, of the *San Francisco Chronicle*, was friendly with both men during all this family dysfunction, although he gravitated more toward Phil. He said, "These two brothers could fight. They refused to do joint interviews and only posed for photographs together by appointment. Their contract not only called for separate dressing rooms, but separate stage entrances."

> The two brothers couldn't have been more dissimilar. When they were out on the road together, Don was a raucous, outgoing, life-of-the-party type, while his brother was a quiet, cordial and soft-spoken Southern gentleman. A mutual friend, songwriter Sharon Sheeley, sent me to meet Phil Everly backstage at a show at the Circle Star Theatre in the late eighties. A loud party spilled out of one dressing room into the hallway.
>
> A bunch of biker-types and their ladies crowded into the room, drinking bourbon out of Styrofoam cups. In the center of the throng was Don Everly. Down the hall, at the far end of the corridor, in another dressing room, sitting on an upended suitcase and looking at a magazine all by himself was Phil Everly. He was glad to have company.

Meanwhile, Dave Edmunds, a doyen of the British music industry and a fully paid-up member of the Everlys' fan club, jumped at the chance to oversee their comeback album. He wasn't immune to the whispers of fraternal infighting but hoped that middle age had infused a mellowness into both men's lives.

This optimism quickly foundered when both singers insisted on, in the main, recording their vocals separately, shielded from the other man's judgmental gaze. Only constant coaxing by Edmunds brought them to sing side by side for the sessions at Maison Rouge Studios in London. He recalled,

> My preferred hours for recording usually stretch from noon until ten or 11 p.m., and these were the hours we agreed.
>
> The band and I would show up at noon and work on the arrangements, as far as we could without Don and Phil's input and participation. Don would arrive at about 3 p.m. and could be persuaded to sing a guide vocal and discuss arrangements but would usually prefer to sit in the control room relaying humorous anecdotes from his legendary career, as though deferring the awful moment of commitment.
>
> While I was quite happy listening, enthralled by his stories of the early recordings they had made, the methods they employed, and the impressive musicians they had available to them, along with many hair-raising tales of their early touring years, we were making slow progress in the vocal department.
>
> Phil would arrive at the studio even later than Don, and, both having made prior dinner arrangements, would consequently leave the studio around seven in the evening. It was even more problematic coaxing Phil up to the microphone.
>
> At first, he suggested that Don should sing his part first, and that he would add his harmony later. It was like trying to separate yin from yang. We tried this approach once, but I found it to be a miserable experience, with Phil becoming frustrated and throwing the occasional prima-donna fit.
>
> Eventually, after some prodding, I persuaded them to share the microphone, with some magnificent results, once they warmed up and became familiar with the songs. Something that struck me about Don and Phil was that I have never encountered such a disparity of personalities and opposing values in two brothers. You get on well with one at the cost of not getting on well with the other. I never met anyone who was close to both. While Don and I hit it off so well, I never managed to unravel Phil and vice versa.

Nevertheless, an unsteady truce held firm as the comeback album, EB84, turned a respectable dime in world markets, proving yet again the Everlys' enduring popularity. The lead single, "On the Wings of a Nightingale," an excellent song Edmunds managed to coax from Paul McCartney, captured them in harmony heaven just the way it used to be back in those halcyon Kentucky days.

Aware of the financial high stakes in play, Phil and Don eventually agreed to stop picking over old scabs long enough to maintain an image of brotherly love. Remarkably, a precarious truce stayed in place to allow them to play more than 320 shows over the next 20 years—an average of 16 shows a year that self-evidently tells its own story.

The Everlys' bandwagon eventually stopped rolling in November 2005 in the inauspicious surroundings of the Regent Theatre in the touring backwater of Ipswich. As the applause faded and the safety curtain came down, none of those present could have known they were witnessing the final Everly Brothers' performance.

A few years earlier, there had been one last moment where they took center stage before huge crowds. In 2003, Paul Simon and Art Garfunkel unexpectedly, given their own dysfunction, reunited for a world tour and threw out a surprise invite for their boyhood heroes to go on the road with them, a long-overdue thanks for the harmonies that had indeed propelled their own adolescent musical hopes and dreams.

The amusing irony of the situation—two couples whose music had often been eclipsed by stories of brutal fallouts and free-for-alls—was not lost on Simon. He told *Rolling Stone*,

> It was hilarious that the four of us were doing this tour, given our collective histories of squabbling. And it's amazing, because they hadn't seen each other in about three years.
>
> They met in the parking lot before the first gig. They unpacked their guitars—those famous black guitars—and they opened their mouths and started to sing. And after all these years, it was still that sound I fell in love with as a kid. It was still perfect.

Still, before a note had been played, family members fretted over the fear of the siblings rekindling the bitterness of old, even though both men were now in their seventies. Phil's son Jason, who had taken over as his father's de facto manager, has his own take on the origins of a lifetime of feuding.

> They became world famous and wealthy and all the things that go with that. Everybody gets their own agent, their own lawyer, accountant and managers, and bad things happen. When you add in the professional side, you have room for gossip like crazy, from band members or hangers-on. But at the end of the day, you've walked the same path, and so you know there's no one you love more.
>
> That's how they work. You can run into a lot of problems with that, but at the end of the day there's zero question they loved each other. Zero. When

Paul Simon asked to bring them on board for the Old Friends tour, I said, "Paul, you know them. They're brothers. If they're getting along, then the answer is yes. If they're not getting along, then the answer is no."

Phil Everly had been a heavy smoker all his life and, from 2010, the effects of his habit were becoming all the more self-evident. Suffering from pulmonary disease, his health slowly deteriorated until he finally succumbed on January 3, 2014. He was seventy-four and time had finally killed off any hopes of a last-ditch rapprochement between the brothers.

But the obituaries that flashed all over the world paid warm and genuine homage to the immortality of the sound they created. Bob Harris said,

> I could walk over to my record shelves and pull out three or four albums of new groups doing their best to emulate the sound of the Everly Brothers. It's not just that they were of their time. Their sound is one that present-day artists are still trying to emulate.
>
> It's very interesting in country music there are so many artists, female artists, who would love to sound just like Kitty Wells, and there are so many dual male voices who strive to sound like the Everly Brothers. They have a present-day legacy but their music very much provided a pathway for groups like the Beatles to begin to experiment with the harmony sound.

No one felt the loss of Phil more than the brother with whom he had literally a love-hate relationship for much of his life. Don noted,

> I loved my brother very much. I always thought I'd be the one to go first. I was listening to one of my favourite songs that Phil wrote and had an extreme emotional moment just before I got the news of his passing. I took that as a special spiritual message from Phil saying goodbye. Our love was and will always be deeper than any earthly differences we might have had. The world might be mourning an Everly Brother, but I'm mourning my brother Phil Everly.

In a rare interview months later, however, he summed up their complexities in seven words: "We had a very difficult life together," before adding dolorously, "I think about him every day. I always thought about him every day, even when we were not speaking to each other. It still just shocks me that he's gone."

These words would normally have provided fitting closure to decades of entropy between Phil and Don. However, not even death's sting could lay to rest the animus that had stalked them across the years. For all his proclamations of grief, Don was not averse to punching a dead man. In 2017 he sued his late brother's family to reclaim his copyright interests in the duo's 1960 U.S. #1 hit "Cathy's Clown," which initially carried a joint Don and Phil song imprint. In a case that once again pitted family member against family member, he asked a federal judge to declare him the song's sole author, and block Phil's widow Patti and sons Chris and Jason from claiming half of the lucrative U.S. songwriter royalties.

Don insisted he and Phil had been credited as coauthors of "Cathy's Clown" from 1960 to 1980 at which point Phil then signed a release giving up his rights to the song and acknowledging Don as author while keeping half the royalties to that point. The case was eventually settled in late 2018, with Don awarded the kind of bragging rights that could only really have smacked of a hollow victory. The Everlys were eventually reunited on another astral plane when Don died at the age of eighty-four in August 2021.

The story of the Everlys may have contained a bitter but not surprising postscript, but Phil, befitting the more pragmatic of the two, always had a more rounded view of the complexities that bound them together inside an enclosure from which, ultimately, there seemed no escape.

He once said, "Don and I are famous for our split, but we're closer than most brothers. Harmony singing requires that you enlarge yourself, not use any kind of suppression. Harmony is the ultimate love."

The Clash: Paul Simonon, Topper Headon, Joe Strummer, and Mick Jones
Epic Records/Photofest © Epic Records

6

THE CLASH

Punk rock was already rotting in the grave when Joe Strummer delivered the ignominious last rites to "the only band that really mattered." By the autumn of 1983, the Clash were indeed The Last Gang in Town, post-punks at an existential crossroads. The Sex Pistols had shot their bolt; the Stranglers had found commercial comfort in lachrymose pop; Sham 69 had hoisted the white flag after labeling their fourth album "a load of shit"; and the Buzzcocks had simply burned out.

Across the pond, the Ramones and the New York Dolls, apex groups whose template, arguably, had done more than any other to codify punk's nihilistic aesthetic of rebellion and social change, had fallen victim to drug and alcohol overload and an inability of band members to stand each other's company one day longer.

Strummer was now facing the same kind of entrenched disconnect with Mick Jones, a founding member and the Clash's lead guitarist, whose innate and pop-savvy musicality so easily gave life to Strummer's punk-driven, fundamentalist lyrics. But for months their once-easy comradeship had given way to malign sedition over the band's future musical direction.

The embers of previously dormant divisions had left them dancing on an active volcano during sessions for *Combat Rock*, the band's fifth album. Jones was determined to plow an adventurous new pathway that would find eclectic common ground between rock music, dub reggae, and the nascent American hip-hop sounds; Strummer, in contrast, wanted the Clash to remain true to the realpolitik, right-on stridency, and lyrical satire of their West London roots.

There was, of course, more to it than just that age-old bromide "musical differences." Punk posturing had given way to rock star grandiosity. Jones, by his own admission, had been seduced by the kind of hedonism that comes hand in glove with being shuttled around in limousines, being feted by flunkies, with drugs on tap, and playing giant arenas.

Untethered, he would channel his inner Keith Richards by frequently turning up hours late—occasionally mildly toked—and throwing recording sessions for the album into chaos, a habit that infuriated Strummer, drummer Topper Headon, bassist Paul Simonon, and the band's newly re-installed first manager Bernard Rhodes. And when disagreements erupted over songs, Jones flicked his plectrums out of the pram. He was more likely to be found, detached and morose, tinkering with beat boxes and synthesizers while his Les Paul guitars collected dust in the corner of the studio. Jones wanted to be a rock star; Strummer wanted to be a punk rock star.

It was a subtle but important genre-defining difference. It led, literally, to a clash of personalities, one that ultimately prompted Strummer to deliver a memorable no-holds-barred takedown.

"Mick was intolerable to work with by this time. He wouldn't show up. When he did show up, it was like Elizabeth Taylor in a filthy mood." There was only one way out of the impasse—and on September 10, 1983, the tipping point arrived when Strummer pulled the guillotine chain after Rhodes had helped erect the scaffolding. "We had to change the team because the atmosphere was too terrible," Strummer later said in *The Rise and Fall of the Clash*, before adding, "We got so much work to do that we can't waste time begging people to play the damn guitar!"

The fallout was ultimately mushroom-shaped, a fracturing of friendships and alliances. One friend who had a foot in both camps recalled an acrimonious conversation just hours after Jones was issued with his demob papers. "I got this incredibly vitriolic phone call from Joe, saying, 'I fuckin' sacked the stoned cunt! Whose side are you on, mine or his?' And I was like, 'Uh-uh-uh . . . yours, Joe, yours!'"

It was a turf war with only one winner. The divisions between Strummer and Jones had been a cancer at the heart of the Clash for months, and now Joe had taken action to cut out the tumor by employing the kind of directness the situation required. In time, however, it would be seen as an incredible act of self-immolation, not least by Strummer himself, who would wrestle with the guilt of the decision for the rest of his life.

The band's tour manager Johnny Green was just one of many eyewitnesses to the walls that came tumbling down and the slow-burning fuse that eventually exploded between Strummer and Jones. "It worked on affection and competition," he recalled. "While they were really fond of each other and close to each other, like the best love affairs it could spark up with passion at times. It could spill over in any direction—it was strong emotions. It wasn't cool and calculated."

Tensions were, understandably, not confined to the studio. Amid the claustrophobia of life on the road, pent-up feelings could understandably boil over. During one early gig at Sheffield, Jones refused to go back for the encore. Strummer promptly let his fists do the talking and left his bandmate with a busted lip.

Neither was it the last time the two men would come to blows. But it was a clear—and early—example of the chest-beating power struggle being waged behind the scenes for the soul of the Clash. Jones's expulsion also wasn't the first time Strummer had carried out a preemptive strike to oust a member of the band.

Eighteen months earlier, just days before *Combat Rock* hit the shelves in May 1982, Strummer had bulleted Headon, punk rock's most seminal percussionist, over the drummer's unchecked cocaine and heroin use—a move that, in hindsight, would be seen as the beginning of the end even though it was done to preserve the band as a functioning unit.

"Punk was an attitude, not a music or a fashion," argued Strummer, whose fidelity to the truth was absolute. "If I see a situation, I'll fucking cut right to the heart of it. That's a punk attitude and I've got it inbred."

Buried between the lines, however, was an inescapable axiom; without Topper Headon, and especially Mick Jones, the Clash, once the quintessential standard bearers for youthful rage in the late 1970s and early 1980s, were a busted flush. A glorious band doomed to an inglorious death rattle. But the end of the Clash owed as much to a litany of more self-inflicted wounds caused by deepening financial pressures, business breakdowns, record company conflicts, prima donna attitudes, bizarre walkouts, and the Machiavellian mind games being played out behind the scenes by Rhodes, a man who reveled in internecine chaos.

Rhodes, of course, was in at the ground floor of punk alongside Sex Pistols manager Malcolm McLaren. He was in the middle of the Venn diagram that interlocked London squatland, pub rock, and youthful insurgency in a common cause. He was also the big bang theorist whose networking first brought Jones and Simonon together with Strummer through a series of fateful meetings to form the Clash and give birth to that blistering three-guitar forward line, two neurons and a proton. Original drummer Terry Chimes—Tory Crimes—would soon make way for Topper Headon to form punk's alchemist's stone.

Together, they set off a musical chain reaction that made other bands look like first-year pupils trying to work a Bunsen burner. Between 1977 and 1982, they released five albums—*The Clash, Give 'Em Enough Rope, London Calling, Sandinista!,* and *Combat Rock*—that established them as the kings of British punk rock and the band that launched a million dreams for those punk wannabes in bedsit land.

Without the Clash, there would have been no U2, no Nirvana, no Primal Scream, no Manic Street Preachers, and no Rage Against the Machine. "White Riot" wasn't a song—it was a clarion call to arms against the looming threat of Thatcherism and the onslaught of destructive right-wing politics. Writer Charles Shaar Murray venerated them as the third spoke in the Holy Trinity of punk bands alongside the Ramones and the Pistols. "No rock band before or since ever explored the conflicting imperatives of left politics and hunger for rock stardom to a greater extent, or put that contradiction to better use as a source for their creative engine," he declared.

"They were everything they said they were, and much that they said they weren't. They were also, between 1978 and 1980, the greatest rock band in the world on more wild nights than anybody else."

That view is shared by many, including Bono, who has acknowledged his own road-to-rock-n-roll Eureka moment after seeing the Clash with the rest of U2 in Trinity College, Dublin, in 1977. "The Clash were the greatest band in the world," declared Bono. "They wrote the rulebook for U2."

But Strummer's single-minded banishment of Mick Jones put that rulebook through the shredder. And it was the critical act in a drama that had shades of Shakespeare woven into the narrative—*et tu, Brute* and *render unto Caesar?*—and at that point left Strummer and Simonon as the last men standing of the original lineup that was formed in 1976. Sadly, Strummer's tragic early death at the age of fifty in 2002 has only brought into sharper focus the incredible legacy of the Clash and a sense of "what if" over the bitter estrangement between him and Mick Jones. Former *Mojo* editor Pat Gilbert, whose book, *Passion Is a Fashion* remains essential reading for students of the band, is an avowed champion of the Clash's musical heritage.

They wouldn't have reached the heights they did without the quality of the music. It's kind of very melodic and very original and quite quirky. Especially the way Mick writes music. And on top of that you have Joe's kind of street radical political lyrics.

So I always see them as a kind of musical militia, a guerrilla unit. Which is why they were so exciting, I think. They did have a kind of morality. The Pistols were trying to stir things up, but the Clash were trying to educate people and make them think.

They may once have been united under a punk flag, but Strummer and Jones straddled two different musical worlds from the start. Strummer's angst rose up from living in a London squat and listening to the likes of Woody Guthrie; but Jones was a closet old-school rocker who lionized Mott the Hoople and the Rolling Stones.

It didn't necessarily mean the two men didn't share the same vision politically, but in terms of musical progression, they were often running on separate tracks. Increasingly, they found themselves trapped between a punk rock paradox and a rock star's paradise. These differences were, in the beginning, however, swept under the carpet to maintain an integrated unity. But when inflamed, they were the source of constant flashpoints.

Strummer once said, "It's like having a split personality. I want the Clash to get bigger because you want people to hear your songs, you want to be successful . . . but on the other hand I'm pretty wary of that, of having to get too big to handle."

Jones's departure came just as the Clash's popularity crossed the great divide between indie rock and international mass acceptance. Propelled by the monster appeal of radio-friendly tracks such as "Rock the Casbah" and "Should I Stay or Should I Go," *Combat Rock* was the commercial pinnacle of the Clash's career.

The album climbed to #2 on the UK charts but, more pertinently, peaked at #7 in America, where the band was hailed as rock's revolutionary conscience.

Behind the lines, however, the lives of Strummer, Simonon, Headon, and Jones were locked into a form of mortal combat that only internal chaos foments. The reasons were multilayered and complicated. Strummer had forced a split from their management company and lobbied hard for the return of Rhodes, a man he regarded as a Svengali/mentor but who he had also fired in 1978.

Fearing a musical ennui had set in, Strummer was convinced Rhodes could help them rekindle the incendiary spirit and musketeer mantra of 1976. Jones, in contrast, dreaded a return of the divide-and-conquer approach, which was Rhodes's modus operandi.

He had long harbored an acute mistrust of the band's original manager, who he was sure had wanted him out of the band during his first stint as capo de capo. Those suspicions were further aroused when Rhodes invited Pistols' guitarist Steve Jones to sit in with the band during sessions. Then he started "appearing" for encores during a UK tour in the early weeks of 1978. Mick was convinced that Strummer and Rhodes, a close ally of the Pistols, were conspiring to replace one Jones with another.

Simonon was also acutely aware of the musical chairs taking place. "There was stuff going around about individuals swapping between groups," he recalled. "Mick felt uneasy because Steve Jones used to turn up all the time. He may have felt that Steve was going to oust him." Mick, however, found himself in a minority of four over the return of Rhodes, who swiftly set about resurrecting the Stalinist regime he had fostered during the early years.

Pat Gilbert remains convinced that Strummer's decision to bring Rhodes back into the fold accelerated the unrest that was already brewing.

Was it a problem for Mick Jones? Yes it was. There was never any love lost between Mick Jones and Bernie and it often inflamed the tensions even more with Joe. No one was ever quite sure what Steve Jones' unscheduled appearances were all about, but they certainly stirred things up between Mick and other members of the band. And Bernie knew it would unsettle Mick.

He was going through what at the time the others called his "poodle" stage. To say he was unpopular within the group at this time is to misunderstand the whole dynamic of the Clash. The others have all admitted he was becoming a bit difficult, but now he found himself in the role of a punk Cesare Borgia, fearing that there was a plot to depose him.

During *Sandinista!* And, to a certain extent *London Calling*, for those two records Mick was really in the driving seat. The management they had at the time, which was Blackhill, didn't interfere creatively or really between the band members. But when Bernie came back, he had a vision, which clashed with Mick's vision, and that is a very, very important ingredient in the whole thing as well. Bernie is brilliant, no doubt about that. But he is just a very, very difficult man, forever testing your commitment and your abilities and your loyalties, and also playing silly buggers really and stirring things up and being very difficult to deal with. And that made life in the Clash difficult for everyone but especially for Mick Jones. And it definitely drove Mick away.

Rhodes's ongoing role as agent provocateur only added to Jones's creeping sense of paranoia when, in late autumn 1981, sessions began at New York's famed Electric Lady studio to begin work on an album with the working title *Rat Patrol from Fort Bragg*. Jones had already been seduced by the Big Apple's cultural and musical heartbeat and was keen to spend as much time as possible with his American girlfriend Ellen Foley, whose raucous vocals had left an indelible footprint on Meat Loaf's classic "Paradise by the Dashboard Light."

In fact, the choice of studio had already provided an early standoff between Jones and the rest of the band, which in itself shone a light on the parlor games being played. Kosmo Vinyl, the band's sometime press officer, sometime part-manager, recalled, "Mick said if we didn't produce *Combat*

Rock in New York, he wouldn't be at the sessions. So we cart everything to New York and make the record there. One day there's an argument and that gets brought up and Mick goes, 'Oh I didn't mean it.'"

Right from the onset of beginning work on the album, Jones and the band were on different pages. Mick, his antenna tuned into music's shifting sands, was anxious to avoid repeating the kind of self-indulgent tosh that had ripped holes in their previous album, the sprawling thirty-six-track, three-record set *Sandinista!* And that meant leading the Clash down a road paved with rap, funk, and even disco. "I was keen to go forward with a more contemporary approach," he said.

The main points of friction weren't just about musical joie de vivre as the length and format of the songs. A form of détente was agreed when the band set off for a tour in Far East Asia. Cloistered together on a tour bus, however, only widened the cracks. Photographer Pennie Smith, a long-term ally of the band whose time-frozen image of Simonon hurling his bass guitar to the floor adorned the cover of *London Calling*, accompanied them as the tour wound through outposts like Vietnam and Cambodia. And she easily picked up on the smoldering bad vibes between certain individuals, fissures now exposed through a lens.

One day she took the band to the side of a railway track, ostensibly to shoot a cover image for the forthcoming album. "Halfway through the shoot something happened and the whole band seemed to dissolve in front of my eyes." When they picked up the threads of the album—now retooled as *Combat Rock*—in the spring of 1982, mild disagreements quickly morphed into bitter discontent. Having mixed the tracks himself, Jones was convinced there was enough musical muscle to warrant a double album like *London Calling*. CBS executives felt differently. They had indulged the child when the Clash turned in *London Calling* as a double album, front-loaded as it was with brilliant songs. But when the band insisted that the highly experimental *Sandinista!*—it was largely recorded with a cast of outside musicians—warranted triple album treatment, curtains on the top floor began twitching. More so since Strummer and Rhodes especially were adamant it should be sold retail for the price of a single album.

The upshot was CBS caved on condition that the Clash waive a huge chunk of their royalties. This only served inevitably to ensure the members of the band remained cash poor despite their status as punk's most totemic band. And shoveling more salt into gaping wounds was the fact the album was largely derided by critics and fans—leaving Strummer, a man long burdened with feelings of insecurity and inadequacy, standing on the end of an emotional precipice. One reviewer in the wake of *Sandinista!* had asked, "Seriously: what the fuck are the Clash any more?"

It was a question Mick Jones had also been asking himself at the outset of recording tracks for *Combat Rock*.

Meanwhile, CBS had other questions about the album. With one eye on the bottom line, the label's head of A&R Muff Winwood—brother of Steve—feared *Combat Rock* in its current "lightweight" form would stiff.

Enter then at Bernie Rhodes and Strummer's invitation legendary producer Glyn Johns, whose stellar curriculum vitae was franked by, among others, the Rolling Stones, Led Zeppelin, the Who, the Eagles, and the Beatles. Handed the job of paring the mixes down to single-album length, Johns quickly trimmed the excess fat, jettisoned the rubbish, and delivered an album that passed the Strummer and Winwood smell test. Having stared down the likes of John Lennon, Keith Richards, and Glenn Frey, Johns had no worries about locking horns with the new kid on the block.

No stranger to rock-star egotism and armed with a fuck-you attitude, Johns was comfortably prepared for awkward conversations with Jones, who felt he was the back-stabbing victim of record company politics and group chicanery. Rather than go head-to-head with Johns, however, Mick's solution was to simply remove himself from the fray. Recalling the sessions, Johns told *UNCUT* magazine,

> It was a hell of a mess. I started with Joe at 10am and he was happy for me to get stuck in, edit and chuck stuff out. It was like fighting through the Burmese jungle with a machete. Was Mick Jones miffed that the album largely got recorded without his involvement? That's a bit of an understatement.
>
> Mick didn't turn up till 7pm and I'd already mixed four or five tracks. He came in and I said, "I'll play you what we've been up to today." I played them all back and he sat there with a pencil and pad and was making notes and he went, "Okay, these are the changes I want you to make." I said, "I'm not making any changes, I've done it." I said, "If you'd have been here at 10am I'd have been very interested to hear what observations you had while I was doing it. If you think I'm going to do them all again for you because you can't be bothered to turn up till seven in the evening, you're wrong, mate."
>
> He got pissed off and left. There was a big row the next day, and then I just got on and finished it with Joe, who was very supportive. It was rather sad, but there are some classic performances on it, and they would have been classics whether I'd mixed them or not. I think Mick liked the album in the end.

That, though, was to miss the point. Jones felt Strummer had meddled with his art—an unforgiveable crime. At the same time, Strummer later made clear his disdain for Jones's habit of brooding when he didn't get his own way. "I can't stand this sulking business. It's like being in a group with a load of old women. Sulking is pop-starism. I couldn't believe we turned into the kind of people we were trying to destroy."

In another interview, he trained his sights directly on Jones's main complaint.

Mick was accusing me of ruining his music because I got Glyn Johns to remix *Combat Rock*. It isn't all good, but he shook some rock 'n' roll out of that record. It sold a million and a half records in the States and Mick calls it ruined music. I was trying to save this guy from embarrassment, but he wanted all the attention. That was Mick's whole problem—he wanted all the attention for himself.

Pat Gilbert, though, has plenty of sympathy for Jones's position while understanding Strummer's determination to hold true to the band's musical ethos.

Mick was the de facto producer of the band after *Give Enough Rope*. There was always some sort of antagonism between all of them and it was there from the start.

They were all quite capable of being brutal to each other. They would gang up on Mick, undoubtedly, but at the same time when you think of the *Sandinista!* sessions Mick and Joe went off and recorded a whole album's material without Paul. I think that's just how they operated. There was always a kind of creative brutality between them.

The idea was that they were all committed to the idea of the Clash rather than being best mates. But I think the problems were exacerbated after Glyn Johns was brought in. That was indicative of the fact that musically they didn't know what the Clash should sound like in 1982 and 1983. You have to think of the times and the fact that music was becoming dominated by sequencers and synthesisers. Where do you go if you're a punk rock band?

Paul and Joe were very beholden to the idea of rock 'n' roll and rockabilly, stripped down kind of soul music and reggae music. It's all to do with authenticity and earthiness and swagger. How do you relate that to what Mick was trying to do with beat boxes and the sound that he eventually found with Big Audio Dynamite? But to make that leap with the Clash would have been difficult.

Having won the battle over the album's sound and length, however, Strummer faced a war on other fronts. By 1982, the Clash were seriously in debt, mainly as a result of their entrenched stance over the cut-price release of *Sandinista!* Much, then, was riding on the success of the new album and the UK tour scheduled for April 1982 that was intended as a show reel for

Combat Rock. Tickets, however, were piling up unsold in box offices across the country—a worrying sign that Strummer justifiably feared suggested their time in rock's spotlight was dimming.

Meanwhile, Topper Headon's spiraling drug use—he had graduated from coke and smack to speedballs—threatened to make him a lame duck drummer. In December 1981, he had been busted for heroin possession at Heathrow Airport and fined £500. Months earlier, the tell-tale signs of Topper's addiction were on full show when he threw up on a carpet at Vienna airport. Cornered by a posse of hacks, Headon shifted uncomfortably in his seat. But Strummer, summoning up a Clash esprit de corps, waded into the journalists and loyally defended his bandmate's behavior. Deep down, though, he knew the drummer was unraveling at breakneck pace and so did Bernard Rhodes.

Strummer recalled, "Bernie said, 'He's a junkie, he has to go.' Ignorance ruled the day. We knew nothing about heroin." Headon's self-destructive plunge into substance abuse was seriously at odds with the band's shaky but long-held anti-drug ethos. He loved being on the road, but when the other band members were not performing, they would retire to their hotel rooms to read or write songs alone. As their laissez-faire punk roots gave way to mainstream musicianship, they became more critical of Headon's behavior.

"I could see their logic," he told *The Independent* in a 2014 interview. "But at the same time I thought, 'Well, I can't hang out with you guys because you just come back and go straight to sleep.'" Headon, by contrast, had reached the point where he was taking drugs on stage to get through a gig. "Every three numbers I used to go . . . [he mimes a final drum roll] and the lights would go off and my drum roadie would be there with a mirror." Headon would snort a line of cocaine and be ready for the next song.

"The band were getting the hump with me using on stage. I'd think we were getting out of it every night," he recalled. "One night Joe would come down and we'd get drunk, the next night Paul would be down, and I'd get out of it with him, and the next night it would be Mick. I'd be thinking, 'This is great, we're all partying.' I wouldn't realize that only I was there constantly."

But Strummer's ethics on the road didn't extend to monogamy. While Headon was balls-deep in drugs, Joe was similarly active with the drummer's girlfriend. It was a libidinous red line, which he crossed with uncaring abandon. Headon recalled, "There were parts of Joe's character I didn't like. I had my girlfriend on the road with me, and we had a big argument, and I said, 'Right, you're not sleeping in my room.' I woke up the next morning to find she'd spent the night with Joe. That kind of thing really hurt. I felt betrayed. He did it with me and he did it with other people."

Caught in the middle of all these overlapping and self-inflicted crises in the spring of 1982 was the Clash's heat shield. Strummer, though, could no longer absorb all the internal friction that by now threatened to overwhelm him. He was barely on speaking terms with Jones, was staring down the barrel of a tour catastrophe—and *Combat Rock* was due out within weeks. He was already consumed with guilt over Headon's brutal but necessary dismissal.

"I don't think we ever played a decent gig again," he declared. The power struggle, which pitched him and Jones in opposite corners, had also taken a terrible toll on his psyche. What followed next is perhaps the most bizarre episode in the history of any rock 'n' roll band. Rhodes, in a bid to stoke some hype for the tour and album, hatched a comical PR stunt for Strummer to simply pretend to vanish—which he did, only for real.

Just days before the tour was due to kick off in Aberdeen, Scotland, Strummer did a bunk to a secret address in Paris where he remained incommunicado for almost a month. He stayed off the grid except for an inexplicable decision to suddenly run the Paris Marathon, which he completed despite allegedly a liquid lunch the day before. Back in London, panic set in as the tour was shelved amid speculation that the Clash had split.

Kept in the dark, Jones, Simonon, and Headon were left cooling their heels in frustration. Simonon later theorized that it was Strummer's attempt to wrest power from Jones. But the singer had a more simplistic rationale. "Well . . . it was something I wanted to prove to myself: that I was still alive," he would later tell the *NME*. "It's very much being like a robot, being in a band. . . . Rather than go mad, I think it's better to do what I did even for a month. I think I would have started drinking a lot on the tour, maybe. Started becoming petulant with the audience, which isn't the sort of thing you should do."

Coaxed back into the fold after being tracked down by Kosmo Vinyl, Strummer reunited with the Clash in time to play a festival in Holland on May 20. Eyewitness accounts say the show was shambolic, with Strummer phoning in his own performance. Reconciliation, however, would carry a nonnegotiable toll—and Topper Headon would pay the price. Minutes after the gig, Strummer told the drummer his Clash P45 was in the post. The final straw came when Headon ignored previous ultimatums by going nose deep in cocaine before and during the gig. It didn't matter that Topper was in Mick and Paul's camp—he was out. Seen through time's prism, this was the moment for many—not least Strummer himself—that spelled the unofficial end of the Clash. He declared, "When Topper became addicted [to heroin], I knew we'd had it."

In the mind of Pat Gilbert, however, they had no choice. "It was a massive problem for the band," he said.

> More so than is acknowledged or recognised. It just becomes a practical problem if somebody is being arrested and they are being fined. There was a genuine possibility at the end of the *Combat Rock* sessions, and before the Clash went to Japan, that Topper would be given a prison sentence for his arrest at Heathrow at Christmas for bringing heroin into the country. Imagine then the problems you get with visas.
>
> Once a band member is publicly deemed to be a liability in a sense you get all sorts of problems. It's not much fun being around people who are stoned all the time. Topper always thinks that he got a bit of a bad rap, but they didn't get rid of him for nothing. But again, you're a punk rock band and you're not like the Rolling Stones; you're not a bunch of old junkies.

An easy-going character, Headon was also accomplished on other instruments, notably piano and bass. The best example of his virtuosity can be found in *Rock the Casbah*, perhaps the band's most commercially successful track. Arriving at the studio early one day, Headon laid down all the backing tracks himself, leaving Strummer to write the lyrics.

But that adroitness was not enough to prevent him from getting the boot. And it sent him headlong into years of addiction, bankruptcy, busking outside Tube stations, squatting—and for a short time, prison—before he eventually and admirably hauled himself out of the morass.

In later years, he blamed no one but himself for his drug-addled downfall. "Joe wouldn't have sacked me if I hadn't been a raving heroin addict, trashing hotel rooms, throwing up, late for rehearsals. He had no choice. . . . I was in a state," he confessed. So, too, were the remaining members of the Clash. *Combat Rock* climbed the charts on both sides of the Atlantic, bringing the kind of acceptance they had been striving for since their first few, mesmerizing gigs in west London, and which was now a financial necessity.

Success, though, found Strummer and Jones impaled on the horns of an old dilemma. Commercial kudos meant a further drift from their roots. A fact underlined by Rhodes's quixotic decision to accept an invitation by the Who for the Clash to support them on their farewell tour of America in late 1982. Jones was happy to hang out with Roger Daltrey and Pete Townsend and watch the dollars roll in; Strummer was left grappling with his conscience over fears that this was simply another sellout and a further distillation of hard-won principles in favor of stadium rock—the very antithesis of the punk rock orthodoxy. Jones, for all he and Strummer were in opposite corners, recognized the dichotomy.

He told *GQ* magazine,

I know it was particularly hard for Joe, above all. I was slightly more OK with it, I'd say, than Joe, because it was what I'd dreamed of. I did understand what Joe's concerns were, especially in terms of what our material was saying. But I thought it was an interesting thing in terms of seeing how far we could go with it, you know? Listen, it's a contradiction; obviously, you want to be the biggest band in the world—all bands do. But you want to retain your integrity and credibility and do it on your terms. And that's very hard to do. I'd be lying if I said that we didn't want to be the best group, or that we weren't trying to be the best group, because we were. But obviously, with that comes money and success, and we weren't very adept; we were pretty naïve in terms of all that stuff. We were open; we were vulnerable. And then we were under massive pressure, and in the end we couldn't deal with it anymore, couldn't even talk to each other, I guess, because it was so massive.

Press-ganged into service for the rescheduled UK tour and the U.S. dates as a replacement for Headon was Terry Chimes, the band's original drummer who had played on their first album before stepping off the page. "It had become a 24/7 thing and every day it just seemed to be me arguing with everyone else," he recalled of those tempestuous early days. "The band, Bernard, the roadies . . . they all bought into that Stalinist-nonsense and I didn't. But, funnily enough, when I came back in 1982, it was quite nice to realize that I was going to find out how it would have eventually been. Of course, the trouble then was that other things had changed, and they were all arguing with each other in different ways."

Specifically, it didn't take him long to sniff out the bad vibes between Jones and Strummer. "The problem with Joe was that he would feel guilty if he was comfortable," offered Chimes. "He had a vision that his life should be about helping people, doing meaningful, profound things. He thought he should be out there fighting for a cause." In many ways, though, he was, the one cause that was closest to his heart—the binary battle with Mick Jones for the heart and soul of the Clash. Yet they would soldier on.

Penciled in for late May 1983 were several shows at the Us Festival in California—the sun-kissed refuge of hippydom—which would see them share the bill with artists as diverse as Van Halen, David Bowie, Stray Cats, and remarkably, a Flock of Seagulls. In many ways, it was the epitome of rock capitalism—and its greed-is-good creed naturally ran counter to Strummer's punk principles.

Jones, though, had long ago inked a Faustian pact over his motives for being in the Clash. It was yet another example of the personal and political differences that by now seemed irreconcilable. They would turn out to be the last gigs Mick Jones would play as a member of the Clash. In September that year, with Clash activity mothballed by indolence, Jones attended what he thought was a routine band meeting only to be handed his jotters by Strummer.

Blindsided, Jones was bewildered and stunned. "It came as a bit of a shock, I have to admit, because it was my band, wasn't it? It didn't feel great." The official line opaquely hinted at the conflict behind the scenes but was nevertheless typically blunt. "Joe Strummer and Paul Simonon have decided that Mick Jones should leave (the Clash). It is felt that Jones drifted away from the original idea of the group."

As Simonon later attested, however, alternatives seemed at that pivotal point in short supply. In a joint interview with Jones sitting beside him in 2014, he broke his own vow of omertà over the dismissal of a key band cornerstone and harbored zero regrets. He told *GQ*,

> When me and Joe decided that Mick had to go, I think we knew we were cutting off our right arm, but we had to, and so what? At least, we have a certain control and a certain self-respect for not doing it all again. I mean we are all guilty, but Mick did go overboard, and it was just too much for me and Joe, and we thought rather than play safe and go, "OK, well let's placate Mick all the time," and, "OK, Mick wants to go on holiday now and maybe we should have gone on holiday," or whatever, but it wasn't like that. The fact is that we had just had enough of Mick and we just said, "Well, that's it." And we did that and it did start to fall apart and fair enough, great, that's the way it is, and in some ways we're better people for it because we felt we needed to do that rather than keep the charade going.

When the tumbleweed eventually cleared, Jones adopted a different perspective, while acknowledging his own failings. "There were a lot of things behind it. I made it easy for them because I wasn't in a good mood about things not going my way. I fell into the trap, but by that time we were all pretty fed up with each other. It's inevitable that groups split up. But the real shame was that we lost our friendship."

Meanwhile, convinced the band still had a future, Strummer pressed the reset button and drafted in several new musicians to record *Cut the Crap*, which hit the airwaves in November 1985 to a fusillade of flak. The album's title only served to underline the mockery that the music—largely created by Bernie Rhodes who had decided to join the band—generated.

The album, top heavy with electronica, was as far away from *London Calling* as you could get and stands as a cardboard tombstone to a band that had redefined music and fired the hopes and dreams of a new generation of kids desperate to finally break with the chains of hippy idealism and comatose rock. Contrast that with the reception for *This Is Big Audio Dynamite*, the first offering from Jones's post-Clash band, which was hailed for its diverse and stimulating soundscapes. Unlike many feuding rock bands, however, the Clash would swiftly replace internal friction with external friendship. Bridges so quickly torched were repaired within months. "We actually became friends again very quickly," said Jones who, nevertheless, found himself forced to rebuff pleas by Strummer to reunite the old gang one more time. There was no going back, despite the occasional cross-band collaborations—Strummer had a big part to play in the genesis of Big Audio Dynamite's second album.

Life-changing sums were dangled before them to reunite but never was there a moment when all four members of the Clash's classic cast were in alignment. The speculation, however, was ramped up in November 2002, when it was announced the band would be inducted into the Rock & Roll Hall of Fame the following March. A week later Strummer and Jones shared a stage for the first time since that moment a hole was ripped in the Clash's own time continuum at a charity gig for striking fire fighters in London, performing three Clash songs under the umbrella of Strummer's band the Mescaleros.

They looked delighted to be sharing the moment. A week later Joe Strummer, the great seer of British punk rock, was dead as the result of an undiagnosed congenital heart defect. Devastated, Mick Jones, Paul Simonon, and Terry Chimes—Topper, still in the throes of addiction, declined the invite—used the band's Rock & Roll Hall of Fame induction to pay warm tribute to their mercurial friend and front man.

It was a time for glancing back and looking forward, certain that Strummer's legacy would be forever enshrined in amber. Strummer, punk rock's greatest troubadour, once presciently said of the Clash's fundamental lineup, "Whatever a group is, it's the chemical mixture of those four people. It's some weird thing that no scientist could ever quantify or measure, and thank God for that."

Equally philosophical, Simonon would delineate some irony from the name of a band whose name held up a mirror to the era they defined more than most. "We were in a confrontational situation all the time. There was a clash of colors, clash of people—it's kind of self-explanatory."

Guns N' Roses: Izzy Stradlin, Steven Adler, Axl W. Rose, Slash, and Duff McKagan
Photofest

7

GUNS N' ROSES

Peering out at the edge of darkness, W. Axl Rose stomped around the front of the stage, brandishing his microphone stand like a pump action shotgun—and he was spitting bullets. Behind him, the other members of Guns N' Roses paused the introduction to "Mr. Brownstone," the heroin-laced adventure that was supposed to kick off their set.

Like everyone else inside the LA Coliseum, they had no idea what was coming next. Two hours late in arriving, it had already been a night where anger and frustration had collided. "I hate to do this on stage," announced Rose as he prowled the boards, "but I tried every other fucking way. And unless certain people in this band get their shit together, these will be the last Guns N' Roses shows you'll fucking ever see. 'Cause I'm tired of too many people in this organization dancing with Mr. Goddamn Brownstone."

Was he serious? Was it some typically ersatz attention-seeking ploy to wind up the audience? Was it really a threat to break up the world's most notorious rock band over their industrial and routine intake of drugs? Was this the last copter out of Saigon? Shuffling awkwardly, at least four people knew it was no idle threat. Slash, the band's imperious lead guitarist, bassist Duff McKagan, drummer Steven Adler, and rhythm guitarist and Guns N' Roses cofounder Izzy Stradlin, each of them aware a Rubicon had just been crossed.

Slash later said, "I knew it was directed at me, because I was real strung out at the time. But it was probably one of the things that made me hate Axl more than anything." Standing in the same dock was McKagan, his eyes burning a hole in the back of the singer's head. "I shrank; I was so embarrassed," McKagan said. "Once Axl took his concerns public, the times of being a gang—us against the world—were over. We played the rest of the show, but it was a half-hearted effort at best. Afterward, and really for the remainder of our career, we just went our separate ways. That night officially rang the bell for the end of an era in Guns N' Roses."

Resentment was also bubbling up with Adler: "Axl was so gone. I'm hiding there behind the drums thinking, 'I don't know this guy.'" It was only one of many battlefronts to open up in the internecine war of the Roses. And the main combatants were usually Axl and Slash, two musicians constantly at odds with each other for control of a band that formed the bridge in American music between punk, the underbelly of rap, and the hard rock of Led Zeppelin.

Each one was the embodiment of Guns N' Roses, colt idols with a screw-you attitude. Rose's cocksure Jagger swagger elevated him to the rock god throne long vacated by the Rolling Stones' kingpin; Slash's mesmerizing and sinewy solos gave him an unchallenged pathway to the guitar hero status long abandoned by Jimmy Page. And the rest of the band provided the oscillating tempo of a high-speed train with no brakes.

Their ascent to music's Mount Olympus was accompanied by laurel leaves and a belief that here at last were rock's new messiahs. But when the train came off the tracks, everyone was caught up in the wreckage. Amid the carnage, friendships were fractured, and millions of dollars were sacrificed on the altar of rock's bonfire of the vanities. And the ties that once bound Slash and Axl Rose were ripped apart by music's omnipresent destructive forces—personality clashes, a never-ending money pit, drug intake on a colossal scale, management bust-ups, and musical differences. At its lowest point, the bad blood had thickened into a toxic clot.

Rose once declared, "There is the distinct possibility that having his intentions in regard to me so deeply ingrained and his personal though guarded distaste for much of [debut album] *Appetite* [*for Destruction*] other than his or Duff's [McKagan] playing, Slash either should not have been in Guns to begin with or should have left after [1988 mini-album] *Lies*. In a nutshell, personally I consider him a cancer and better removed, avoided—and the less anyone heard of him or his supporters the better."

It was a long way from the band that began life as a group of sewer rats who honed their hard-edged sound while living in drug-addled squalor in downtown LA, crashing out in a flat that was ground zero for debauchery. Stradlin was already vein deep in junk when he joined the band, thanks chiefly to his part-time scam as Aerosmith's official heroin dealer. The only thing that stopped them flatlining was their belief in music as "The Great Escape."

Led by the guitar pyrotechnics of Slash and the venomous angst of front man Rose, Guns N' Roses developed a stellar sense of song craft with a vocabulary that conjoined vintage Rolling Stones' attitude, Zeppelin muscle, and punk nihilism. *Appetite for Destruction*, their visceral debut album, released in 1987, was a middle-finger riposte to the years of poodle-haired rock spearheaded by the likes of Bon Jovi, Def Leppard, and Whitesnake. The record landed with all the megaton potency of a cobalt bomb and single-handedly rescued rock music from the torpor of Dire Straits.

"Welcome to the Jungle" blared the first track, and millions of fans around the world headed into its dense undergrowth. On tracks such as "Nightrain," the aforementioned "Mr. Brownstone," "It's so Easy," "Anything Goes," and "Rocket Queen," Rose sang of the drug, booze, and sex-fueled existence of their lives in cinematic detail. And then there was "Sweet Child O' Mine," the breakout single that placed Rose alongside Robert Plant and saw Slash become rock music's new guitar Godhead.

"It was a joke," said Slash of the song that garnered their first U.S. #1 single. "We were living in this house that had electricity, a couch, and nothing else. The record company had just signed us, and we were on our backs. We were hanging out one night, and I started playing that riff. And the next thing you know Izzy made up some chords behind it, and Axl went off on it. But let me tell you, I used to hate playing that sucker."

Within months of firing their first shot for Geffen Records, Guns N' Roses was both the biggest and most dangerous band on planet rock. In a few short years, they went from traveling in a Transit van to a custom-fitted Boeing 727 borrowed from the MGM Casino in Las Vegas. On the first flight, Slash and McKagan smoked crack in the toilet before it had even left the ground.

"I remember thinking of course we can smoke on here . . . it's our plane," recalled McKagan. Eldorado was theirs for the taking. Domination on a global scale. And it promised the world's last great rock 'n' roll band the kind of eye-watering bounty that would make each of them richer than Croesus. Ranged against all that, however, was Guns N' Roses' own appetite for self-destruction—crack, smack, cocaine, or booze.

Take your pick from the various execrable addictions that gripped Slash, McKagan, Adler, and Stradlin, each of them as a result walking that fine line between life and death. During the notorious 1992 *Use Your Illusion* tour, Slash "died" nine times. Their manager carried a *Pulp Fiction*–style

Narcan shot to bring him literally back from the dead. Slash eventually had a defibrillator inserted to stop his heart bursting.

At the end of the tour, McKagan's pancreas exploded, the result of bingeing himself on half a gallon of vodka a day for weeks on end. He was in so much pain he begged his doctors to let him die. And then you had the menacing megalomania of Rose—Tony Montana in tattoos, a backward baseball cap, and scrotum-hugging shorts—an idiosyncrasy that often pitted him violently against the rest of the band, a mongoose in a nest of vipers. Slash summed it up thus: "Axl is just another version of the Ayatollah."

And nowhere was that self-absorption more on view than that night in October 1989 at the LA Coliseum when they first opened for the Rolling Stones. It was supposed to be the occasion when rock's nuevo young pretenders would topple rock royalty. Guns N' Roses were, however, badly bent out of shape and Rose knew it. Their warm-up gig at a tiny club a few nights earlier was the first time they had played live in eight months and the rust clung to them like winter's chill.

On the night of the Coliseum gig, Guns N' Roses duly assembled at the appointed hour. All of them except Axl, who remained holed up in his hotel nursing a deep-rooted psychosis and a humungous temper. As the clock ticked down, and the arena started to fill, the band's then manager, Alan Niven, was forced to take the nuclear option. After calling in a favor from the Stones' camp, he dispatched two LA cops to "do whatever is necessary" to haul Rose to the arena.

By the time Axl got there, his anger was off the grid. Factor in a racially charged bust-up with Living Colour, one of the other bands on the bill, and the perfect storm was not long in arriving. In the post-mortem that followed, Rose followed through on his ultimatum to walk away unless Slash apologized onstage the next night for being a heroin addict. Adler, whose ingestion rates easily matched those of Slash, dodged the bullet.

"I understand why Axl singled me out rather than Steven. I am the stronger of the two of us and Axl relied on me more. My presence was important to him . . . but it was still a bitter pill to swallow." The guitarist, fearing he was about to lose the keys to Aladdin's cave, meekly complied rather than be blamed for the whole house of cards coming crashing down. "I didn't actually think the smack was the problem," said Slash. "And even if it was, that wasn't the right moment to make an issue of it. I didn't actually apologize. I went into some rap about heroin and what it could do to you. It was more amusing than anything else because I didn't want to bring the audience down. So that pissed him off even more."

McKagan's memories of the Stones gigs turned out to be eerily prescient. "We got down there and the Stones each had their own limo, their own trailer, their own lawyer—you know, Mick has one, Keith has one. Charlie has one. I remember turning to Izzy and saying, 'Man, we'll never be like that.' Of course, six months later that was us." In some ways, their lives as rock stars were a natural extension of their lives as gutter kids. Only the purity of the drugs had changed. But following the success of *Appetite for Destruction* and the hasty follow-up *GN'R Lies*, fortunes were now on the line. On tour, Rose habitually refused to be on stage at the required time set by promoters, who promptly hit the band with astronomical fines as a punishment for the singer's egotism. Sometimes he would be as late as three hours.

"Axl cost us an absolute fortune by simply refusing to play the game," said Slash.

> Yes, we did a lot of drugs, but the four of us were always ready to play when we were supposed to. And then he leaves us to cool our heels for hours in a tiny backstage dressing room while he's lying around in a hotel room. He thought he was a fucking Roman emperor, and we should have confronted him about it. But he kept threatening to walk away. We should just have let him. It's hard to have respect for a guy who treats the band so badly.

McKagan now shudders at the millions of dollars frittered away on epicureanism.

> It must have added up to the gross domestic product of a small country. We didn't know anything about the business side of being in this huge band. We let other people take care of that. But Axl's behavior cost us a fortune. And it definitely put him in a different corner to Slash and I. It was tough being in the same room as him sometimes never mind having to play nice on stage.

Separation and disenchantment had set in at the same time as rock star grandiosity became part of their daily ritual. By the time they came to start the laborious sessions for what became *Use Your Illusion I* and *II*, Rose cut an isolated and morose figure within the Guns N' Roses camp. Wrestling with inner demons—a legacy of being abused as a child by his demonic preacher of a stepfather—he sank deeper into self-isolationism.

He was also dealing with the bitter aftermath of his brief and tempestuous marriage to Erin Everly, the daughter of Don Everly and herself no stranger to the vicissitudes of a rock 'n' roll lifestyle. In the studio, Slash, McKagan, Stradlin, and Adler worked on the music, leaving Rose to fit his lyrics to the songs. But he got into the habit of overdubbing his vocals on his own, contributing even further to the sense of what could have been mistaken for aloofness or sheer mania.

Weeks morphed into months as the sessions descended into indifference and chaos. Progress sometimes quickened to a crawl, but more often tracks stalled on the grid. He frequently only communicated with the other four through messages passed on by management. "Duff and the rest of us were only informed about what was happening through phone calls and faxes. Guns N' Roses had officially become a dictatorship," recalled Slash. Paranoia was increasingly rampant, with the singer convinced the others were planning to supplant him.

"Everybody hated each other in the band with the exception of me," declared Rose, long after he was the last man standing of the original lineup. "Slash was fighting for power with Izzy because he wanted to take control of the band and destroy it. They were trying to take me down."

Running on twin tracks with this psychosis was Rose's tempestuous relationship with Adler, a childhood friend of Slash, which had been unspooling for years. When Rose recorded his vocals for the *Appetite* track "Rocket Queen," he felt the song lacked a special something—the sound of two people having down-and-dirty sex. He quickly remedied the situation by putting the suggestion to the nearest woman to hand, Adriana Smith—who just happened to be Adler's lover.

Bizarrely, Rose proposed to Smith that they have sex in a vocal booth so that the sounds Smith made could be recorded and put over the bridge of the song. Smith replied that she would do it "for the band, and a bottle of Jack Daniel's." She later admitted it was an act of revenge against the drummer for allegedly cheating on her.

But the upshot of this dangerous liaison and permanent betrayal was to send Adler, arguably the band's worst junkie, further down the rabbit hole of heroin and crack cocaine. By the time the 1980s morphed into the nineties, and Guns began the monumental sessions for *Use Your Illusion I* and *II*, Adler was a junkie write-off.

As the band recorded their epic track "Civil War," more than fifty takes were discarded because Adler's drumming was not fit for purpose. Incandescent, Rose sent up a red flare to management and told them to get a shot of the gunner who was by now seriously misfiring on every level.

Adler recalled the time of his fateful execution:

> Slash called and said, "We're going in the studio to record 'Civil War.'" And I said, "Dude, I'm so sick. Please, can we just wait one more week? I'm so sick."

And he said, "We can't waste the money. We've gotta do this song." So I go in at A&M Records to record, and I'm so weak and sick. I did my best, but I had to play, like, twenty-five times. So they were getting frustrated. And I kept telling them: "I'm sick." And they kept saying, "No, you're not. You're just fucked up." And I said, "I'm not fucked up. I'm sick." And I got kicked out.

His final gig took place in the spring of 1990 at Willie Nelson's Farm Aid, a show that was so removed from Guns N' Roses's fan base it might as well have taken place on the moon. Filmed for TV, the concert captured Adler in all his unraveling glory, starting with his stumble into his drum kit at the start.

"If his playing had been fine, I don't think anyone would have cared what he was doing to himself—at least I wouldn't have," Slash later claimed in his 2008 biography. "We weren't really concerned for Steven's health as much as we were pissed off that his addiction was handicapping his performance and, therefore, the rest of us."

Blind to his own foibles, Adler was convinced Axl Rose had deliberately set him up to fail. "They wanted me to fuck up on live TV; that would be their evidence. By branding me as an ill-equipped, crappy drummer, they'd be armed with a sound reason for kicking me out." Adler's summary dismissal was, however, the first serious sign of the tyrannical clout Rose held with the band's management power brokers, Alan Niven and Doug Goldstein.

"Doug Goldstein called me into the office about two weeks later," recalled the drummer. "He wanted me to sign some contracts. I was told that every time I did heroin, the band would fine me $2,000. There was a whole stack of papers, with colored paper clips everywhere for my signatures. What these contracts actually said was that the band were paying me $2,000 to leave. They were taking my royalties, all my writing credits. They didn't like me anymore and just wanted me gone."

Watching through the cracks in his fingers was Marc Canter, a boyhood friend of Slash who had a ringside ticket to the various drag down fights that beset the band. But he is quick to defend Rose's behavior up to a point. In an interview with Legendary Rock Interviews (https://legendaryrockinterviews.com), he said,

Axl is a perfectionist to the extreme, it had to be right or not at all. Somewhere along the line he had to start eating some of that and realize he couldn't control everything. Interestingly, they never argued amongst themselves or fought over how a song would be written though, the songs always just happened, and it wasn't any type of power struggle or control trip in that regard. A lot of the songs would start with some idea from Izzy like "My Michelle" or

"Nightrain" and then Slash would come and punk it out or rock it up, like the spooky intro part of Michelle was total Izzy, but without Slash we wouldn't have gotten the harder riff that followed it.

Axl would hear these unfinished songs and just know exactly how to work within them. Duff and Steven would then make the songs truly swing and really flesh them out with their ideas. You could say, as some have, that Axl was the most important because he was the singer, but even then I don't think Axl would agree with that. If you took any one of those guys out of the equation, it would have drastically changed all of those songs. It was truly a democracy in the beginning, at that time in 1985 or 1986 they were all on the exact same page.

Adler's dismissal, however, was enough to send shudders of insecurity through Slash, McKagan, and Stradlin who, especially, was at the end of his rope. "Axl had this power thing where he wanted complete control," said Stradlin, the man widely credited as being the musical heart of Guns N' Roses. But he was fed up with the desultory life cycle of drugs-record-drugs-tour-drugs. Near the end of the *Use Your Illusion* tour, he handed in his dog tags, blaming his decision on Rose's unpredictable whims and his refusal to at least adhere to some kind of structure.

"I tried talking to him, during the *Illusion* albums: 'If we had a schedule here, come in at a certain time.' . . . And he completely blew up at me: 'There is no fucking schedule,'" Stradlin told *Rolling Stone*. "There was one song on that record that I didn't even know was on it until it came out, 'My World.' I gave it a listen and thought: 'What the fuck is this?' But Axl made it clear that he was going to do things his way, and there was no space for debate. So I had to make it clear to everybody that that was the end of the line for me."

But the real reason to jump ship came from Rose springing a contract on him that relegated him to the position of being a hired gun instead of the real thing. "I was like 'Fuck you, I've been there from day one, why would I do that?' It was utterly insane." Months later, with Stradlin out of the picture, Rose hit McKagan and Slash with the same autocratic demands—give up your claim on the band's name or you're history.

It came minutes before they were due on stage in Barcelona and left both musicians dumbstruck. It was couched in the usual and oh-so-familiar menacing tones—sign or I won't go on. Fearing a stampede of bandana-clad señors and señoritas, they penned their signatures to the documents.

McKagan later declared,

With the crowd outside already getting rowdy, the guy then implied Axl wouldn't go onstage that night unless we signed the documents. I pictured people getting hurt if a riot started—at least that was my fear. And I was so exhausted—it felt as though I'd been dragging a house around behind me for the last two years. Besides, at the time I never thought Guns N' Roses could possibly exist without us. I signed and so did Slash. The idea seemed ridiculous and in that case, maybe the documents didn't need to be fixed?

Slash admitted he had been worn down by a war of attrition waged by Axl and his legal infantrymen. "He pushed this contract issue on us with so much pressure to the point that Duff and I just gave in. I signed it and let it go. Needless to say, my trust in Axl was gone. That entire contract situation was the antithesis of Guns N' Roses. I was being forced into a secondary role, while Axl was now officially at the helm."

By 1993, Guns N' Roses were shot to pieces. They had replaced one drug-addict drummer—Adler—with another in Matt Sorum, who was fired in 1996. Gilby Clarke also only lasted a short period as a Stradlin guitar clone before being shown the door. With Guns N' Roses mothballed, Slash formed a sideline project called Slash's Snakepit, which included among its ranks McKagan and Clarke.

Their debut album was well received as was the supporting tour and gave Slash a glimpse into an alternative life free from Axl's controlling tendencies. Guns N' Roses remained his day job, however—until the day he arrived at the studio to record a band cover of the Stones' "Sympathy for the Devil" for the film *Interview with the Vampire* only to find another lead guitarist holding a plectrum and wielding a Les Paul. Paul Huge was a school buddy of Axl's from Lafayette whose primary function was to copy Slash's soul-burning riffs.

Huge wasn't in Sash's musical league. It was an inevitable standoff, which could only end one way. "Axl and I have not been capable of seeing eye to eye on Guns N' Roses for some time. We recently tried to collaborate, but at this point, I'm no longer in the band," revealed Slash. He elaborated on the split in a later TV interview: "It wasn't even me necessarily leaving the band. It was more not continuing on with the new band that Axl put together, that he was now at the helm of the new Guns N' Roses. I was given a contract to basically join his new band, and it took about twenty-four hours before I decided this was the end of the line."

Marc Canter is adamant that Slash's decision to have no part in a recalibrated band took Rose by surprise.

I know that Axl was really upset that Slash quit and that Slash took those particular songs because those were songs that were written explicitly for Guns

N' Roses. Just because Axl didn't want all of them didn't mean he didn't want to work with some of them.

I mean, at that point Slash was a little big headed after being out on the road and playing in front of hundreds of thousands of people. But Axl pretty much never forgave him for leaving. He's also angry about some things Slash said in the wake of leaving and about some things said regarding signing the name of the band over.

It's really a story of miscommunication more than anything because they're both really, honestly telling the truth but unfortunately there are two different stories and therefore two different truths.

Years later, having finally gotten sober, Slash insisted his decision to leave owed as much to his dalliances with the grim reaper as to his allegiances to Guns N' Roses. "There's no doubt that if I'd stayed with the band under those circumstances, I'd surely be dead by now because of too much unnecessary drama. I definitely would have found junk again or it would have found me."

McKagan's role as the honest broker between Axl and Slash became redundant when the lead guitar meister picked up his plectrum and left a spoiled brat hurling his remaining toys out of the baby stroller. "I left the band two weeks before my daughter was born," recalled the newly clean bass player.

It wasn't fun. Guns had been paying rent on studios for three years now—from 1994 to 1997—and still did not have a single song. The whole operation was so erratic. It didn't seem to fit in with my hopes for parenthood, for stability. . . . I told Axl, "It's your band now. I'm not interested in you as a dictator." He had hired Paul Huge, his best friend, for the band. I couldn't play with Paul.

McKagan's decision to remove himself from the play left Rose as the only original cast member left. But the stage lights had by now long dimmed on Guns N' Roses. As was his right as retainer of the band's name, Axl hired a revolving door of new players to keep the name up in lights.

The most notable of them was a lead guitarist called Buckethead, whose gimmick was to take the stage sporting a mask and wearing a KFC bucket on his head. He embarked on recording *Chinese Democracy*, an album that would ultimately take more than thirteen years to make and end up as, financially, the biggest white elephant in rock history. Slash, meanwhile, got clean, formed the ill-fated "supergroup" Velvet Revolver (apparently no one saw the obvious pistol correlation to his old band) with McKagan,

Soren, and former Stone Temple Pilots front man Scott Weiland, a junkie with even more social hang-ups than Axl Rose who was doomed to die at the age of thirty-eight in 2015.

Adler continued wrestling with various demons while Stradlin slipped quietly into obscurity, making music when the mood took him but more than happy to live the life of a millionaire rock hermit. Recluse was also a tag equally appended to Axl Rose, who rarely gave interviews and stayed largely below the radar as *Chinese Democracy* stalled on the grid while garnering almost mythical status.

When he did break cover, the storied history of the original Guns N' Roses lineup was never far from discussion. Journalists were happy to throw out juicy pieces of bait about Slash or Duff, confident enough that Axl would be easily reeled in.

Inside the court of public opinion, Guns N' Roses fans had already held Rose accountable for high crimes and misdemeanors. Egotism was no defense in the eyes of a loyal following that had in the main mobilized behind the two guitarists. Between Slash and Rose, however, there was only sniping from the sidelines.

The two wouldn't speak for many years to come, even when issues about the music they made together came up. "He hates my guts," Slash said. "It's over a lot of different stuff; I don't even know. There's just no communication between us. I talk to Duff and Steven, but when it comes to old Guns N' Roses, there really isn't anybody that makes decisions."

Axl even took to trying to ban fans at Guns N' Roses shows from entering the venues wearing Slash T-shirts. Gradually, the beef became an albatross "because there was so much attention on the breakup," Slash told *Esquire*. "It got built up into this monster that led to a kind of animosity that wasn't the focus for me. Neither one of us wants to be down each other's throats for no reason. At this point, I'm trying to put it to rest. So I try to avoid the subject."

Except he couldn't. Eventually, he and Duff took it upon themselves to dive deeper into the tangled legal papers they had signed during the foggy days of the early nineties that gave Axl full custody of the band's name. In 2006, ten years after they left the band, Slash and McKagan took their revenge in a Los Angeles courtroom, accusing Rose of swindling them out of a multimillion dollar fortune. The central thrust of their claim was that the singer had recently—and secretly—changed the publishers of the band's copyrighted songs and kept the royalties for himself.

The two guitarists charged that Rose had deliberately "omitted and concealed" the new arrangements to cream money off the top. The courtroom scenes tore apart old wounds while creating a new media circus around the band's three central characters. Rose hit back at the "baseless" allegations through his lawyers and claimed Slash and Duff were trying to rewrite the history of the band.

> The Federal lawsuit Hudson and McKagan filed was based on a faulty premise from the start. What Hudson [Slash's real surname] and McKagan attempted to portray as egregious misconduct by Axl was in fact—as Slash and Duff have learned—nothing more than a clerical error committed by ASCAP. Had Slash and Duff or their representatives bothered to pick up the phone, the clerical error could have been easily sorted out without the need for filing an utterly baseless lawsuit which one can only assume had been filed for the purposes of self-publicity at Axl's expense.
>
> For over 10 years Slash, a consummate press, photo and media opportunist and manipulator, has attacked Axl Rose on a number of levels. Slash's actions, whether in or out of Guns N' Roses, have been a complete betrayal across the board of his alleged friendship and business relationship with Axl and the so-called brotherhood and band loyalties that are supposed to have existed.
>
> Instead, Slash has publicly attempted, by soliciting public and media support, to take credit for something that was not his or anyone else's to take, notwithstanding that Slash played a major part in the success of the band as Axl has continually acknowledged.

The feud even lured Weiland into its web, with the Velvet Revolver singer at one point challenging Rose to an all-out fight over his remarks about Slash. "We toured our album over a year and a half. How many shows have you played over the last ten years? Oh, that's right—you bailed out on your long-awaited comeback tour, leaving your remaining fans feeling, shall we say, a trifle miffed. I won't even list what I've accomplished because I don't need to," he vented in true scorched-earth fashion. "What we're talking about here is a frightened little man who once thought he was king, But, unfortunately, this king without his court is nothing but a memory of the asshole he once was."

It wasn't hard to imagine Slash doffing his trademark top hat in appreciation. It wouldn't be the last time Slash and Axl would face off in court. In 2010 the singer gave the makers of the video game *Guitar Hero* permission to use "Welcome to the Jungle"—on one solemn condition. That any imagery of a certain curly-haired lead guitarist would be nowhere in sight.

Imagine then his unbridled rage when he checked out the game only to see a digitally enhanced Slash dancing his way along the fretboard. It no longer really mattered. Rose had been left way behind in the battle of the bands, becoming a graceless irrelevance compared to his former bandmates.

Nowhere was this better summed up than when Guns N' Roses were inducted into the Rock & Roll Hall of Fame in 2012. As industry rumors swirled over who exactly would show up, all ultimately became clear. Slash, Duff, Izzy, and even Steven Adler duly took their bows at the ceremony in Cleveland but Rose was a not unexpected last-minute no-show.

In a statement, he explained his reasons for sitting out a reunion of the classic lineup. And rejected any attempt to place him in the pantheon of rock greats. "Let sleeping dogs lie or lying dogs sleep or whatever," he wrote. "Time to move on. People get divorced. Life doesn't owe you your own personal happy ending especially at another's, or in this case several others' expense."

Rose's Hall of Fame snub looked to have finally closed the door on a reunion even though the odd shaft of daylight continued to emerge. Slash once mentioned the prospects of a reunion, stating, "It's not even something I like to dwell on. I don't even like to make comments because you end up with quotes that sometimes exacerbate the issue. I've got other things going on. I'm very, very proud—endlessly proud—of everything the band stood for and everything that's gone on with it."

The loudest reunion cheerleader was Duff McKagan, who maintained a discreet back channel with Rose during those long years when the singer's career was in the toilet. Speaking in 2015, the bass man, who even occasionally guested at live Axl gigs, admitted, "I think it would be wonderful, one day, if we reconciled, first and foremost. That alone would be cool."

Later that same year, the latest iteration of Guns finally imploded—and McKagan played his peacekeeper part to perfection, pitching his belief that the time was now right to put down the gloves. Surprisingly, though, the icebreaker was Axl Rose, who made the first move in a call to his estranged guitarist.

I had asked for [Slash's] number. And then I had called him, and he was on tour or something, and then we set up when we were gonna see each other, and I think something happened to both of our plans and that didn't happen. And then eventually in October, we got together and we had a dinner at my house.

And then Duff and I went and hung out right after that—like a week or so after. And then it was just kind of talking and planning. We initially were gonna do some kind of promos and stuff, and then other things came up that got in the way of that.

And then it was rehearsals. And I went down to rehearsal, and everything just sounded right. And we just went to work. It was time to sing, see what the sound sounded like and stuff and get ready for the show, and it was all working.

Speaking with *USA Today*, Slash recalled reconnecting with the singer. "It was nice that it happened," he said. "I don't know if I would have had the wherewithal to call him, just because I'm introverted and it might have been hard for me," Slash admitted. "Not during that initial phone call, but after that, it was really good to be able to get rid of some of the negative baggage that we'd been carrying around for a long time. It had been 20 years of not talking and letting this bad blood continue to be perpetuated by the media. It turned into something way bigger than what was really going on, so it was good to get past that."

In December 2015 came the announcement that Duff and Slash were rejoining Guns N' Roses, a declaration that was accompanied by news of a headline appearance at Coachella in January and a North American tour. Using the same dark humor employed by the Eagles, the swing through twenty-one cities was billed as the Not in This Lifetime tour—a reference to Axl's repeated insistence that he would never again share a stage with Slash and Duff.

Their first proper gig featuring all three was at LA's famed Troubadour, one of the key rungs on the rock 'n' roll ladder they had first climbed almost three decades earlier. Slash said, "We really got our start in this particular venue. I remember that gig pretty well. At that point, we were selling out these venues and had a really big word of mouth going and had a really eclectic demographic coming to see us—from hardcore punk rockers to metalheads and glam and surfers. It was a very mixed-up kind of audience, but it was great."

The gigs were a critical success and set in motion a worldwide touring cycle that continues to the present day. By the end of 2018, the Not in This Lifetime tour had grossed an incredible $563 million, a figure only eclipsed by U2's 360° tour. The fact that Slash and Axl, both bloated by the early onset of middle age, now looked like caricatures of their former selves didn't matter a damn to the faithful who, high on nostalgia, longed to hear "Sweet Child O' Mine" and "November Rain" played live one more time. More chilled out this time around, each party—Duff, Slash, and Axl—had early staked out their respective positions in order for the thorns to be removed from the Roses. In short, Axl was required to grow up—and show up on time. Gone were the drug-addled dramas of their wild youth. Inevitably, there were expectations of a new Guns N' Roses album.

In turn, Slash and Axl, now the best of buddies again, threw their fans a bone, but at the time of writing no new product has emerged from the supposedly hundreds of studio sessions that have taken place. This naturally underpins the legitimate acceptance that Guns N' Roses are now happy to take their place alongside the likes of the Eagles, Aerosmith, Fleetwood Mac, and other iconic bands on the dollar-laden heritage trail. Especially now that everything is apparently coming up roses again.

The Rolling Stones: Keith Richards and Mick Jagger
Atlantic Records/Photofest © Atlantic Records

8

MICK JAGGER AND KEITH RICHARDS

It was, by Keith Richards's own account, "a terrible fucking day." Outside, the autumn rain lashed the windows of the Mayfair apartment smothered in Moroccan drapes and cheesecloth scarves. Overhead, flashes of lightning lit up the dark, brooding skies over London's west end as passers-by dashed for shelter. The grim weather was a perfect match for Richards's black disposition, a mood shaped in no small way by the heroin coursing through his body.

But it wasn't the climate that was causing him to sink deeper and deeper into drug-induced desolation. It was simply the deep instinct that, three miles away at a house in Lowndes Square, his lover and muse at that precise point was seducing his best friend in full view of a camera crew and a manipulative and voyeuristic film director. The more he tried to blank out the licentious images exploding in his mind's eye, the more the mushroom clouds formed behind dilated pupils.

As always, music provided the best—the only—therapy. Reaching for his Maton Supreme guitar, Richards hit on the open-tuned chords for the first time, and the metaphoric words simply tumbled out: *"A storm is threatening, my very life today. . . . If I don't get some shelter, Oh yeah, I'm gonna fade away. . . ."*

A Rolling Stones riff inspired by a Rolling Stones rift. An end-of-the-world song rooted in a personal apocalypse. No one really knew for sure if the erotically charged scenes in *Performance* between Mick Jagger and the bewitchingly alluring Anita Pallenberg had crossed the line from fake fumbles and giggles beneath the covers to the real thing. They didn't have to—but Richards suspected it had, didn't he?

Deep down, he knew. And there wasn't a damn thing he could do about it. If he did, it would probably have brought the curtain down on the Rolling Stones, ladeez and gentlemen, the world's greatest rock 'n' roll band. But this was 1969, the final year of the decade that set the parameters for free love. And hadn't Richards rescued Anita from the sadomasochistic clutches of his former bandmate Brian Jones, meaning he was in no position to demand blind loyalty—from Anita, or for that matter Jagger, a man with a rampant libido who, like some Roman potentate, felt that no woman was off limits.

"I didn't find out for ages about Mick and Anita, but I smelled it," said Richards years later. "Mostly from Mick, who didn't give any sign of it, which is why I smelled it. I never expected anything from Anita. I mean, I'd stolen her from Brian. What do you expect?

"You've got an old lady like Anita Pallenberg and expect other guys not to hit on her? I heard rumors and I thought, if she's going to be making a move with Mick, good luck to him. She probably nearly broke his back." Anita repeatedly denied going the full nine yards with Mick. Jagger, for his part, only ever added to the layers of intrigue surrounding his ménage-a-trois scenes with Anita and French actress Michele Breton.

"All the stories around the filming of those scenes are so good, I'm not going to deny any of them," said Mick enigmatically when interviewed for a book chronicling the making of a movie that became a byword for sexual decadence.

Six months later, when the Stones reconvened to begin work on their next album, *Let It Bleed*, the song of ultimate doom Keith Richards had begun that stormy day, now titled "*Gimme Shelter*," was among the first he and Jagger worked on. It was the height of the Stones' golden run of albums that also took in *Sticky Fingers* and the peerless *Exile on Main Street*. Collaboration, however, could never allay suspicion or that horrible sense of betrayal bordering on incest. And the did-they-or-didn't-they vignette produced a wound that kept bleeding. Richards declared, "It probably put a bigger gap between me and Mick than anything else, but mainly on Mick's part, not mine. And probably forever."

Mick Jagger was "Jumpin' Jack Flash," an ambisexual demon, happiest with his arms draped round someone exotic. Keith Richards was the guitar-toting pirate, happiest when holed up with a kif pipe and a line of something narcotic. Together, they represent the core mythology of the Rolling Stones and rock music's most complicated and conflicted partnership—camp versus cool, status-seeker versus street-fighting man.

Anita Pallenberg was, ultimately, just one of several butterflies broken on the wheel. Richards's revenge, when it eventually came, was devastating for Jagger. In 2010, he published his biography, a weighty tome titled, with no small amount of self-parody, *Life*, and hit rock music's greatest lothario right where it hurts—in the crotch.

Spite leaped from the page as Richards, acknowledging Jagger's alleged affair with Anita, mocked the size of his friend's manhood, a barb that held Mick up to worldwide ridicule. He wrote, "She had no fun with his tiny todger. I know he's got an enormous set of balls, but it doesn't quite fill the gap, does it?"

And, just for good measure, he dropped another bomb, claiming he had once slept with Jagger's then lover Marianne Faithfull, a disputed act of reprisal that brought both of them more than an ounce of mutual smug satisfaction.

Jagger reportedly demanded a face-to-face apology in order to keep the Stones rolling into their sixth decade. It was, he argued, a sacrosanct condition for their continued existence. He declared, "Well, I think it was a good thing he got together with me and said that. Yes, it was a prerequisite, really. You have to put those things to one side; you can't leave them unspoken."

Jagger's alleged performances with Anita set the scene for the first serious rupture of the Stone Age between the band's two alpha males. But all the did-he-or-didn't-he imputations did, really, was light the fuse on a feud that would occasionally erupt with volcanic intensity over the next five decades. Richards once threatened to "slit his throat" when, in 1988, Jagger embarked on his first solo tour with a set list that grew more Stones-heavy with every gig.

And Mick's decision to accept a knighthood from British prime minister Tony Blair in 2003 was seen by Richards as the ultimate sellout, his childhood friend kowtowing to the same establishment that, thirty-six years earlier, had locked them up for being a subversive danger to the world's youth.

"I went fucking berserk when I heard," Richards raged. "I thought it was ludicrous to take one of those gongs from the same people who did their very best to throw us in jail and kill us at one time."

Another public apology was required in 2018 when Richards said Jagger should get the snip after the singer, at the age of seventy-five, fathered his eighth child. "Oh, those poor kids," lamented Richards. But any attempt to unravel the Gordian knot that has bound Jagger and Richards together for so long is an exercise in futility. Equally, it would be disingenuous to point a fish-eye lens at their lives and zoom in on the distortions.

Yet it is these same ripples that symbolize the choppy waters of rock 'n' roll's most tempestuous bromance. The truth is this; the Glimmer Twins have long been marked by their unpredictable affinity. Genuine love mixed with naked loathing is often caught in a crossfire hurricane of their own making.

Throughout the 1970s, Richards and Anita descended further into heroin hell, two junkies elegantly wasted by addiction. At the same time, the Stones kept on producing albums of steadily diminishing quality, while at the same time maintaining the myth of the world's greatest rock 'n' roll band. During that decade, though, it was Jagger who kept the ship afloat, despite the band's slow retreat from critical relevance with albums like *It's Only Rock 'N' Roll* and *Black and Blue* before the disco groove of *Some Girls* clawed back a modicum of street cred.

And it was Jagger, combining his keen business acumen with a desire for establishment acceptance, who most took advantage of Richard's druggy passiveness to turn the Stones into a multimillion-dollar conglomerate with its own private jet fueled by sold-out tours and a back catalog that continued to pour money into the band's coffers. Yet it was this period that did most to delineate the personalities of Mick Jagger and Keith Richards in the eyes of the public.

Craving acceptance by the nouveau riche, Jagger took his first proper steps on the rung that led to high society. In 1971, he had married Blanca (Bianca) Pérez-Mora Macías, a stunning Nicaraguan actress and model whose grand social appetites were never in question. Richards hated her from the off, but meanwhile was powerless to halt his own mythology, which was picking up speed with every arrest and every bust.

While Jagger scaled the social ladder, Richards stayed on the streets, a ghetto outlaw. He was the only member of the old order to be held in awe by the newly emerging punk rockers who saw in him that sense of rebellion that still burned deep. But by 1979, he was facing jail in Canada, having been busted again and charged with trafficking. And the Stones were literally facing the end of the road.

At the time, Jagger never chastised Richards in public, preferring always to throw a protective arm round his friend's shoulder. In private, however, he seethed at Richards's "weakness," despite being far from an innocent himself where drugs were concerned. "How did I handle [Keith's drug problems]? Oh, with difficulty. It's never easy."

"When someone is always on drugs, you never get anything done," he declared.

> When Keith was taking heroin, it was very difficult to work. He still was creative, but it took a long time. Anyone taking heroin is thinking about taking heroin more than they're thinking about anything else. That's the general rule

about most drugs. People have different personalities when they're drunk or take heroin, or whatever drugs. I don't find it easy dealing with people who have drug problems.

Neither man spoke at length about it, even though the issue threatened to break up the band permanently. Touring had become a major headache. Richards's rap sheet for drug convictions and other legally challenging misadventures meant serious negotiations were required to allow him a visa to travel to, especially, Canada and the United States, a land of milk and honey in terms of concert revenue streams. By the end of the seventies, the Stones had arguably become rock's most notoriously dysfunctional band, a state of decay driven by Jagger and Richards's ever-growing hostility to each other.

Ronnie Wood's recruitment quickly established him as Richards's dope buddy, an alliance that only served to fuel further Jagger's antagonism. Conceding the band's future was on a tightrope, Richards eventually cleaned up in 1979 to avoid jail time in Canada.

The band released *Emotional Rescue*, their seventeenth album, and set off on yet another lucrative world tour. But hopes for rapprochement quickly faded. Offstage, they rarely spoke. Jagger demanded his own dressing room well away from the pre-gig "rituals" adopted by Richards and Wood.

When the curtain came up, only the stage served as Switzerland, an area of mutual neutrality. Disagreements between them erupted mainly over the future musical direction of the band. Richards was adamant the Stones stay true to their R&B roots; Jagger insisted their sound had to evolve to embrace new audiences and to keep them "current." Richards was also looking to have a bigger say in the band's musical output having, he believed, finally emerged from his chemically induced cryogenic chamber to help share the burden going forward into a new decade.

"I thought it would be a way of saying to him, 'Thanks, I know you had everything on your shoulders but I'm back now.' But by then the ego genie was out of the bottle. He had become an even bigger control freak."

Behind his back, Richards began to bitchily refer to Jagger as Brenda or Her Majesty, and said he was suffering from LVS—lead vocalist syndrome. He said, "Onstage, you have to believe you're semi-divine. The problem comes when that belief sticks with you off stage."

This latest animus sounded the starting gun on a race to the bottom that persisted through the entire 1980s, a period Richards characterized as "World War Three." Meanwhile, Rolling Stones Records' distribution deal with Atlantic had expired and CBS Records, now owned by Sony Corporation, was aggressively pursuing the band, despite their fading status.

The Stones' value as a superstar group was still hailed as a feather in the cap of label president Walter Yetnikoff, one of music's most egotistical and deranged figures. A man, it is said, who began his day with a glass of vodka and a cigarillo while his barber dyed his beard and stuck cocaine up his nose (simultaneously). Yet he presided over the most profitable and prestigious stable of artists of all time, a roster that simultaneously included Michael Jackson and Bruce Springsteen.

Jagger, a former London School of Economics student, took it upon himself to deal directly with Yetnikoff, and it wasn't long before all the mutual backslapping paid off. In August 1983, the Stones signed a new deal with CBS reportedly worth a reported $28 million, an eye-watering sum for a band that was clearly mired in a midcareer crisis.

But buried between the lines was a secret pact that included a three-album solo deal for Jagger. Yetnikoff burnished Mick's already monstrous narcissism with a promise of world domination, a vanity-appealing pledge to make him as big a solo star as Michael Jackson. Richards, he said, was a drag on Jagger's talent.

But the alliance only served to take the Stones to the brink of a permanent split. Richards wasn't slow in venting his anger when he discovered what he considered to be underhanded chicanery.

> I personally would lay a lot of the Stones current non-communication and this current break at the doorstep of Yetnikoff in particular. He thought Mick was the Rolling Stones, and he encouraged and greased him up, led him to believe he was really all that counted. I don't think that was good for Mick to hear at the time. Because that's what he wanted to hear and to believe.
>
> And as far as I'm concerned, if you want to say who broke up the Rolling Stones, I'd say CBS. It's fairly obvious when you think about it. Why sign a band for twenty-eight million bucks and then steam straight away into breaking them up?

Elsewhere he noted, "We didn't build this band up to stab each other in the back." Jagger, typically, thought Richards was turning a minor costume drama into a constitutional crisis. "When we signed the recording contract with CBS, I had a provision to make a solo record. Keith knew all about it, so it wasn't a bolt from the blue," he retorted. "I don't want to excuse what happened; it was a very bad period. Everyone was getting on very badly. Keith just liked to mouth off about it. He became very upset and overreacted when I wanted to do a solo record, which in retrospect seems a natural thing to want to do."

Running on parallel lines amid this latest round of warfare, sessions had nevertheless been continuing for the album that would become *Under-*

cover, but the displacement between Jagger and Richards in the studio had become even more noticeable.

The album, the follow-up to the outtake-laden *Tattoo You*, was recorded in Paris in an atmosphere of open hostility—and in shifts—with Mick in the studio between noon and 5 p.m., and Keith working typically vampire hours from midnight to 5 a.m. Producer Chris Kimsey had worked with the band on *Some Girls, Emotional Rescue*, and *Tattoo You* but saw the temperature between the two chief Stones plummet to arctic levels during sessions for *Undercover*.

> That was the worst time I'd ever experienced with them. I would get Mick in the studio from like, midday until seven o'clock, then Keith from like, nine o'clock till five in the morning. They would not be together. They specifically avoided each other. Mick would say, "When's he coming in? I'll be there later." After about a week, it was killing me. And it was such silly things, like one would say, "What did he do?" And I'd play a bit, and the other would say, "Get rid of it."

Jagger point-blank refused to tour the album and instead directed all his energies on his first solo album, *She's the Boss*, which came out amid much fanfare in February 1985. By the time the band regrouped to work on *Dirty Work*, their first album for Columbia—and with that huge advance already in their bank accounts—the game was up. Drummer Charlie Watts and bass player Bill Wyman, fed up with the constant infighting, both largely stayed away from the sessions.

Jagger, morose and disinterested, pitched up with little material, having used all his best songs for his solo debut. Furious, Richards instead formed a songwriting pact with Ronnie Wood, who received an unprecedented four writing credits on the album. Tracks such as "Fight," "Had It with You," and "Winning Ugly" told their own stories. But the video for "One Hit (to the Body)" took the Stones' internal feud to DEFCON 1.

The footage, spliced with clips of real boxing fights, showed Jagger and Richards circling each other like two snarling bare-knuckle bruisers, staring each other down and, at times, nearly landing real-time punches. Slashing, aggressive guitar chords only ramped up the tension. Method acting might have been in play, but Richards admitted it was hardly a stretch for them both to ham it up as two men seemingly at each other's throats.

"That video more or less told the story of where we were as a band," recalled Richards. "We nearly literally came to blows over and above our acting duties." Another who was caught up in the internecine Jagger/Richards schism was Steve Lillywhite, then rock music's most in-demand producer.

Lillywhite was stoked to be working with the Stones but soon became dismayed by the state of internal relations. He said, "I produced the worst-ever Rolling Stones album. There wasn't a great tailwind with the Stones at that point. There was too much bitterness."

With *Dirty Work* virtually stillborn, Jagger was in no mood to spend months on the road with the Stones, and especially Richards. For Mick, it was easier to walk away from *Dirty Work*—and maybe even necessary. "The album wasn't that good, it was okay," he told *Rolling Stone*.

It certainly wasn't a great Rolling Stones album. The feeling inside the band was very bad, too. The relationships were terrible. The health was diabolical. I wasn't in particularly good shape. The rest of the band, they couldn't walk across the Champs Elysées, much less go on the road. So we had this long, bad experience of making that record, and the last thing I wanted to do was spend another year with the same people. I just wanted out.

Later, when tempers had eventually cooled, he insisted his decision to keep the band in mothballs saved them from splitting for good. "I was completely, 100 percent right about not doing that tour," Jagger said. "The band was in no condition to tour. It's as simple as that."

Speaking earlier to the *Boston Globe*, he clarified things. "If we had gone out after *Dirty Work*," Jagger said, "we'd have never finished the tour, which would have been the end. It would have been hard to come back from that." Instead, he plowed on with his second solo album, *Primitive Cool*, and began to put together his own touring band as he prepared to go it alone.

Picking up the gauntlet, Richards then formed his own breakaway group, the X-pensive Winos, and released his first solo album in 1988. Lauded by critics, *Talk Is Cheap*—a clear jibe at Jagger—underscored Richards's credentials as a true rock kingpin. Between the R&B grooves lay a brilliant track called "You Don't Move Me." The best song the Stones never recorded, it was an undisguised lyrical assassination of the man who now considered the Stones a "millstone round my neck."

Richards's antipathy toward his songwriting partner was laid bare in lines such as "Why do you think you got no friends? You drove them all around the bend." It was Richards's "How Do You Sleep" moment, an echo of John Lennon's notorious takedown of Paul McCartney. "Half of me is saying I don't want to rub the guy's nose in it," Richards told the *Washington Post*, "but, of course, you're also human, so you stick the knife in and turn it one time."

James Fox, the esteemed *Sunday Times* journalist who so magnificently captured Richards in his biography *Life*, reckons Jagger's dismissive comments cut Richards to the quick. Fox told the *Rock's Backpages* podcast,

"There was the moment when Mick's head is turned; I don't know exactly what happened."

> But Keith feels a sense of betrayal and a terrible sadness. And then it is compounded by Mick making fatal remarks like the Rolling Stones are a millstone round my neck. This will be a moment when you cannot restrain Keith from saying exactly what he thinks, that (Mick) should not have gone and done this music, almost broke the band up, I really mind about it, and so on.
>
> People thought it was very unfair but within the Rolling Stones' world, all the people who knew Keith, they would have thought he had copped out because it was such a big story inside the band. That's how relations were.

After battling it out on *Billboard*, Jagger and Richards took their push-and-pull solo duel into the concert arena. In March 1988, Jagger enlisted musical hotshots such as guitarist Joe Satriani—whose main job was to channel his best Keith Richards—as he kicked off his maiden solo tour in Japan.

But despite having two solo albums under his belt, Mick still frontloaded his set with Stones classics such as "Gimme Shelter," "Tumbling Dice," and "Bitch." This presented Richards with an open goal to give Jagger and his "ersatz Stones" an easy kicking.

> I thought it very sad that a high percentage of his show was Rolling Stones' songs. If you're going to do something on your own, do stuff off the two albums that you did. Don't pretend you're a solo artist and have two chicks prancing around doing "Tumbling Dice" . . . that severely pissed me off. If Her Royal Highness had her way, we'd be playing in fucking panto.

Jagger preferred to pull his punches rather than get involved in a public slanging match over the quality of his solo output. "He was very rude," said Mick of the media potshots taken by Richards. "Keith just doesn't have any manners. I tried to play off saying what I thought about Keith because it's potentially damaging. You don't like to say, 'Well, my brother is an idiot but I have to get on with him.' I just thought Keith was an unnecessary loudmouth."

The press tended to side with Richards, by then reveling more and more in his image as a gentleman junkie and the gypsy king of twelve-bar rock 'n' roll. He frequently arrived for interviews clutching two bottles of Rebel Yell and kept a Smith and Wesson gun in his bag—just in case.

Betting against the house, Jagger's tour bombed, the American leg being scrapped due to poor ticket sales. It was an incredible knock to his self-esteem, especially coming so soon after *Primitive Cool* had received a critical mauling. It had barely scraped into the *Billboard* top fifty while peaking at twenty-six on the UK album charts. In contrast, the Winos uncorked a Beaujolais Nouveau from an unexpected vineyard—and went down a storm with audiences in North America. It was the final step in a personal vindication.

The Stones hadn't toured since 1982, easily the longest performance hiatus of their career. The Jagger/Richards codependency had long ago morphed into a schoolboy standoff. Unofficially or not, the band was dead, although no one was yet ready to administer the last rites.

Former *Sunday Times* journalist and author Robert Sandall said, "The Stones had lost their mojo in the late 1980s, no question about it. And this album was Keith's way of saying to Mick, 'Look, I know what the Stones should sound like—they should sound like this.' Keith was saying this is what rock 'n' roll is about with my garage band behind me."

Then suddenly two things happened: (1) the Stones received an invitation to be inducted into the Rock & Roll Hall of Fame—and (2) Ronnie Wood took it upon himself to try and heal the rift between Jagger and Richards. "It looked like Mick and Keith weren't ever going to talk again, but I did manage to get them talking on the phone," said the spikey-haired guitarist. "I wasn't going to let the institution of the Stones fall down."

Barbados was chosen as the location for the Stones' own version of the Yalta conference. For the first hour, Mick and Keith screamed at each other before realizing all this petty name-calling had casually slipped into comedy. Weeks later, they stood side by side at New York's Waldorf Hotel as Pete Townsend eulogized "the only band I've ever idolised." During the buildup, the Stones' anticipated appearance at the Hall of Fame dinner in Cleveland was the talk of the music biz. Would Mick and Keith show up together in spite of their recent press feuds? Would the Stones play? Would this be the official kickoff for a reunion?

Well, yes and no. Jagger and Richards did show up, draping arms over each other's shoulders, digging elbows into each other's ribs, and cackling like errant schoolboys at the jokes in their respective acceptance speeches. A beaming Ronnie Wood was there, along with ex-Stone Mick Taylor.

Looking directly at Richards, Jagger told the audience, "I'm very proud to have worked with this group of musicians for twenty-five years. The other thing I'm very proud of is the songs Keith and I have written."

It was the signal, greeted with loud applause, that détente had, finally, broken out. The band reformed and, in short order, had compiled enough songs for an album, The release of *Steel Wheels* was followed by the biggest tour of the Stones's career—and set in motion a pattern that has, by and large, continued at the point of writing. The Stones comfortably settled into an album-tour cycle, becoming their own tribute band, while Jagger and Richards maintained an uneasy armistice as they stumbled into official, wrinkly, old age. Looking back at the apex of their dueling days, Richards occasionally effected twinges of regret.

Denying their feud was a publicity-generating put-up job, he said,

> Mick and I would not go in for stunts. Unfortunately, it was for real. Maybe I should actually say fortunately. To me the unfortunate part is that this was a family squabble that was carried out via the world's press. And then you're getting into something else. Fleet Street loved playing us off against each other. We should have known better. The squabble was about making solo albums on the back of Rolling Stones record deals.
>
> It's ok to do solo stuff but cut your own deal. If you want to go deeper, maybe that was only the trigger. The Rolling Stones had got too big to be any good as a band. It was two years on and two years off, and I couldn't handle that. If you want to be the world's best rock 'n' roll band, you have to be able to play at least once a week. Because, otherwise, it takes months to crank up that machine again.
>
> Mick and I were aware of this thing as a problem but figured we could handle it. It was basically frustration over stopping and starting, stopping and starting. But this is a rock 'n' roll band, and they're only any good if they play regularly.

It was a glib summing up of the discord that still bubbled up between the Glimmer Twins. Even as the shadows of middle age lengthened, hostilities still occasionally erupted across various media platforms. Jagger's 2003 knighthood acceptance from Tony Blair reopened old fissures over Mick's craven courtship of the establishment—the very same establishment that once was hell bent on sending them both to Wormwood Scrubs for a long spell at Her Majesty's pleasure. Insurgency, such as it had ever really been there, was now officially replaced with elitism.

"I don't want to step out on stage with someone wearing a coronet and the old ermine," mocked Richards. "I told Mick it's a paltry honour, it's not what the Stones are about, is it? They didn't offer it to me because they knew I'd turn it down. It's bollocks. You have to kneel and I'm not going to kneel for anyone. Mick came to me and said, 'Tony Blair insists I accept this.'"

Richards continues: "I said, 'Well, you can always turn it down.' You know, Mick wanted one, so he got one. He is a power freak and there's nothing we can do about it. I don't want to do anything about it. Let him bugger about. It doesn't make any difference to what we do." Richard's biography, aside from the vengeful size-matters taunt at Mick's manhood, often shone a difficult light on the twists and turns of their lives together. In 2018, he was forced into an embarrassing public climbdown after delivering his own barbed congratulations over Jagger fathering a child with ballet dancer Melanie Hamrick at the age of seventy-three.

"Mick's a randy old bastard," Keith told the *Wall Street Journal*. "It's time for the snip—you can't be a father at that age." With yet another billion-dollar tour in the planning stage, Jagger insisted on an apology. "I deeply regret the comments I made about Mick in the *WSJ*, which were completely out of line," Keith tweeted. "I have, of course, apologized to him in person."

It's hard to imagine the unrestrained Richards of old groveling like this to Jagger. Through it all, however, an undoubted friendship endured, a beautiful mystique neither man can properly explain. James Fox comes closest to unraveling the riddle. Recalling his conversations with the guitarist for Richards' autobiography, he told *Rolling Stone*,

> Underneath, what Keith was saying was a terrible sadness—of two lost friends. I think he really minds that he can't be close to Mick. He keeps on looking and searching for the Mick when they were so close that they wouldn't even have to speak to each other about music. The frustration of somebody he found unapproachable—it hurts him.
>
> There are a couple of photographs in the book of Keith with his parents, when he's twelve. He looks so forlorn, only-child-y. Therefore, the betrayal thing would be even more painful. He believes a lot in loyalty. As he says about people, "With one look, you can tell." And he won't give up on them until they give up on him.

Richards, perhaps surprisingly given his outlaw image, has often seemed the most nostalgic of the two, and regrets the personal and professional distance that had over time set in between them, saying wistfully, "I used to love Mick, but I haven't been to his dressing room in twenty years. Sometimes I think, 'I miss my friend.' I wonder, 'Where did he go?' I love the man dearly; I'm still his mate. But he makes it very difficult to be his friend."

Keith once described the relationship as like "two very volatile brothers—when they clash, they really clash, but when it's over." But that kind of glib comparison has never sat easily with Jagger.

> People always say things like that. But I have a brother [Chris Jagger], you know? My relationship with my brother is nothing at all like my relationship with Keith, which is someone you work with, completely different. With a brother, you have parents in common, families in common.

We don't have that, Keith and I. We work together. If you didn't have a brother you might say that it was like being a brother. But being in a band is another kind of relationship.

Perhaps Marianne Faithfull, that elfin-like symbol of the Swinging Sixties, summed it up best: "Of all Mick's relationships," she declared, "the only one that really means anything to him is with Keith."

In 2016, the Stones' touring machine was once again revived from its mummified state for an excursion that rolled its way across South America, a swing that saw the band play before 1.3 million fans and rake in an astonishing $91 million through the turnstiles. Much of it was filmed for a new rockumentary about the band.

But the best footage came when Jagger and Richards, their faces gnarled by time, turned back the clock to their days as adolescent R&B lovers sat across from each other in a squalid London flat, Keith especially having no qualms about ripping off yet another Bo Diddley riff.

Perched nonchalantly on a pair of chairs in the middle of an empty room, there was still no disguising the easy-going camaraderie between Jagger and Richards. Suddenly the silence is broken by the oh-so-familiar opening riff of "Honky Tonk Women" followed by Jagger's oh-so-faux-southern drawl. And for the next few minutes, something spellbinding this way comes, a magic that defies time's unforgiving advance.

As the last notes from Richards's acoustic guitar melt into the ether, both men break out in huge, wrinkly grins. It's a moment that owes plenty to nostalgia, and an acknowledgment of the almost spiritual ties that will bind them together until death do they part. Richards's obituary has been updated many times, but he simply refuses to dance with Mr. D. while Jagger's heart scare in 2019 only served to reinforce the truth that mortality is constant.

"That's the way it went," says Richards in his trademark gravelly wheeze. Two rock legends raging against the dying light of their glory days but simply refusing to accept the final curtain. For Mick and Keith, it really is only rock 'n' roll in a world where there's always been, as writer Rich Cohen so memorably put it, the sun, the moon, and the Rolling Stones.

The Police: Stewart Copeland, Andy Somers, and Sting
AF Archive/Alamy Stock

9

THE POLICE

We didn't go to school together or grow up in the same neighbourhood. We were never a tribe. We care passionately about the music and we're all strong characters, and nobody would be pushed around. We fought over everything. —Sting

Blinking into the blackness of the packed bleachers at Shea Stadium was the point of greatest illumination. It was a light bulb moment of clarity lit up by the realization for Sting that this was his fork on the road to Damascus. This was the career crossroads for himself and the Police, at that point in the summer of 1983 the biggest pop/rock band in the world. And for the group's singer, the master builder behind their biggest songs, there was only one way to turn.

It was time to put some healthy distance—professional and personal— between himself, Stewart Copeland and Andy Summers, the powerhouse drummer and pioneering guitarist who were also part of the Police's force majeure. Once upon a long ago, theirs had been a tense and complicated marriage of musical convenience. Copeland, the son of an American CIA agent brought up in relative prosperity in Beirut, and the band's founder, was brash, opinionated, and aggressively uncompromising when it came to music; Sting, a fiercely working-class former phys-ed teacher from Newcastle, charismatic and a gifted songwriter, was self-centered, ambitious, and aggressively uncompromising when it came to music.

Diplomatically perched in the middle was Summers, ten years older than the other two and a man whose experience as a jobbing musician playing in bands on both sides of the Atlantic made him acutely familiar with internal group politics, where machismo often ruled. Strangers to begin with, they had managed to set aside the serrated differences in their personalities to create an indomitable axis that formed the bridge between punk rock and new wave.

Roped together, their journey over almost thirty years together would see them set off from music's base camp, traverse some tricky terrain, sever these same ties, and then regroup for one final climb for old times' sake. Now here they were, five years after emerging from the scattered ashes of punk, having reached their own personal "Everest." But for Sting, scanning the packed, horseshoe-shaped aisles at Shea, home to the legendary New York Mets baseball team, and the venue where, twenty years earlier, the Beatles had been drowned out in a tsunami of screams, the view from the top meant just one thing—the only way was down. And that would also mean continuing unhappily on a familiar record-tour-record-tour rut with a band that, for him at least, had run its race.

"I made the decision on stage that this is it," said Sting in *Rolling Stone*. "This is where this thing stops. Right now." There was never an infinity clause in their contracts. Their most recent album, the sublime *Synchronicity*, had been their most successful yet. It had spawned hits such as "King of Pain," "Wrapped around Your Finger," and, of course, "Every Breath You Take," a song that bathed its creator Sting in permanent luminosity even as the shadows lengthened on the Police.

It had, however, been a joyless experience. One in which their fragile democracy had finally collapsed under the weight of Sting's autocratic ego. Beckoning in the distance was the siren call of solo stardom. The first two Police albums formed an equilateral triangle, but the next two—1980's *Zenyatta Mondatta* and 1981's *Ghost in the Machine*—saw the geometry twist out of shape. "Since *Regatta de Blanc*, I [had] wondered how long Sting would play this game," recalled a frustrated Summers in his autobiography *One Train Later*. "He's not a team player. He doesn't want to share credits, and he makes comments in the press to that effect. . . . It is obvious he doesn't want to be in a band. It sure feels like the sun has set."

Summers called *Synchronicity*, their fifth album, the Police's Cinderella moment and this tour would see the clock strike midnight. Copeland declared, "At the end of the *Synchronicity* tour, we just couldn't stand the tension anymore. The work we were doing was really great . . . but life outside the band was beautiful. Somebody loves me . . . just get me out of this cocoon and the others felt the same way."

Yet the dysfunction that clearly lay at the heart of the Police was rarely in plain sight. The Police are a textbook example of how the very thing that makes art successful can also be its undoing. It is a strange affair. Scant evidence exists that the friction between them was ever sorted the old-fashioned way—behind the chapel at dawn deploying Marquis of Queensberry rules. But little hints have emerged of intermittent Police brutality.

Copeland used humor to allude to physical confrontations. No film of this exists, but the drummer, who taped much of their early days, says that's because "Sting works out. He used to run, like, twenty miles a day then. If you're trying to squeeze the life out of him, it takes two hands, with no free hand to film. So I never got that shot."

Meanwhile, Summers described one notable incident in which Sting "totally blew up on him," apparently bursting out with a string of insulting comments that left "everyone in the room white-faced and in shock." This, by itself, does not obviously speak to a wider pattern. But it was important enough to remain imprinted on Summers's memory. In another instance, Copeland told one interviewer that "we were in this state where any little incident would turn into World War III."

Ironically, Sting was painfully nursing a broken rib at Shea after an altercation a few days earlier with Copeland. But that was more the result of horseplay than any display of alpha male decorum. On other occasions, however, especially after subpar live performances, no one was holding back.

"We would take the anger backstage," recalled Copeland. "So many nights we'd be screaming at each other unintelligently." But was all this talk of internal strife a public relations invention? A mythical backstory hatched by record company executives in smoky rooms to add a layer of mystique? The short answer is no. And the evidence can often be found in real time, in almost every interview they gave. There was no need for scandal-hungry journalists to tease out salacious tidbits over the internal dynamics of the Police.

Depositions for the prosecution often came unprompted from their own lips, as if interviews were a kind of therapy. Neither Sting, Copeland, nor Summers would hold back in making public the disdain they held for each other when on Police duty. Copeland described being in the band as "like wearing a Prada suit made out of barbed wire."

Set against this, however, was the group assurance that they were only joshing, that they could always hug it out. Away from the studio and the stage, they really were a band of brothers—provided music was off topic. Yet they arrived at the point of *Synchronicity* where there was none. The early bonds of fraternity that had taken them from cheap dives and playing for buttons to the likes of Shea Stadium had long been broken.

Recalling the moment they regrouped to begin the album fresh off the back of a short U.S. tour, Summers admitted they felt like distant strangers eyeing each other suspiciously. "It seemed as though Sting was at the North Pole, I was at the South Pole, and Stewart was in the Tropics," he later recalled. "We were the emotional opposite of when we recorded *Outlandos* [their first album]."

The problem was not in creating new music; the problem lay in simply being able to find common ground without a loose remark or thinly veiled criticism providing the spark that caused tempers to erupt. Looking back on the difficulties of recording their fifth album, Copeland reflected, "We used to walk up to the studio whistling a happy tune, but once we started working together it turned into a dark, bitter dirge. It was miserable, we all hated it. We didn't hate the music; we all stand by the music. But the experience of making it was very painful for all of us."

The groundwork of putting down basic tracks for the album started against the idyllic backdrop of the Caribbean sun on the island of Montserrat following the same pattern that had been used for *Ghost in the Machine*. But the sessions at George Martin's Air Studios almost immediately descended into ugly verbal sparring, habitually between Sting and Copeland. All three recorded their basic tracks in separate rooms—a practice that was symbolic of their fractured working relationship.

The upshot was that two weeks into the sessions, progress had virtually stalled and there was a serious danger of the album being canned as indifference and lethargy took hold. The Police had arrived at their *Let It Be* moment. At one point, Summers, close to breaking point, schlepped halfway across the island to seek out the wisdom of the one man who knew more than most about the difficulties of working with egotistical musicians. But George Martin could only offer a cup of Darjeeling and a very British solution to the infighting. "It's typical group stuff," he told the guitarist, while advising them to patch up their differences. "Seen it all before."

The impasse was only broken when their manager Miles Copeland—the chief of Police and Stewart's brother—flew in for a make-or-break summit to ensure his officers got back in line or quit the force. Manning the board at Montserrat and Quebec, where the album was eventually mixed, was Hugh Padgham, the decade's uber producer who had worked wonders with the likes of Peter Gabriel and Phil Collins. This was his second time on the Police beat, having worked on *Ghost*. So he was only too aware of the time bomb constantly ticking, particular between Sting and Copeland. And the Kissinger-like qualities required to keep everybody happy.

"They were getting on so badly at that time that they didn't even want to be in the same room together. It was difficult for me to do anything about the fighting. Relative to their being a band, I knew them for a very short space of time and their attitude was 'You can't tell us what to do . . . stay out of it.'" But even Padgham was shocked by the fault lines that had developed in just two years from *Ghost in the Machine*, rifts that now left him traversing tricky group terrain.

"It was shocking," he told *Classic Pop* magazine (http://classicpopmag .com). "Sting and Stewart were infantile. Poor old Andy was left piggy in the middle, though he could be pretty grumpy himself. It was scary, too, because it was my job to get the record made." And he recalled Miles Copeland's caustic ultimatum that if they couldn't put the gloves away, the band was finished.

> After two weeks we still had nothing on tape and everybody was fighting. I remember ringing up my manager and telling him I wanted to come home. One of the problems was that part of the deal involved Stewart and Andy having one song each on every Police album. So we had to leave off some great Sting songs, like "I Burn For You," to include things like Mother and Stewart's "Miss Gradenko," which Sting hated and didn't want to sing. We ended up having a crisis meeting.
>
> Miles Copeland flew out from London and we sat around the pool and seriously discussed whether we should just pull the plug on the whole thing. In the end, Miles said, "Get your shit together, all of you." They respected that and we got back to work, but it still wasn't easy.

Sting had inevitably arrived with enough songs to make the album on his own and was convinced they could take the band to a new level. Many of them, such as "King of Pain," ventured into a heart of darkness, reflecting his recent divorce from actress wife Frances Tomelty. In fact, all three suffered marital heartache during their time together as relationships were sheared by the rock 'n' roll lifestyle.

This, however, led Sting to muse that his latest batch of songs were, in fact, perhaps too personal to take their place on a Police album, a view that soon served to further stoke smoldering cinders. He declared, "I realized that I couldn't involve this kind of personal work in a democratic process, at least not about the issues. So it was very clear to me during the making of this record that this was the end of the Police."

Their new work, he insisted, should be an unvarnished display of honesty that the game was up. "I felt very strongly that this album should say to the world that we are individuals." He said, "We don't have to breathe the same air. We are not joined at the hip; we are not a three-headed hydra. We were very much thrown together by accident and we're very distinguished by strong egos."

Copeland and Summers, meanwhile, also brought material they thought deserved equally serious consideration. No one, though, could seriously argue they were on a par with Sting's songs. It resulted in the kind of awkward standoff that happens in almost every band. But every Police hit so far had been crafted by Sting. Balanced against this was Copeland and Summers's justifiable belief that their musical eloquence had helped define Sting's songs—witness "Roxanne," "Walking on the Moon," and "So Lonely," to name just three—and, in turn, the band's idiosyncratic fusion of punk, reggae, ska, and new wave.

Respected music magazine writer and broadcaster John Aizlewood, a veteran of publications such as *Q* and *Mojo*, understands the dichotomy that conflicted internal relationships.

> Pop bands work better as dictatorships and Sting was a dictator. But, while he didn't trust the others to write songs, he gave them musical leeway and so Police music always sounded like a democracy. That shouldn't be confused with "letting them do what they want."
>
> I think that's why it worked, rather than the diverse backgrounds they came from musically. If a band doesn't happen, their fault lines don't matter. If they do happen, then the exhilaration and grind of that success first hides and then exacerbates those fault lines. Everyone feels invincible and everyone feels more responsible for the success than they're given credit for, even if the objective evidence says otherwise. Ergo, the other two felt undervalued.
>
> From what I can gather, non-confrontational Summers held his tongue— he'd had success and then failure, so he knew how fragile it was—and tried to mediate. Sting and Stewart Copeland were both alpha males, Sting passive-aggressive, Copeland more outspoken. Rightly or wrongly, Sting knew the success was all down to him and Copeland believed Sting saw him as Sting's drummer.
>
> Copeland could not accept that: he'd had a privileged upbringing, was used to getting his way and was frustrated that he wasn't acknowledged more.

This age-old dilemma was quick to resurface on Montserrat when Sting debuted "Every Breath You Take." Straight off the bat, it was clearly a monster song: The Motherlode.

"I knew it was the biggest hit we would ever have," said the song's creator. "Which is why it was so easy to put it on the album, despite cries from the others that it was too simplistic. That's no disrespect to Stewart and Andy, it was just the climate at the time; very contentious and very bitter."

Summers especially argued it was far from the finished article. It needed "Policifying." Initially, the song had been smothered in keyboard textures, but Summers was adamant the Police were still a guitar band. As they wrestled for days with the dilemma on how to raise the song to its full potential, Sting's patience eventually snapped. He gave Summers rare carte blanche to make good on his criticisms. "Go on then, make it your own," he told him.

The result was the arpeggiated acoustic pattern, produced in one magical flourish, that gave "Every Breath You Take" its signature and almost stalkerish sound. Of course, it was still Sting's song. The royalties from a song that became the most successful track of the eighties flowed in perpetuity into his bank account. Uncredited for his input, Summers was left eating cake.

A victim of schadenfreude, he said, "Without that guitar part, there is no song. That's what sealed it. My guitar completely made it classic and put the musical edge on it." Years later, one of Summers's children alerted him to a track by American rapper Puff Daddy called "I'll Be Missing You"—a mash-up tribute to murdered rapper Biggie Smalls—which sampled "Every Breath"—or at least it sampled the guitar riff.

Sting's publishers sued and won a settlement that guaranteed all the song's royalties came to the song writer—a corona-watering $2,000 a day. Not surprisingly, Summers was incensed. He declared, "I went into his room and listened to his radio, and I was like 'This is me; what the fuck is this?' That was the major rip-off of all time. He actually sampled my guitar, and that's what he based his whole track on. Stewart's not on it. Sting's not on it. I'd be walking round Tower Records, and the fucking thing would be playing over and over."

Meantime, back in the studio during the *Synchronicity* sessions, Copeland threatened to dynamite the fragile détente brokered by his manager/brother. He was the drummer in this band but neither he nor Sting could reach an accord over the rhythm for "Every Breath," a song Padgham claims Copeland disliked from the off. The esteemed producer recalled a typical incident when the album was being mixed:

> One morning Stewart came in and said, "I've got an idea. I want to overdub a hi-hat on 'Every Breath You Take.'" We got the hi-hat out; it's played on the song. Then later Sting comes in and I played him the new version of "Breath" with the hi-hat and Sting went, "That's fucking awful, get rid of it." I told him if you don't like it, shouldn't you talk to Stewart about it? The response came: "No, it's my song. I hate it. Get rid of it. Now." And of course Stewart comes in the next day going, "Where's my fucking hi-hat?"

Pragmatism eventually won out over egotism, according to Miles Copeland: "They listened to advice and Stewart shut up and did what he's supposed to do."

For some observers, Miles Copeland's alliance with Sting was the most pivotal in the Police. *Synchronicity*, with the exception perhaps of the Beatles' swan song *Abbey Road*, remains the greatest example of a successful band turning entrenched attrition into great art. By the time they took to the stage at Shea Stadium, only Michael Jackson's *Thriller* shared equal billing to the album's global domination. They were also the early king surfers of the wave generated by MTV.

The *Synchronicity* tour wrapped in Melbourne in March 1984; the Police were no longer reporting for duty. There were, however, no major Police-split headlines. Just a weary tripartite cognizance that, for now at least, time apart was essential to repair broken nervous systems. For all that was left now of their brittle three-way union was the astringent smell of burning bridges, leaving each one to kick over the embers of their once-convenient alliance. *Synchronicity* could have been the intersection toward something new. Instead, it was the end.

"It was awful, it was murder," was Copeland's summary of the sessions. "We don't make music to hurt each other and be miserable."

Within a year, Sting had flown out the traps with his excellent first solo album, the jazzy-toned *Dream of the Blue Turtles*, which included a supporting cast of some of the genre's most stellar musicians. The move wasn't entirely unexpected since Sting had played with jazz and progressive rock bands in his youth, but the result was considerably more nuanced and diverse than any Police record. With songs such as "If You Love Somebody Set Them Free" and "Fortress around Your Heart" reaching the American Top Ten, the album became an international hit, establishing Sting as a towering commercial force outside of the Police.

In July 1985, Bob Geldof created the "Global Jukebox" with Live Aid. But, despite being the biggest-selling group in the world at that time, the Police did not join the rank and file of all those doing their bit to help the starving millions in Ethiopia. Sting happily signed up for the charity single, forging an instant blokey affinity with Phil Collins, but he doggedly drew the thin blue line with Geldof over reforming the Police for the show played before an audience of 100,000 at Wembley. This was a non-negotiable stance that said everything about the glacial permafrost that now isolated him from Copeland and Summers.

Instead, he was happy to team up onstage with Collins for a number of collaborations that included Police classics such as "Roxanne," "Driven to Tears," "Message in a Bottle," and a joint version of "Every Breath You Take." He also appeared alongside Dire Straits to add his famously breathy contribution to "Money for Nothing."

Blessed with photogenic Slavic looks, a muscular frame, and onstage charisma, Sting effortlessly oozed rock-god magnetism. When he inevitably delved into acting, securing roles in the likes of *Quadrophenia*, he seemed to be on the kind of upward curve that often sees the enmity of others arriving unchecked at the gate. By the time of their third album, Summers and Copeland were already beginning to feel like spare parts.

The Police were gradually transitioning into a one-man band. But it was that one man, the one with three jobs, who was mainly driving the bus. "I'm out for myself," he once said. "And they know it." It was difficult to know if his tongue was lodged firmly in his cheek when he made the remark. By 1984, Copeland and Summers knew they were staring at an unavoidable truth—they needed him more than he needed them.

"Sting was completely within his right to be a musician and to complete the songs he'd written in the way he'd envisioned them," said Copeland. "He didn't have to wait for the percussion section—i.e., me—to tell him how the rhythm should go. But from mine and Andy's side, we weren't playing in a band just so that we could realize someone else's fait accompli." Sting's prodigious writing output ensured his name was attached to the bulk of the songs on every album. By extension, this meant cornering the lucrative singles market.

Contractually, Copeland and Summers were thrown the odd bone, but Sting carried the most clout and he wasn't afraid to weaponize his influence against record company executives to the detriment of the other two. Summers only found out after the group had disbanded that bigwigs at A&M wanted his track "Omega Man" to be the lead single from *Ghost in the Machine*. But the plan was kyboshed when Sting spat out his dummy.

"'Omega Man' was a really strong piece," said Summers. "A&M wanted to put it out as the first single. But Sting, who was feeling his power at the time, was freaked out. He didn't want it out. He refused. He got very upset, but A&M didn't want to upset him for all the typical reasons, so it didn't get put out. I didn't know that until much later. I wasn't told that at the time."

The biggest flashpoints, however, always erupted between songwriter and drummer. Copeland was not the type of person to back down from an argument if a musical point of principle was at stake. Compromise was not a word that sat easily with him. Especially since he could only watch as the power shifted in the band he had formed. "Stewart used to remind him quite forcibly that the Police was his band," recalled Padgham.

Their conflict sometimes went beyond the boundary of normal disagreement. On one tour Copeland made clear his feelings by daubing the slogan "Fuck Off You Cunt" on his drums—a less than subtle message directed at only one person. Every fill seemed to carry extra potency. "For Sting, music was a balm, an anesthetic, a way to escape from the evil, harsh, grim world to a place of celestial, unblemished beauty," he said. "For me, it's a celebration: let's light up this room and let's have fun. This can overlap—we made five albums as the Police. But the conflict grew and grew out of that diversity of purpose. . . . We are trying to do two completely different things. And since it's kind of important, and we take it seriously, we are going to clash."

A few months before Live Aid, the Police received a Brit award for outstanding contribution to music and all three, each of them suited and booted and wearing incongruous bow ties, pitched up at London's Dorchester looking the very essence of music establishment. Long gone, perhaps inevitably, was the punk ethos and outlaw tendencies that had fired their early days. Jokingly, Sting offered the award to Miles Copeland for safekeeping so the band wouldn't end up solving the thorny question of possession inside a boxing ring.

Further illustration of Sting's growing detachment came through his growing interest in human rights issues. He signed up for Amnesty International's 1986 groundbreaking Conspiracy of Hope tour alongside Peter Gabriel, U2, Joan Baez, Bryan Adams, and Lou Reed. Suddenly, he was elevated to new levels of stardom. He managed to persuade Copeland and Summers to don their Police uniforms once again to play the last three dates of the tour—ending a two-year band hiatus.

But the onstage tensions between them were hiding in plain sight to those who had a ringside seat. *Billboard* magazine Canadian bureau chief

Larry LeBlanc was in the wings for the show in Chicago and could feel the tension swirling throughout their set. "I thought Sting was going to get a drumstick in the back of the head," he said. "There was no communication between them, and it was ferocious watching them play. You could feel the anger in the music. And it was brilliant."

The shows, nevertheless, raised the prospect for Copeland and Summers at least that the Police could yet go back on the beat. "I thought we still had a lot more in the tank," said the guitarist. "It just seemed crazy to quit when we were at the peak of our powers."

A month after the Amnesty gigs, they regrouped in the studio for the express purpose of making a new album. But the wheels came off right from the start. Portentously, Copeland arrived on the first day with his arm in a sling, having broken his collarbone in, remarkably, a polo-playing accident. So they had no drummer. They also had no new material. From day one, Sting was a reluctant conscript and, in truth, had no desire to rejoin the gang of three.

Rather, he was intent on keeping his stockpile of new songs for his second solo album, *Nothing Like the Sun*, which was already taking shape inside his head. The entire enterprise was doomed from the outset. Summers explained: "The night before we went into the studio, Stewart broke his collarbone falling off a horse, and that meant we lost our last chance of recovering some rapport just by jamming together. Anyway, it was clear Sting had no real intention of writing any new songs for the Police. It was an empty exercise."

Collaboration was maintained just long enough to record bizarre new dance mixes of "Don't Stand So Close to Me" and "De Do Do Do, De Da Da Da" for a greatest hits album, the traditional harbinger that often shutters a band. Summers later detailed the whole unhappy experience of rerecording "Don't Stand So Close to Me." "This version took three weeks to record. I did my guitar part on the first night and the rest of the time it was Stewart and Sting arguing about whether the Fairlight or the Synclavier was better. The whole thing was absolutely tortuous."

With the band now clearly on life support, they reached rare common ground to privately pronounce the Police dead. Unlike, for example, the Beatles, there was no media frenzy or fans going into meltdown. Rather, the Police slipped gently off the page and handed over their crown to the likes of U2 and REM.

"The Police never actually broke up," said Sting. "We didn't feel like having an official divorce. We didn't take ourselves that seriously." Their solo careers veered down expected paths. Summers and Copeland ventured into recording albums that rarely found much traction. Sting, meanwhile, saw his tides rise and fall in line with the surf of most ageing rock stars. Albums like 1993's *Ten Summoner's Tales* yielded monsters hits like "Fields of Gold" and "If I Ever Lose My Faith in You." Over time, however, he suffered the same natural decline in sales and mass appeal that afflicted many of his contemporaries.

There were occasional cross-pollinations with Summers and Copeland. Largely, though, each band member kept a respectable—and friendly—social distance. There were exceptions. At Sting's wedding to Trudie Styler in 1992, all three were persuaded to clamber onto a makeshift stage to raggedly play a few songs for old times' sake.

Then followed a more formal reunion when the band was inducted into the Rock & Roll Hall of Fame and old tensions were swept aside long enough to perform "Roxanne," "Message in a Bottle," and "Every Breath You Take." Predictably, their appearance sparked the usual clamor for a full-blown reunion. Summers and Copeland, haunted by loose ends, made it clear they were on board, but Sting continued to play the part of outlier. Then a series of events took place that, in stark contrast to the name of their last album together, owed quite a lot to synchronicity and happenstance. Puff Daddy's Police-sampled track—the one that so enraged Andy Summers—arrived out of leftfield to suddenly burn up the airwaves.

The American rapper's mawkish tribute to fellow rapper and record company client Notorious B.I.G. unwittingly made the Police cool again and plowed the field ahead not with gold but with dollar signs. The band's record company immediately cashed in on the whiff of filthy lucre by assembling a new Greatest Hits collection that now blended Sting's work with the Police and his solo career. At the same time, all three found themselves in the U.S. city of Sundance for the famous film festival and began hanging out socially.

This time they could see the fiscal sense in one last roll of the dice. They also agreed, collectively, to fire Miles Copeland as their manager. Industry rumors of a permanent reconciliation followed yet another coming together for the forty-ninth Grammys in Los Angeles. The next day, all three took to the stage at the city's famous Whisky a Go Go for a carefully choreographed—and chummy—set to announce a gargantuan 153-date world tour. Even though Sting was the main instigator, the decision to get back on board the carousel seemed to surprise him.

"If you'd asked me a week before I made this decision," he says, shaking his head in lingering disbelief, "I would have said, 'You're crazy. I'm not doing that.'" "What clinched it," he told *Rolling Stone*, "was thinking, 'What would surprise people? What would surprise me?' Surprise is everything. It certainly surprised the guys."

By now, Sting and Copeland were in their midforties, with Summers, obviously, a decade further down the river. Each of them went out of their way in interviews to suggest a much more mellow approach to ironing out any local difficulties. It was a massive undertaking, easily the biggest of their time together, and one that would test the tolerance boundaries of any band, let alone one where fireworks were never far from being lit.

But whenever things became fractious, all they had to do was count the noughts at the end of their respective bank balances for proof of Dylan's famous mantra—"money doesn't talk, it swears."

The tour would go on to become, at that time, the third highest grossing one of all time, raking in an astonishing $350 million. To begin with, however, old wounds inevitably started to reappear like a form of stigmata. Now, though, they were able to impose their own form of social distancing to keep relationships on a more even keel.

Sting later confessed that the stress at the time was almost on a par with the old days. "It was more difficult than I thought it would be," he told *Mojo*. "Psychologically speaking, that is. It was like going back to a dysfunctional marriage where all the old problems were still there. The truth is I got ill, I got physically ill. I got through it but it wasn't easy."

Summers, often the most emotionally articulate of the trio, concurred as he pulled back the curtain to reveal a familiar tableau. "Some discussions are more heated than others. We are not falling apart—the motor is purring nicely. But at the same time, we are a rock band and by definition you have to be somewhat at the edge. There's nothing wrong with having an ego."

No more thought, however, was given to recording new material. "We appreciate each other but we don't get each other musically," said Copeland. "We totally get along socially, but we realize the effect Sting has on me and I have on him. It's not comfortable." The tour was naturally a swing through their best-known songs—and why not? Nostalgia is always a great place to hang out and relive youthful days of yore. But none of them was prepared to detonate their newfound accord by blowing up in a studio, despite strong hints from Copeland that they did indeed try out new songs.

We were very close. We tried, but I think Sting just dried up. He tried to write some songs and, needless to say, we are surrounded by people for whom the idea of a new Police record would probably be a great idea. Andy and I didn't get as much pressure from that because we were not the front of that new song. But ole' Stingo, oh my god, he's gotta write something. And understandably the juices or the gift of creativity did not occur in that environment. To the extent that there is a Police now, it wouldn't be about new material. It'd be about the listening. That body of songs have real emotional power because they've been here for thirty or forty years. Sting writes a great song. The wrong place for it, is the Police. Why should he be arguing with Stewart about this or Andy about that? Why should he be struggling with that when he knows exactly how to make a record. That song that he's got, he knows exactly what to do with it.

Time, it appears, has finally proven to be the ultimate chill pill for the Police. "What we do understand," said Copeland at the end of the reunion tour, "is that whatever we do with each other seems to work. But we're all getting kind of nervous now, 'cause on the last leg of the tour, we're looking at each other every day and saying, 'What part of this sucks?' And none of us can seem to think of anything, really."

That view, though, was not shared by the band's front man, who later conceded that it was no more than a schlock-driven, self-serving—and lucrative—exercise in schmaltz. He told *Readers Digest* in 2021, "That was simply how I felt and is still how I feel today. I think it's OK to be honest about your feelings and that was the way it went for me. That's not a slight on the people I was with or the way things panned out, it's just how I saw it by the end, and let's be honest, that's not how I wanted to remember it. If I thought that would be the emotion I'd be leaving with, I wouldn't have done it in the first place."

Since disbanding for the last time, the Police now occupy an odd ranking in rock 'n' roll. Lauded for groundbreaking, radio-friendly hits but at the same time derided for their faux punk roots. John Aizlewood has his own take on a band whose music has blended seamlessly into the parched badlands of rock without ever being a derivative for those who followed. He told me, "They're widely accepted as near-great, they were massive commercially but, like, say Joy Division, their catalog is complete."

Their hermetically sealed world while they existed, allied to their lack of presence since the split, adds to the myth, but concomitantly it reduces their influence and so very few acts cite the Police. It's as if nobody ever picked up a guitar because of Andy Summers or wrote a song because of Sting. The reunion showed how loved they are, but it's a silent majority love. I can't see it changing: the comparison isn't exact but it's similar to the Moody Blues and Jethro Tull, who sold millions across the globe, but influenced few.

It's a myth about conflict breeding good art: conflict tends not to work for bands. In fact, it almost always (Jagger/Richards, the Kinks aside, perhaps) destroys them artistically and commercially. A split would, of course have happened soonish, but in the short term the conflict directly brought the Police to an end. That's a good thing since their recorded legacy is perfect: there was no decline, no albums with missing/additional members, and no chance of an album to go with the reunion. That makes them unique amongst global acts where nobody has died.

The Police file has been closed since they exited stage left at Madison Square Garden on August 8, 2008. But charges of breach of the peace and the occasional assault rap remain on record.

The Eagles: Bernie Leadon, Glenn Frey, Don Henley, Randy Meisner, and Don Felder
Photofest

10

THE EAGLES

THE FIRST ACT

The stage at California's Long Beach Arena had become a cage for Glenn Frey and his fellow Eagle Don Felder as they glowered at each other with murderous intent. "When this show is done, I'm going to kick your ass," said Frey, his hooded eyes narrowing.

Throughout the show, a political benefit for Democratic senator Alan Cranston, the clock ticked down. "Three more songs until I kick your ass, pal," said Frey. "I can't wait," replied Felder. "You're a real pro, Don, all the way. The way you handle people. Except for the people you pay, nobody gives a shit about it." Frey responds, "Fuck you. I've been paying you for years, you fuckhead."

Hostilities unleashed, this was the moment for the Eagles when the fuse finally met the keg. A chain reaction ignited by rock star machismo, years of mutual loathing, and levered by financial envy. And it was absolutely the real deal. Two men irrevocably driven crazy by the sound of their own wheels.

"We're out there singing 'Best of My Love,' but inside both of us are thinking, 'As soon as this is over, I'm going to kill him.' I definitely wanted to kill him," said Frey years later. Engineers scrambled to mute Frey's microphone in case the audience picked up the threats.

Meanwhile, the rest of the band—Don Henley, who had cofounded the group with Frey a decade earlier; bassist Timothy B. Schmit; and guitarist

Joe Walsh—were watching open-mouthed. And they all knew that a line in the sand had been breached. "When that kind of thing happens on stage in front of people, you have problems," declared Walsh.

Equally shocked was Schmit, who feared his future as a member of the Eagles was crumbling before his eyes. "We got through the show and then all hell broke loose backstage," he recalled. The moment the curtain came down, Felder reached for his guitar and hurled it against a wall, sending splinters flying in every direction as roadies ducked for cover. Likewise, Frey threw a Budweiser bottle in another direction.

Knowing Frey was right behind him, Felder ducked the inevitable confrontation by heading for the nearest limo and hightailing it as fast as possible into the darkness of a west coast night. Left choking on diesel fumes as the Lincoln sped away was Frey, with paparazzi pictures showing him raising his clenched fists in uncontrollable rage.

It was by any measure of rock 'n' roll combat an extraordinary sight. The next day Frey called Henley and said the Eagles, America's most commercially successful band of the 1970s, were grounded. It was, however, only the end of the first act. An interlude that would, nevertheless, last for fourteen years before the frozen waters of the River Styx melted and signaled a reunion that, for Felder at least, would eventually end in a bitter, messy, and costly courtroom face-off.

"I knew I had to get out. That was the straw that broke the camel's back," said the guitarist. Yet, there had been no foreshadowing the volcanic events to come twenty-four hours earlier ahead of the reelection benefit gig for Cranston. Felder, however, was a reluctant conscript when it came to charity shows, partly because he believed these gigs provided him with no financial benefit whatsoever.

Politically distant from many of the social causes backed by his more liberal-minded bandmates, Felder was already brooding when he was introduced to Cranston's wife before the show. As she thanked the Eagles for agreeing to play, Felder replied, "You're welcome," before muttering under his breath the words, "I guess."

He recalled, "I was very uninformed about politics. I didn't know or care who Alan Cranston was." Two feet away, Frey caught what he considered to be a sarcastic aside and erupted. "I heard it and got really mad," said Frey.

> By the time we went on stage I was seething. I wanted to kill Felder. Felder didn't like us doing benefits. He felt that was money that should be going into his pocket.

There were a lot of things building up and a lot of things I overlooked for
the good of the band. But then I just couldn't look past it anymore. It finally
came to a head at Long Beach.

It was hardly the first time the two men had butted heads. They had been
locked inside their own personality struggle almost from the time they first
met, each one the mirror to the other's moods: Frey, the founding member
whose twelve-inch stare broached no argument, and Felder, the virtuoso
guitarist whose music for the anthemic track "Hotel California" alone guaranteed him a place on the band's own musical Mount Rushmore.

Viewed in isolation, the incident immortalized in Eagles folklore as the
"Long Night in Wrong Beach" may seem superficial when seen through the
prism of band politics. Life inside the bubble of a band is easily pricked by
friction and fractious disagreements. But for the Eagles this was the simmering tipping point that followed years of abrasion, drug-induced chaos,
touring burnout, creative slowdown, and the plain fact that this was a band
destroying itself from the inside. They had even stopped referring to each
other by their first names.

Work on their most recent album, *The Long Run*, had gone on for eighteen morale-sapping months, leaving them creatively barren and psychologically wasted. The result was a jaded record, which in no way matched
the majesty of 1977's *Hotel California*, the album that set a bar that, ultimately, was too high to reach.

"*The Long Run* was the beginning of the end," said producer Bill Szymczyk, who had a ringside seat at the sessions that came to symbolize the
last rites for a band already on life support. "A lot of friction had entered
into the band by that point. Instead of the old 'all for one, one for all,'
everybody had their own car and their own this and their own that. Everybody even had their own handler, and everybody was kind of selfish
about certain things."

The final split, accelerated by Felder and Frey's onstage meltdown, had
in truth been years in the making. By 1980, only Frey and Henley remained
of the fledgling Eagles that had first taken flight in 1972.

Augmenting that original four-piece lineup was Bernie Leadon, a country music buff whose bluegrass guitar chops helped give the band its early
signature sound. On bass was Randy Meisner, a gifted musician whose
vocal delivery of the iconic "Take It to the Limit" would give the band
their first American #1 single in 1975. Felder, a guitarist whose skillset
had brought comparisons with Jimmy Page, was a high school friend of

Leadon's and was brought into the nest in 1974 on his recommendation as Frey and Henley decided the band needed to gravitate from their country roots and develop a rockier edge.

But both would be discarded along the way. "Not everyone stayed on the train for the whole journey," said Frey acidly when asked once about the treatment of jilted band members. In the Eagles, Frey and Henley would always rule the roost with self-righteous justification.

As the band's principal songwriters and vocalists, they were naturally viewed by record company suits, first manager David Geffen and then his successor Irving Azoff, as the money tree. For the first three albums, *Eagles*, *Desperado*, and *On the Border*—each of them million sellers in the United States—their esprit de corps held firm. But by the time *One of These Nights* hit the shelves in 1975, initial cracks, between Frey and Leadon especially, were turning into fissures.

The success of *One of Those Nights*—the album yielded three hit singles and was the Eagles' first chart-topper on *Billboard*—and the subsequent spike in the band's media profile and fan popularity only encouraged Frey and Henley, relishing the first flush of fame and fortune, to redefine the internal pecking order.

And Leadon especially felt he was being relegated to the status of an economy-class Eagle, despite his profound musical abilities and having been a key architect of the band's sound. And also, crucially, having been a signatory to Eagles Ltd., an agreement that not only bound him to Frey and Henley as a bandmate but as a business partner as well.

Marc Eliot, author of the excellent *To the Limit: The Untold Story of the Eagles*, reckons the band's transition from having been Linda Ronstadt's barroom backing band to California musical kings turned two of them into rampant Eaglemaniacs and broke the early camaraderie that can sometimes be an accelerant.

He wrote, "For all the buddy-buddy boy celebrating, the Eagles were in reality four distinct personalities, with different takes on everything from the type of music they liked to listen to and play to the brands of cigarettes they preferred. Except for being in a rock group that made hit records, they probably would never have sought each other's company for any length of time."

Leadon's disenchantment was rooted in familiar territory. More and more he found his song offerings choked off by the Frey-Henley power axis. An Anschluss that deprived him of a share in the financial motherlode provided through song royalties and music publishing. Despite having contributed several cowritten songs to Eagles albums—notably "Witchy

Woman"—Leadon was beginning to play the victim card. Between 1974 and 1975, he was romantically involved with Patti Davis, the rebellious daughter of future Republican president Ronald Reagan, at that time the governor of California.

Davis soon began attending band sessions with Leadon, a habit that gradually got under the skin of Frey and Henley, who, according to Eliot, caustically referred to her as "Yoko" in hushed tones. During sessions for "One of These Nights," Leadon road tested a track he and Davis had written together called "I Wish You Peace."

Henley dismissed it as "smarmy, cocktail music" and argued it had no place on an Eagles record. Leadon, a man known to settle disputes using bare knuckles, had a different view. "I let it be known that if we didn't record the song, I was going to break his arm," he declared.

The song made the final cut as the album's final track. But Leadon's time as an Eagle was drawing to a close. By 1975, he was running on empty, reluctantly stuck on that eternal record-tour-record-tour treadmill. He was also facing a hard fact. Felder's edgier rock 'n' roll credentials signposted a move away from the band's country roots, a transition that left Leadon feeling he had become an outlier in the band he had helped take flight.

Factor in unwanted media attention and a man uncomfortable with stardom, and it's easy to hear the sounds of wheels coming off. A healthy bank balance didn't necessarily bring happiness to a musician who embraced that old cliché about a band selling out.

"I hated the idea of travelling in limos. I felt we were thumbing our nose at the audience," he said. Matters came to a head during one band meeting when Frey animatedly mapped out a future that consisted simply of nonstop touring. Standing in a corner, Leadon simply got up, walked over to Frey, and tipped a glass of beer over his head before walking out of the room and out of the Eagles, with the words, "You need to chill out."

Leadon recalled, "I kept asking are we going to rest next month? I suggested we take some time off. They weren't excited about that idea. I was afraid something inside of me was dying. Leaving was an act of survival."

Years later, time's arrow allowed Leadon to demonstrate a degree of regret over the incident, which he said was disrespectful. "It's not something I'm proud of, but it did illustrate a breaking point." Notably, no one—not even his friend Felder—tried to talk him out of quitting. And Henley, in particular, felt an obstacle to band harmony, and its upward trajectory, had been fortuitously removed.

He said, "Glenn and I always wanted the band to be a hybrid to encompass bluegrass, country, and rock 'n' roll. There was a part of Bernie that really resisted that. After a while it became a real problem, particularly be-tween Bernie and Glenn." Frey acknowledged he and Leadon often butted heads. "We had our problems with Bernie, and he had his problems with us. Some of it was based on him having a voice in the Eagles and that meant recording the songs he wrote the way he wanted to but you can't work like that in a band. At least you couldn't work like that in our band."

Unfortunately, Leadon had stepped out of the Eagles elevator just as it began its ascent to rock's penthouse, an upscale suite reached by only a handful of bands in history.

By 1975, the cumulative effect of four hit albums had made the Eagles America's premier group. And the subsequent release in 1976 of their *Greatest Hits* album—a record that would become the biggest selling of all time—only further propelled them into the cultural stratosphere. Existing on the same kind of plane as the likes of the Rolling Stones, the Who, and Led Zeppelin, they reinvigorated rock 'n' roll for a weary post-Woodstock generation and established Los Angeles as an unchallenged musical mecca.

Leadon's departure barely caused a ripple of interest. More so since their calculating manager Irving Azoff—he may be Satan but he's our Satan, declared Henley—largely maintained a media blackout on the band, hoping it would cloak them in a Zeppelin-style mystique. Frey and Henley, naturally enough, were the only members of the band to have any kind of public profile.

Ascendancy in rock circles, however, brings with it a curious form of hedonism. Hand in glove with success came that familiar cliché about sex, drugs, and rock 'n' roll and the Eagles took it to the max. On the road, the Eagles didn't so much as burn the candle at both ends as put a blowtorch in the middle. At the time of Leadon's exit, they were easily rivaling Zeppelin in the debauchery stakes. Backstage, cocaine abounded like confetti. And it also provided constant stimulus during recording sessions.

One group who followed the Eagles into a Miami studio were shocked by the amount of blow that had been left on desk consoles and amps—and it took a lot to shock Black Sabbath. Then there were the groupies. Henley and Frey devised the Eagles' notorious "Third Encore," with roadies hand-ing cherry-picked girl fans a special lapel button, which gave them access to the band's hotel where they would be expected to provide some post-gig gratification at the Fellini-like good-time emporium.

In certain cities, where supplies ran low or didn't come up to scratch, the Eagles would fly in company from LA by private jet, a band practice jok-ingly referred to as "Love 'em and Lear 'em." More and more, the band's private lives came to reflect Frey's lyrics for "Life in the Fast Lane," a song inspired by a high-speed drive he took with a dope buddy that perfectly captured an attitude of excess in all areas.

Health-wise, there was already a price to pay for men still in their twenties. Meisner and Henley both suffered stomach ulcers, while Frey was struck down by a number of intestinal problems. Perfectly suited then for this epicurean tableau was Leadon's quixotic replacement on guitar.

Joe Walsh was the unbridled wild man of west-coast rock, a star who fancied himself as a cross between John Bonham and Keith Moon. Off the road, though, he was mellow and someone who provided a balm to any internal tensions. No wonder Frey described him as "an interesting bunch of guys."

His favorite on-tour party trick was to take a chainsaw to hotel rooms while drinking as much tequila as his body allowed. Walsh, though, was no rival to the Henley-Frey arbor and was happy to play his part as a spectacular lead guitarist instead of fomenting internal unrest.

Felder, on the other hand, was not content to be a bit part player and was growing more and more resentful toward the two men whose autocratic impulses were by now unchecked. The Eagles, all five of them, were ruled by Henley and Frey. When the band regrouped in March 1976 to start work on their fifth studio album, Felder, who had submitted around fifteen songs for their last album only for them all to be rejected by "The Gods" as he later called Frey and Henley, was determined to fight for more needle time. And he had an ace up his sleeve.

He had handed Henley and Frey cassette tapes of an instrumental guitar track he had worked up during the band's recent downtime as well as another track called "Victim of Love." For once, Henley didn't dismiss the extended guitar track, written on a twelve-string with the working title of "Mexican Reggae."

Weeks later he returned to the studio having added arcane lyrics to the song that was now officially rebranded as "Hotel California." When Frey, Meisner, and Walsh added their parts, a legendary song was born. "Hotel California," and the album of the same name, was a serious game changer for the Eagles.

The eponymous title track, with its shimmering-mirage opening, was a song that occupied the same adult-oriented rock space as "Stairway to Heaven," "Freebird," and "Shine on You Crazy Diamond." Felder hoped the song, which he would receive a music credit on, would finally see him being treated as some kind of musical equal. Brimming with confidence, he tried his luck a second time with "Victim of Love."

This time, though, he insisted on singing it himself. Felder, by his own admission, was no match for either Henley or Frey in the lead vocal stakes. And none of the takes with him at the mic came up to snuff. According to Eagles folklore, Felder was invited out for dinner one night by Azoff while, back in the studio, Henley secretly put down his own lead vocal for "Victim of Love."

The next day, listening to playback, Felder realized he had been done up like the proverbial kipper, but years later conceded it had been the right decision. "It was a bitter pill to swallow," he admitted. "I felt like Don was taking that song from me. I had been promised a song on the next record, but there was no real way to argue with my vocal versus Don Henley's vocal."

Henley offered no remorse over the stealth tactics used to usurp his bandmate.

> "Victim of Love" was not brought to the band as a complete song; it was just another chord progression that Felder brought in. It had no lyrics, no melody, no title. Glenn and I and JD Souther sat down and hammered out the rest of it. We did originally let Mr. Felder sing it. He sang it dozens of times over the space of a week, over and over again. It simply didn't come up to band standard.

It was, however, far from being an isolated incident. By the time recording for *Hotel California* got underway, civil war had virtually broken out on all sides, turning the group into an emotional combat zone, one intensified by a copious drug intake. Paranoia and insecurity was rife inside and outside the studio. And it also began to slowly drive a wedge between Frey and Henley.

Frey often used Henley's house as a long-term crash pad, but one particular explosive row saw him move out and move in with Azoff. It was like a rock band version of the Borgias. Henley became irked at Frey's growing friendship with Walsh and gravitated more toward Felder just to wind him up.

Factionalism wasn't just confined to the band. Even the band's road crew were forced to choose sides between Frey and "Massa" Henley as they had started calling the dictatorial drummer. Squeezed in the middle of this creeping silo mentality was Randy Meisner, the introvert from Nebraska who by now was suffering serious rock star burnout. And he recognized that *Hotel California*—and the subsequent year spent on the road to promote it—represented a turning point for the band.

The bassist told writer Eliot,

> We were [all] real close, more or less, up until the year of *Hotel California*. I just didn't feel like I was part of the group. Success changed everything. When we first started we were really close, like brothers. We'd sit around, smoke a

doob together, drink beer, and have a good time. By 1976 it just wasn't the same. It was all business. The friendships were kind of gone at that point.

Fueling Meisner's ill will—and guilt—was a lifestyle that had simply spiraled out of control. He felt no choice but to become a fully paid-up member of the Eagles' cocaine club as well as being a willing participant in the "Third Encore."

Those optics were not good for a man who had a wife and young family back at his Nebraska homestead. When the dime dropped that Randy was indeed happily living up to his name, divorce proceedings quickly followed in the middle of recording *Hotel California*.

Reclusive by nature, Meisner also loathed being shoved under a spotlight every night by Henley and Frey to sing "Take It to the Limit," a song cowritten by him that had become a victim of its own success. It was a form of water torture for him. Something had to give, and it did during a gig in Knoxville, Tennessee, in June 1977. It had long been the custom for the first encore to be Meisner's showstopping signature moment, famous for that high-octave finale. But on this night he simply refused to go back out, blaming a cold but more likely a booze and drug hangover from the night before.

Meisner simply felt in no condition to sing the song. "My ulcer was starting to act up, and I had a bad case of the flu. We were being called back for another encore. 'No way,' I said. I was too sick and generally fed up. I decided I wasn't going back out."

In his face right away was Frey, who accused him of being a "pussy" and soon the two men were swapping punches as gun-toting cops watched nervously on the sidelines. "They were ready to move in when they saw us go at it," recalled Frey. "But Henley turned to the cops and said, 'Stay out of it. This is personal and it's private, real fucking private.'"

It was for Meisner, literally the end of the road for him and the Eagles, the second cofounder to fly the nest. For his few remaining gigs, he was ostracized, frozen out in the same way Leadon had been. Meisner added, "When the tour ended, I left the band. Those last few days on the road were the worst. Nobody was talking to me or would hang after the shows or do anything. I was made an outcast of the band I'd helped start."

Empathy was in short supply, notably from Henley who had barely spoken to Meisner in months and was naturally in Frey's corner when the first bell sounded. In quotes attributed to Henley, he offered this:

> The night of the fight between him and Frey began with Randy complaining as usual about his throat. And he was drinking. After they finished the show,

while the audience was cheering for an encore, Randy was guzzling from a bottle of booze and then said he simply wasn't going back out. That's when Frey called him on it. In truth, Randy had become a major pain in the ass. He was probably looking for a way to leave. That night he found it.

This latest departure put Frey in the center of the Venn diagram that charted the band's most explosive moments. He was also instrumental in Leadon's exit and was now seeing antipathy putting his friendship with Henley under serious strain. But he remained unapologetic and freely admitted he had no interest in group equality. He declared, "The band was like a fake democracy. Henley and I were making the decisions while at the same time trying to pacify, include, and cajole the others. There was always so much turbulence around our band that it made us serious all the time. There was never a day when all five guys felt good. I'd think, 'Who is gonna blow it today? Who's gonna want to fire everybody?'"

Arriving in the teeth of the punk rock hurricane, *Hotel California* was nevertheless a serious game changer for the Eagles, an album that spun gold from surprisingly bleak themes: disillusionment and loss, the end of the sixties, and the Jimmy Carter–era splintering of America itself. It sat atop the *Billboard* summit for eight weeks on its release in January 1977. Within eighteen months, it had shifted a staggering 9.5 million copies in America alone.

Today its worldwide tally is north of 32 million. It was unquestionably a commercial and crucial peak for the Eagles. But in the mythos of this extraordinary band, it also marked the beginning of the downslope, more so when the challenge of repeating the trick loomed large in their rearview mirror.

Soon Henley and Frey, as the self-appointed leaders, were confronting the unspoken enormity of the Eagles and the ubiquity of *Hotel California*. "If you were to ask a struggling, twenty-five-year-old musician, 'How would you like to sell eighteen million albums?' he'd say, 'Yeah! Damn right I would,'" Glenn Frey explained.

"The next question is 'But how would you like to try to make one as good as the one that sold millions and millions of records?' Somebody asked my friend Bob Seger, 'Why do you think the Eagles broke up?' He said, *Hotel California*."

Drained and devoid of inspiration, sessions for the follow-up, *The Long Run*, quickly became an exercise in navel-gazing. Weeks would pass without anything of note being recorded. Neither Frey nor Henley could summon up the inspiration that had yielded classic songs such as "New Kid in Town,"

"Life in the Fast Lane," and the peerless "Wasted Time." While they labored in the studio, record company fat cats were working themselves into a frenzy as the deadline for another Eagles album passed into history. And Henley freely admitted that was the cause of the final schism between him and Frey.

"We got into arguments about creativity, lyrics, and some angry words were exchanged. There were the usual problems that all bands have with ego. . . . In essence, we were all just too strung out. Everything was a drama."

Timothy B. Schmit, Meisner's replacement, soon felt himself tiptoeing through the minefield that was internal Eagle politics. He said, "I knew that there was some squabbling—I mean, it was obvious; it couldn't be hidden—but I had no idea how truly serious it was. To me, all bands fought. Another day at the office in rock 'n' roll. I didn't know how heavy the issues were."

Three tortuous years in the making, *The Long Run* revealed the Eagles, in Marc Eliot's words, as "cynical citizens of a fallen world scoffing jadedly at golden-calf cultists from their bar stools at Dan Tana's," their favorite LA hangout. By the time they reached Long Beach for that most public of ruptures, and with the sun setting on the seventies, their own run was long over.

Forthright as ever, Frey refused to sugarcoat the reasons for the end of the Eagles. His professional relationship with Henley—and Felder—was well past the breaking point. And their personal lives were on different tracks. "We were coming apart at the time of *The Long Run*, but it wasn't even our fault," he said in the 2013 documentary *History of the Eagles*.

> We were in the belly of the beast. There was a tremendous amount of pressure on us. *The Long Run* was going to be judged solely on whether it was bigger than *Hotel California*, and you just can't do that. It had stopped being fun.
>
> We no longer trusted each other's instincts, so there was considerable disagreement as we were for the first time considering what we ought to be doing. Plus, Henley and I had developed drug habits, which didn't help matters. But most importantly, during the making of *The Long Run*, Henley and I found out that lyrics are not a replenishable source. We, Don in particular, said a mouthful on *Hotel California* and a big part of the problem was "What do we talk about now?"
>
> Towards the end, we just wanted to get the record finished and released. None of us wanted to go through that again, so we figured it was the right time to call it a day.

Henley was also of the view that time—and their self-indulgent lifestyles—had finally caught up with them. He admitted, "We had gone from being a band that could make an album in three weeks to a band that couldn't finish an album in three years. In some ways, the success took a lot of the fun out of it. I think Henley took some of the fun out of it for me, and I'm sure I took some of the fun out of it for him."

There would also be one final postscript to the first act. Contractually, they were bound to deliver a final album, so they agreed to compile a live record from their most recent gigs. But neither Frey nor Henley could stand sharing the same space, agreeing it was better for them to be 3,000 miles apart—one on the West Coast and one on the East.

So live overdubs were done separately and then flown into a studio. Frey was in Los Angeles while the rest of the band was in Miami, with Henley overseeing the postproduction sessions. Tapes were sent back and forth between the two locations until the album was completed. Bill Szymczyk said, "I had my assistant in Los Angeles with Glenn, and I had the rest of the band fly to Miami. We were fixing three-part harmonies courtesy of Federal Express."

THE SECOND ACT

"We'll get back together when hell freezes over." Don Henley's brusque and legendary dismissal of an Eagles reunion was absolute. It was a clear-cut response to the ongoing fan clamor for the group to navigate a path back to those carefree days at Dan Tana's. "I just rule out the possibility of putting the Eagles back together for a Lost Youth and Greed tour."

On May 27, 1994—fourteen years after Glenn Frey walked off into the rock 'n' roll hinterland—filthy lucre won out. Of course, it was never just about the money, they insisted; it was about the fans and about showing that time's arrow could, indeed, be reversed.

The lineup was the same iteration of the band as the one that folded during *The Long Run*. This meant Don Felder being awkwardly readmitted to the club. And he was honest enough to admit the motivation for all of them was financial. He admitted, "There was such a massive amount of money on the table that everyone was willing to be on their best behavior in order to play music together, and go back out together and give it a shot to try to have a reunion."

During what Frey called a fourteen-year vacation, only he and Henley had enjoyed any degree of success. Henley by far set the pace throughout the 1980s. His magnificent 1989 album, *The End of the Innocence*, by itself shifted 6 million units worldwide, swept that year's Grammys, and easily held up against his best work in the Eagles. Frey dabbled in acting and enjoyed the occasional solo single success.

Between 1981 and 1991, Joe Walsh took the wrappers of four albums that, for all their musicality, barely caused a ripple. Instead, he slipped more and more into a twilight world of drug and booze addiction. Felder and Schmit simply fell off the grid. Catching the whiff of big bucks, however, was Irving Azoff who continued behind the scenes to shuffle pieces round the board in the hope of brokering some kind of reconciliation. He offered, "The Eagles talked about breaking up from the day I met them. There'd be one mini-explosion followed by a replacement in the band, then another mini-explosion followed by another replacement. You just had to step back and give things time to calm down."

His Kofi Annan–type diplomacy almost paid off in 1990 when Henley, Walsh, Schmit, and Felder rehearsed for several days in a studio in north Hollywood. Despite promising to turn up, Frey was a no-show and the whole thing was scrapped after three days. "It was all about when Glenn was ready to do it all again," said Azoff.

It took an act of synchronicity to get all five in the same place at the same time. Azoff corralled America's best country singers to record a tribute album of Eagle songs, the highlight of which was Travis Tritt's interpretation of "Take It Easy." Tritt then had a light bulb moment to invite all five Eagles to appear in a video for the song—and amazingly they agreed.

Much to everyone's surprise, the feuding former Eagles decided they could set aside their differences long enough to hang out with Tritt on a video set shooting pool—and although it wasn't a true reunion in the musical sense, it proved an important first step in softening some of the hard edges.

"I saw a bunch of guys who got together and really seemed to realize that they didn't hate each other as bad as they thought they did," Tritt recalled. "I got to be an Eagle for a day." Six months later, they embarked on the Hell Freezes Over world tour—no one could miss the self-mockery—which was preceded by an MTV special recorded and released as a live album.

The tour, which was interrupted after Frey required intestinal surgery for the onset of ulcerative colitis, set new records for ticket sales, proving rock 'n' roll nostalgia was a candle that never went out. Henley said, "We realized we had been apart for fourteen years, and maybe we could have that rarest of things, which is a second act, a second chance."

Joe Walsh's "second act" was conditional on an inviolable agreement—he was to check into rehab in a last-ditch attempt to clean up before they went on the road. Henley reportedly drove him to the facility in person. Sober since then, the decision clearly saved him from joining the rock 'n' roll victims club. "I had hit rock bottom," said Walsh. "I knew I was done. I would probably have died if I'd kept going."

The shows were an enormous success. It appeared as if time had cast a spell on all five members, who on stage at least, looked stoked and full of joie de vivre. Behind the scenes, however, old embers were not slow in catching fire, especially with Felder. Frey justifiably insisted he and Henley should be guaranteed the lion's share of the take.

Felder, pointing to his long-term status as a member of Eagles Inc., insisted on equal status. During talks with Azoff and various promoters, Frey refused to budge. "I'm not going to do it unless Don [Henley] and I make more money than the other [three] guys," Frey said.

> We're the guys that have kept the Eagles' name alive on radio, television, and in concert halls. So we came up with a deal I was happy with, Don was happy with, Timothy was happy with, Joe was happy with . . . and Don Felder was not happy with.
>
> I phoned Felder's representative and said, "I'm sorry you happen to represent the only asshole in the band, but let me tell you something. Either sign this agreement before the sun goes down today or Don Felder's out of the fucking band." Felder blinked, having calculated in the short term at least that finance outweighed fundamentals, but the still-burning antagonism between him and Frey was an early red flare.
>
> Felder was never ever satisfied, never ever happy. . . . A rock band is not a perfect democracy; it's more like a sports team. No one can do anything without the other guys . . . but everybody doesn't get to touch the ball all the time. Felder couldn't appreciate the amount of money he was making. . . . He was more concerned about how much money I was making.

Incredibly, this rickety confederacy held until 2001 before Felder was unceremoniously dumped, prompting the kind of legal face-off that had for so long seemed inevitable. Seeking a reported $50 million in damages, Felder filed two lawsuits—one against "Eagles, Ltd.," a California corporation, and the other against Henley as an individual.

Henley and Frey hit back with their own countersuit, alleging breach of contract over a book Felder had written called *Heaven and Hell*, which laid bare the tumult at the heart of the Eagles. In the same way that John Lennon had used a post-split *Rolling Stone* interview to reveal the sexual debauchery of Beatle tours, Felder opened Pandora's box in an act of retribution against Frey and Henley.

Leaping from the pages were the lewd details of the band's "Third Encore" as well as drug use on an industrial scale. Lost in the media frenzy the book created was the undeniable music they had forged in the white heat of the furnace, a cauldron fired in no small part by creative friction. Henley scornfully dismissed it as "nasty little tell-all" by a bitter man who got kicked out the group. Calling the book a "really low, cheap shot," he told *The Guardian*, "A lot of people on the outside believe a lot of the bullshit in Felder's book, and believe Glenn Frey and I are some kind of tyrants. . . . The fact is, we are largely responsible both for the longevity and the success of this band, because we did it our way, and a lot of people didn't like that."

Felder, however, was adamant he had every right to go public on the internal feuding but had not meant for it to come across as someone dishing "the inside trash and dirt on the Eagles." He said, "I wanted to write the book to show how greed, power, and control are corrupting."

As defenses go, it was papery thin. Henley and Frey tried every legal mechanism open to them to try and block the book, a process that ran in tandem with Felder's lawsuit at being axed from the Eagles. Six years went by before Felder's case was settled out of the court, with a binding stipulation that neither party reveal the terms.

In the meantime, Felder's heavily amended book hit the shelves despite attempts by Frey and Felder to bury it. And it did, indeed, set out in coruscating terms, his deep-rooted animus toward the two main Eagles. The band, though, continued to tour—and in 2007 released *Long Road Out of Eden*, their first album of original work in twenty-one years. In terms of song quality, it was a long way from the golden-carpeted floors and white-marble corridors of *Hotel California*—not that anyone was really giving a damn.

The Eagles instead succumbed to rock music's oldest temptation—channeling their younger selves on stage night after night and slowly morphing into becoming their own tribute band. But with Felder having been removed from the play and everyone else comfortable in their parts, there was now a weary acceptance of Groundhog Day. In 2013 the warts-and-all documentary called *The History of the Eagles* featured contributions from members past and present, but it only helped fuel the popular perception of Frey and Henley as two control freaks whose egos were largely uncurbed the more successful the band came—then and now. Even Felder was given airtime to again tearfully air his grievances. Bernie Leadon, by now back in the touring fold and with an eye on the bottom line, was more circumspect in his observations. No point in poking the bear.

THE THIRD ACT

In the end, human mortality killed the Eagles—or should have. Glenn Frey's untimely death in January 2016, at the age of sixty-seven, was perhaps a result of the universal law of cause and effect. Years of rock star excess had taken its toll.

He died from complications brought on by long-term chronic rheumatoid arthritis, acute ulcerative colitis, and pneumonia. He spent his final few days in a coma, having battled various ailments for several years. Only death allows fences so badly ripped up to be repaired by those you met along life's highways. Don Henley spoke for all Eagles past and present when he said it had always been Frey's band.

> He was like a brother to me; we were family, and like most families, there was some dysfunction. But the bond we forged forty-five years ago was never broken, even during the fourteen years that the Eagles were dissolved. We were two young men who made the pilgrimage to Los Angeles with the same dream: to make our mark in the music industry—and with perseverance, a deep love of music, our alliance with other great musicians and our manager, Irving Azoff, we built something that has lasted longer than anyone could have believed.
>
> I'm not sure I believe in fate, but I know that crossing paths with Glenn Lewis Frey in 1970 changed my life forever, and it eventually had an impact on the lives of millions of other people all over the planet. I will be grateful every day that he was in my life. Glenn was the one who started it all. He was the spark plug, the man with the plan.

Sentiment and gratitude were the overriding emotions felt by Leadon who had happily seen his friendship with Frey repaired in the autumn of their years. They last saw each other at the side of the stage after a gig in July 2015, just months before Frey's passing. "He gave me a big, huge thanks for participating," remembers Leadon. "Then he said, 'It's been really awesome to have you back out there. This is not the end.'"

There was no such happy reconciliation for Felder for whom their breach would always remain an open wound.

He said, "Glenn's passing was so unexpected and has left me with a very heavy heart filled with sorrow. At times, it felt like we were brothers and at other times, like brothers, we disagreed. He was the leader that we all looked to for direction and by far the coolest guy in the band. It saddens me a great deal that we were never able to address the issues that came between us and talk them through. Sadly, now we will never get the chance."

A year later Henley, Walsh, Schmit, and Frey's widow Cindy—Felder was pointedly not invited—attended the White House to receive the Kennedy Center Honors for their monumental contribution to American music, a tribute that sat nicely along with their 1998 induction into the Rock & Roll Hall of Fame. And that should have seen the train pulling into the station for the last time. Henley said as much when he declared, "I don't see how we could go out and play without the guy who started the band. It would just seem like greed or something. It would seem like a desperate thing."

The Eagles, it should be noted, continue to tour, happily serving up a peaceful easy feeling to millions of loyal fans all over the globe with a lineup that now includes Frey's son Deacon.

Cream: Eric Clapton, Ginger Baker, and Jack Bruce
Photofest

CREAM

Eric Clapton let Ginger Baker's words sink in slowly. It was, he said in his gruff Cockney growl, an idea, a notion, nothing more. A potential pooling of resources into a mutual admiration society, and we'll call it a band. Let's see where it takes us. The year was 1966.

Clapton was just twenty-one, but his towering talent as an artisan guitarist was already attracting the kind of unsought attention that would soon see hippy graffiti artists anoint him as God on London subway walls. Baker, almost six years older, was an imperious and primordial drummer who had already earned his stripes providing the percussive muscle for several big bands.

He had seen Clapton play with John Mayall's Bluesbreakers, the group that was the birthing pool for many of the era's top musicians. Impressed hardly covered his reaction. Now here they were, sitting in Baker's Rover 3000, the drummer habitually pulling heavily on a cigarette, sitting inadvertently at the crossroads of their lives. Clapton eventually broke the awkward silence: "I'll only do it if we can get Jack in." In Eric's own words, Baker, wild-eyed, a face like thunder, almost crashed his car. "I just thought Jesus, no. On reflection I should have said no right away," declared Baker years later.

"Jack" was Jack Bruce, a classically trained, wiry, truculent, and straight-talking Scotsman, whose adroit bass playing had already marked him out as an extraordinary musician. The reason for Baker gripping his steering wheel tighter over Clapton's suggestion was simple. Just months earlier, Ginger and Jack were locked in as the herculean rhythm section of the Graham Bond Organisation, a group that grafted jazzy overtones onto a rhythm and blues vine.

Until the day, that is, Ginger sacked Jack from the band while brandishing a knife in his face. "Jack's personality was Jekyll and Hyde," said Baker. "If you said the wrong thing, he would suddenly turn on you. One day during my drum solo, Jack began playing a bass thing with me. I was really getting off on it, phrasing with him on the bass drum.

"Suddenly he turned around and said, 'You're playing too fucking loud.' The result was that I nearly killed him. A bouncer had to pull me off. I was the heavy, so it was down to me." By this point, confrontations between them had already become almost a daily occurrence. This, however, was the first time they had used bare knuckles to settle their differences.

"We had got into a fight onstage because he felt I was playing too loud during his drum solo," recalled Bruce. "Some time later we had a meeting, and he pulled a knife on me and said, 'You're fired.' I said, 'You can't fire me. It's The Graham Bond Organisation and I'm a founder member.' But by then poor old Graham was well into smack and he didn't care. But it was very stupid of Ginger because the band was doing well, and I was an important part."

It was the first T-junction of a love-hate relationship that would go on to defy casual explanation for the rest of their lives. A musical marriage that, over the course of almost sixty years was, in equal parts, pernicious and perennial, vituperative and vital. The choice facing Baker in his car that night seemed simple enough. Listen to your gut instinct and resist Clapton's ultimatum or bite back hard on your pride to create the kind of band you always wanted. A group encompassing apex musicians, each man a master of his instrument.

The next day he drove over to Bruce's flat holding an olive branch. "Ginger had to come and ask me—which I thoroughly enjoyed," said Bruce years later, owning up to a dash of hubris. "Jack later said I went there to eat humble pie," said Ginger. "That's crap. We sat down, had a cup of tea, and I said I was getting a band together with Eric. Let's let bygones be bygones."

The band they formed was, of course, Cream, a hothouse of individual virtuosity and a Dada-esque coalition of remarkable talents. The spirited amalgam of Clapton's blues riffs, Bruce's pioneering bass runs, and Baker's monstrous drum fills made them rock's first supergroup.

Over the course of eighteen months—through 1967's Summer of Love—the group released four albums that would leave an indelible footprint on music's shifting landscape and guarantee the three men a permanent seat at rock's top table. At its fiery core, though, was the fractious and fragile accord between the hotheaded, cadaverous drummer and the equally combustible Scot, who was four years his junior.

And sandwiched in the middle of this volatility was Clapton, who during the course of the group's existence would often be reduced to tears by the constant feuding between his two bandmates. "I became the victim in that band," he would later note.

Their mutual antagonism predated the group they would forever be synonymous with and cast a long shadow well after Cream had curdled. Fate first stepped across their paths in June 1962 at the Cambridge May Ball. Bruce was playing bass with the Scotsville Jazzmen but was more curious about the sounds coming from another marquee.

Wandering over, he stumbled on an outfit led by tenor sax player Dick Heckstall-Smith and a wild-eyed, red-haired drummer thrashing away as if his life depended on every backbeat. Bruce's abiding first impressions were as follows: "He looked like a demon in that cellar, sitting there with his red hair. He had this drum kit that he'd made himself. I had never heard drums sound so good. I'd never seen a drummer like him, and I knew then I wanted to play with him."

Gate-crashing the band's set, Bruce won over Heckstall-Smith and within weeks got the call to join Alexis Korner's Blues Incorporated, whose ever-shifting lineup often included Ginger. Musically, Baker and Bruce had more in common than ever divided them; their early passions were rooted in the jazz influences of Phil Seamen and Max Roach.

Clapton said, "Jack and Ginger were musical rebels. They were going after something. I had that, too. I felt like a man on a mission. Then, when I met them, I felt I had found my ilk." Cream's comet shone briefly before burning up in an unavoidable clash of egos, a blizzard of opiate abuse, and ultimately, Clapton's belief that, musically, he was in the wrong movie.

However, when Clapton convinced Baker, already a jobbing veteran of several bands before joining the Graham Bond Organisation, to let Bruce join team Cream, he unwittingly inked a Faustian pact. "I'd heard that there wasn't much love lost between them. . . . But I didn't know if it was a particularly serious issue," said Clapton. It wasn't long before he found out. At their first band meeting, malice swiftly rose to the surface, leaving Clapton wondering what he had let himself in for. In Phillip Norman's *Eric*

Clapton: The Biography, he admitted, "The very first time the three of us got together, in the front room of Ginger's house in Neasden, they started arguing right away. . . . It seemed that they just naturally rubbed each other up the wrong way, both being very headstrong and both natural leaders. But when we started to play together, it all just turned into magic. Maybe I was the necessary catalyst for them both to get along."

There were, however, a few preconditions before all their stars were in proper alignment. Bruce and Clapton demanded that Baker, already vein-deep in heroin and a registered addict, give up the junk; he didn't. Baker demanded that Bruce cut out the windups and turn down the bass volume in the studio and on the stage; he did neither.

Dry tinder also sparked into flame early on after Baker privately told music journalist Chris Welch of this new "supergroup." When Welch made the news public, Bruce was apoplectic. He was at that point contracted to Manfred Mann, while Clapton was still tied to the Bluesbreakers, and Baker officially remained a member of the Graham Bond Organisation. "All hell broke loose," said Clapton. "Jack was furious and almost came to blows with Ginger."

John Mayall was among several who couldn't believe his star guitarist had walked out to join up with two of the most explosive personalities in London's musical melting pot. There were few secrets between bands and most people—Clapton apparently excepted—knew of the loathing that existed between Jack and Ginger. Mayall declared, "I was aware Eric was friendly with Jack and Ginger but no one, absolutely no one, thought of these two in a group. They hated each other."

Bruce was also not surprisingly nurturing a grudge and harbored intermittent notions of revenge against the man who made him appear "difficult" to work with. Still smarting from Baker's decision to bullet him from the Graham Bond Organisation, he occasionally whispered in Clapton's ear that Ginger was the band's weakest link and that the drug-addicted drummer would take them all down.

It was classic divide-and-conquer behavior. Baker recalled one such incident in his own memoir: "We did a gig in Cawley for a guy I'd known in the GBO days. It went really well, and he asked us to do another set, so I said, 'Ok, but for another £45.' He refused, so I got our roadie to pack up my drums and off I went. . . . However, unbeknown to me, Jack had convinced Eric to do another set with just the two of them. He also convinced Eric that they should get rid of me because I wouldn't do another set."

On such flimsy and capricious early foundations was Cream built. Flare-ups would become commonplace, the price Clapton would have to pay for being a member of Cream, the band's name itself a self-heralding reference to their own arrogant elitism. Their first two albums—*Fresh Cream* and *Disraeli Gears*—were released in 1966 and 1967 respectively, right into the teeth of the Sergeant Pepper–style psychedelic storm that was at that precise juncture blowing through music.

Cream, however, was on a separate trajectory to those staring into an LSD-dosed summer. The band was a melting pot of influences drawn from so many areas but grounded mainly in jazz and R&B. "We were never a rock band," was the line maintained by Baker.

In terms of sheer musical brawn, Cream was a breed apart from other blues bands such as the fledgling Fleetwood Mac, the Yardbirds, the Butterfield Blues Band, and Canned Heat. Tracks like "Sunshine of Your Love," "Spoonful," "I'm So Glad," "Toad" (perhaps rock's first drum solo), "Strange Brew," and "Tales of Brave Ulysses" elevated them to an alternative plane of playing.

Only Jimi Hendrix's mastery of the guitar garnered the same of kind of respect and slightly leveled the playing field. By the time they made their third album—*Wheels of Fire*—they had hit their stride before suffering premature burnout. The first LP was the typical mixture of blues covers and self-penned tracks. But by the time *Disraeli Gears* appeared, Jack had emerged as the band's principal songwriter along with Pete Brown, a non-musical performance poet who had worked as a lyricist with Graham Bond. Brown and Ginger had already written a number of songs, so he was inside the drummer's small circle of trust.

Soon, though, Brown formed a more natural writing alliance with the band's bass guitarist. Bruce noted, "Ginger and Pete were at my flat trying to work on a song, but it wasn't happening. My wife Janet then got with Ginger and they wrote 'Sweet Wine' while I started working with Pete."

It was a shift in internal band dynamics that was a red flag for Baker, who was fearful about the potential hit to his bank balance through the loss of publishing money. In his mind, Cream was a cooperative, one in which a group aesthetic was set in stone—which it was until it came to song credits.

Brown later acknowledged the standoff: "I know there was some resentment from Eric and Ginger, but songs were needed and Jack and I were there with the songs—good songs, which have stood the test of time." Baker, naturally, found himself in a different corner.

The problem wasn't that Jack and Pete were writing songs; the bone of contention was whether they should get all the credit for them. It still rankles me that I got no credit whatsoever for contributing heavily to the arrangement of two of Cream's most popular tunes.

The whole way "Sunshine" turned out was totally my input, and I've never even received a thank you for it. Also, the whole introduction to "White Room"—the 5/4 Bolero thing—was my input to the tune. When both songs came out, I wasn't even mentioned. Not a word of thanks. After the first three months together I was dissatisfied with the situation. They wouldn't even try many of the songs I had written. I was informed they were getting a new drummer. Why they didn't, I don't know. But it was just as well they didn't.

It only served to stoke Ginger's lifetime of resentment toward Bruce, especially over what he regarded as an unfair distribution of group wealth. And it never went away as he fought to keep his head above choppy financial waters in later life. "Jack Bruce and Peter Brown made more money out of Cream than Eric and I by a considerable margin," he fumed.

Across the room, Bruce saw no need to redress Ginger's assertions of a financial imbalance. "The point is," he argued, "if someone writes a song they are entitled to get paid for it. The only reason that there were so many Jack Bruce and Pete Brown songs was because, in the beginning at least, that's all there was. Nobody else was coming up with songs and that did lead to quite a lot of friction in the band."

Brown's proximity to Bruce also afforded him a ringside seat whenever Ginger and Jack laced up the gloves as egos repeatedly collided. He said, "As a drummer, no one could touch Ginger. As a human being, not many tried to. It was an incredible scene between him and Jack, though all three of them were oversensitive. There was a minimum of one feud at any given time."

Running parallel to this ongoing hostility was, however, a shared respect for each other's ability as a musician. Never at any time in four decades of intermittently working with each other across a range of bands was there ever a cross word about the music.

"It was as if something else had taken over," Baker explained. "You're not conscious of playing. You're listening to this fantastic sound that you're a part of. And your part is just . . . happening. It was a gift, and we three had it in abundance."

It all boiled down to the fact they simply chafed as individuals. In 1993, Baker and Bruce teamed up with British blues maestro Gary Moore to form BBM (Baker Bruce Moore), a short-lived power trio that inevitably drew comparisons with Cream. Moore, a stalwart of Thin Lizzy, had high hopes of rekindling the musical spirit of his new rhythm section's former band.

He was keenly aware, however, that some delicate diplomacy would be needed to keep things between Baker and Bruce on an even keel. "On the first day we ran through some Cream songs to warm up, and then we started putting down tracks and it was very easy," Moore recalled.

> There was no problem at all. It was really fun, and I got a great insight into the chemistry between Jack and Ginger. It wasn't what I thought at all; they weren't at each other's throats. I think Jack really looks up to Ginger, and Ginger knows it, so he'll never tell him he's any good.
>
> They're like two brothers, just winding each other up. One day I said to Jack, "Can you ask Ginger to play the hi-hat pattern like he did on 'Born Under a Bad Sign'?" "No way, I'm not fucking asking him. You ask him." So I just pressed the button in the control room and asked him to play that pattern and he said, "Yeah, sure, man. No problem." And Jack looked at me speechless. They were just like an old married couple. It's just the way they were.

Less than a year after forming, however, Cream was already experiencing the pangs of a love turning cold. In 1967–1968 they had filled the vacancy caused by the Beatles and (temporarily) the Stones stepping off the concert stage. And their brand of powerhouse jazz/blues easily filled the vacuum as bands transitioned from pop to rock.

Touring, however, created a completely new and ruinous sideshow. At one gig in Denmark, Jack took sharp offense at a remark Ginger made in the dressing room and promptly began heading for the airport before being persuaded to return. Another night, Baker suddenly upped and walked away from his drums in a fit of pique, leaving Bruce and Clapton to carry on as a duo. It wasn't uncommon for drumsticks to be lobbed in Bruce's direction.

On their first American tour, they found themselves playing dingy dives in out-of-the-way frontier towns. This was not the American dream that had been sold to them by their manager Robert Stigwood. Shoehorned into a tiny tour bus that ambled across North America and succumbing to the inevitable sidebars of life on the road, tensions weren't long in bubbling over, pouring gas on the sparking, volatile relationship between Baker and Bruce, who found it difficult to be in such constant and close proximity to each other for any length of time.

The sheer ennui of touring could always be relied on to ratchet hostilities up a few further notches. It should have been a sort of spiritual homecoming. America, after all, was the country from which all their profound musical inspirations had been drawn. It was, however, a miserable first experience. They often found themselves buried at the bottom of the bill and relegated to maybe three songs a night. A year later, they were back across the Atlantic for their second U.S. tour amid a spectacular reversal of fortune.

The Beatles had now officially abandoned the stage and the Stones were moribund. Cream was the band that reaped the prize dividends and for a while could legitimately lay claim to being the world's biggest live band. Their status at the summit of rock's Everest was reflected in the overall package of that second American tour.

The venues were better, the money was better—$500,000 for nineteen dates—and the drugs were also a considerable upgrade. This time, however, all three traveled in separate cars and stayed in separate rooms. Sure signs that, despite massive success and improving financial rewards, Cream was rapidly turning sour. According to Clapton, the personality clashes between Baker and Bruce reached a peak during Cream's tours of the United States in 1967/1968. "Musically they were great, like a well-oiled machine," says Clapton.

"Personally, it was a different matter, they just rubbed each other up the wrong way. It got to the point where we never socialized anymore, or shared any ideas; we got on stage, played, and went our separate ways."

Now marginalized as a writer, Baker's paranoia toward Clapton and Bruce was rampant. Privately, he brooded about being treated as an economy-class subordinate, despite his drumming providing the band's primal center. "Jack and Eric were close musically," he said. "I felt that Jack thought of me as 'merely the drummer.'"

But that was not his main bone of contention now. He could no longer stomach the extended, ear-splitting guitar and bass improvisations that erupted onstage between Jack and Eric. Night after night, solos would be stretched to last up to three or four minutes—sometimes longer—as each man tried to outdo the other in the ramped-up virtuoso stakes. And the huge Marshall amps that were now a routine part of their concert rig only made matters worse.

In the autumn of his years, Baker attributed his painful deafness to the onstage crescendos Bruce and Clapton generated. He elaborated on the issue in an interview with *UNCUT* magazine:

> It got too loud. That was one of the death-knells of it. It was just painful to be on the stage, the volume was so incredible that it damaged my ears. I've

still got a hearing problem from those days. I hate loud volume. Especially loud bass amps.

It's really painful. Because I'm banging the drums hard to hear what I'm playing, because I've got these huge Marshall stacks either side. And Jack would turn up, so Eric would turn up to compensate, and they'd both be turning up all night. It got absolutely stupid. There was one night on the last tour we did where both Eric and I stopped playing for two whole choruses. Jack was playing so loud in front of his stack of Marshalls, that he didn't realise.

He told another publication,

Cream's last year was extremely painful for me. When we started in 1966, Eric and Jack had one Marshall each. Then it became a stack, then a double stack and finally a triple stack. By 1968, I was just the poor bastard stuck in the middle of these incredible noise-making things. It was ridiculous. I used to get back to the hotel and my ears were roaring. That final year damaged my hearing. The incredible volume was one of the things that destroyed the band. Playing loud had nothing to do with music.

The trickle-down effect from all the discord spread out to the road crew, most of whom were left treading on eggshells. Caught in the crossfire most often was tour manager Ben Palmer, a longtime friend of Clapton's. "There was constant and serious disputes between Jack and Ginger every day," he recalled. "It didn't matter what they were arguing about really. It was just that they were at each other's throats, and it was very intense."

Ultimately, America would prove to be the band's downfall. Back home, the flamboyant Australian Stigwood ignored Clapton's frequent SOS's about the band's deteriorating internal dynamics while making a mint in fees. Eric, having long ago laughed off the graffiti proclaiming him as a musical deity, could now ironically clearly see the writing on the wall. And he was fed up being in the middle of a war of attrition between Baker and Bruce, a conflict that showed no sign of an armistice. "The workload was pretty severe," Clapton recalled.

We were playing six nights a week, and I lost weight until I was about nine stone and I looked like death. I was in bad shape. It wasn't so much self-abuse as self-neglect. I think that all added to the psychology of the situation, which was pretty tricky at the best of times. Ginger and Jack were dynamic characters and pretty overwhelming. It felt like I was in a confrontational situation twenty-four hours a day. Half my time was spent trying to keep the peace. And on top of that you're trying to be creative and make music. I was calling home to Robert Stigwood and saying, "Get me out of here—these guys are crazy. I don't know what's going on and I've had enough."

He'd always say to give it one more week. That was bearable as long as there was no visible alternative. But when something came along that showed another way, that was it for me.

That "something" was the music emanating 3,000 miles away from a ramshackle house in Woodstock, the small town upstate of New York where The Band had just recorded their seminal first album—*Music from Big Pink*—in the basement of the property from which the record took its name. A musical cooperative, their roots-driven songs touched a deep chord in Clapton's insecure psyche.

Equally significant, however, was a coruscating *Rolling Stone* review around the same time of a Cream gig, which suggested that the Great Guitar God of Rock was stagnating as a musician by becoming "the master of blues clichés." On reading the review for the first time, Clapton reputedly fainted.

"That confirmed not only what I felt was my role in the group but what would happen to me if I stayed." Broken and jaded, Clapton disbanded Cream literally overnight and instantly retreated from the internecine combat zone manned by Baker and Bruce. For Jack, there was only confusion; for Ginger, there was only relief despite the Cream gravy train suddenly lurching off the tracks. "It was like a great weight off of my shoulders when it was finished. I was bloody tired of it," said the famously acerbic drummer.

"We decided, for different reasons, that it was all over. When Cream died, it died. Short of murder, we couldn't solve a problem between us. . . . The seeds of the breakup were there from the beginning. Many times I had to drink myself into a stupor before I could work with them."

Cream bowed out with a celebrated farewell concert at London's Royal Albert Hall on November 26, 1968. Among the support groups was Yes, whose bass guitarist Chris Squire witnessed a band taking perfunctory to new levels. "There was no eye contact between Jack and Eric throughout the whole set. And Ginger just looked like he wanted to be anywhere else. It was like going through the motions."

One last drop of milk was squeezed from the Cream cash cow three months later—a bittersweet denouement album called, with no sense of self-irony, *Goodbye*. The cover showed each of them dressed in satin suits, with top hats and twirling canes. Cheesy doesn't begin to cover it. It was a cheapskate epitaph, a sad and tatty end to a musical fusion that had redrawn the boundaries of British blues. Cream lasted less than three years from first rehearsal to that final gig. Little more than the blink of an eye when each man's career is looked at as a whole. In their creative wake, however, lay a body of work, the best of which remains eternal in its influence and ageless in its mastery.

They set the bar and then raised it out of reach. But the mystery of why it even lasted that long with Ginger and Jack constantly feuding remained an enigma code not even their nearest and dearest could crack. Ginger Baker was always labeled the most cantankerous man in rock music. American filmmaker Guy Bulger gained rare access to the drummer and interviewed him for a documentary at his farm in Tulbagh, South Africa. But it ended with the drummer breaking his nose with a cane after objecting to some slight hidden from everyone except himself.

Evidence for the defense of the not-so-fabulous Baker boy would, on the surface, seem hard to find. But I uncovered some from perhaps an unlikely source. Jack's son Malcolm, himself a notable musician who is the keeper of his father's musical flame, was able, partly, to gain some insight into the pair's shared and troubled history.

I had spent some time with Ginger over the years, some of which were joyful, some of which weren't so joyful depending on his mental state at the time. Ginger was a really misunderstood guy. He was a really decent person underneath all the gruff, nasty notoriety he is always tagged with. He was a person who didn't suffer fools gladly.

He could smell out people who weren't being authentic with him. He didn't really want to engage with people who would come up and say "I'm your biggest fan." He would go, "Fuck off." But if you talked to him on a human level he was all right. People have this impression of who he was, but I don't think it's the correct impression at all. I think Ginger was a very intelligent and astute human being, but he was maybe someone who went down a certain path, like my dad, that wasn't really the best for him. Ginger was a few years older and was more established.

When they met, he was a heroin addict. My dad was this little spotty Glaswegian, who was trying to make it and was undoubtedly already a stellar musician at the age of eighteen or nineteen when they met.

So I think there was almost like the older brother thing going on. And my dad being the way he was, he's not going to take any nonsense. I don't think anyone will properly understand all they went through to be successful with Cream, sitting on the wheel arch of a transit for 300 days. Baked beans at a truck stop. Smoking reefers, you know.

We've all had these formative years as musicians but I don't think we can quite understand what they went through together. I'm not even sure my mum ever understood the reason for the tension between Jack and Ginger. It was just rivalry, alpha versus beta, male behavior, drug use, women, money, that whole thing of my dad getting the publishing, along with Pete Brown, for the songs that they wrote. Everything that goes to make up a rock 'n' roll life.

Cream was a textbook example of how the very thing that makes art successful can also be its undoing. Yes, the differences between all three band members produced a unique sound, but it also led to tension, battles, and explosions. When the gun smoke drifted on the breeze, the finger pointing started.

"The truth is that we were very different people right from the start," said Baker. "We all wanted to be successful, but in the end success was the only thing keeping us together. And that wasn't enough."

In the immediate aftermath of the band's implosion, Clapton offered his own take.

It is like Cream was a consensus of what we thought we could do as individuals within a group but—because of the nature of the line-up, the different backgrounds, the different points of reference—the conglomeration that resulted was such a vast compromise to what we would all have liked to do as individuals. Maybe we will all get together to play again some time in the future, and there is no reason why we should not appear on each other's records, though it would be a big publicized thing if we did so.

History, of course, tells us that Clapton emerged as the most commercially successful from the Cream Star Chamber. He somewhat reluctantly brought Baker into the fold for Blind Faith, his short-lived first post-Cream band that also included Stevie Winwood in its ranks. Baker then formed Ginger Baker's Airforce, an eclectic amalgam of jazz and rock influences that also weaved African rhythms into its broad tapestry.

Jack Bruce plowed his own distinctive musical furrow away from the mainstream while refusing to compromise his musical principles as he navigated the boundaries, like Baker, between rock and jazz. His first solo album, *Songs for a Tailor*, featured an alliance of like-minded musicians such as George Harrison while still working in lyrical tandem with Pete Brown. But subsequent recordings only appealed to a niche core of fans, ensuring over the years a dwindling financial return. But for all three, there was no real escaping their past.

Ginger and Jack, both still battling various addictions, set aside personal differences to once more be in the same group. In 1998, the drummer sat in for a few shows with the latest incarnation of Ringo Starr's All-Starr Band, which at that point also included Jack on bass. In the same way as the Beatles straight-batted megabuck offers of reunions, the members of Cream also found themselves the recipients of corona-watering sums to reform for a tour.

Clapton, easily the most financially comfortable of the trio, had no wish to try and rekindle his past. Everything, though, changed in 1993 when all three found themselves on the same stage as Cream was inducted into the Rock & Roll Hall of Fame in Cleveland. It was an emotional reunion, the first time they had all been together in a musical setting since 1969. It gave rise to inevitable rumors of a full-fledged reconciliation. But twelve more years would pass before they all decided the timing was right.

"I missed them and I had missed them for a long time," said Clapton.

And I realized deep down that as much as they might want to get together again, it was my call because I had walked from it. At some point, it really just came into my mind more and more and more. I would get up, and I would think about it. I thought, "You may not need to do it, for whatever reason, but maybe they'd benefit."

Not only that, we can. We actually can, because we're all still alive. I thought this is worth it. This is worth whatever grief and stress we may have experienced in the past, to come back to this.

It was widely speculated, at the time, that Clapton had relented in the face of the severe health problems facing his former bandmates. By the turn of the millennium, Bruce was battling liver cancer—he underwent a transplant in 2003 but the organ was rejected, leaving him gravely ill.

But, showing typical obduracy, he eventually recovered after a second operation. Baker was suffering from severe arthritis. More pertinent, perhaps, was the fact that neither man, Baker especially, had nowhere near the amount of cash sloshing through Clapton's bank accounts.

The Albert Hall shows, bringing the band full circle, sold out in a matter of hours, prompting another trio of concerts at New York City's Madison Square Garden in October 2005. This was proof, if any were needed, of Cream's enduring adoration among a fan base that had embraced a legend and watched it grow across multiple generations. The London gigs were a massive success. Each man, having survived a Homer-like odyssey of addiction and excess, appearing thrilled to pay homage to the past while giving thanks for the present. But by the time they moved to the United States, fragile détente had given way to an oh-so-familiar grouchy antagonism between Baker and Bruce. Back in place were familiar rules of engagement, with each man rag-dolling the other offstage over a variety of issues.

"I'd refused to do it first of all," said Baker in 2008.

> Eric phoned me up and convinced me. The reason I didn't want to do it was because of what happened in New York in 1968 when the magic was destroyed. The reason we broke up in the first place reemerged onstage at Madison Square. You'll notice I'm talking about Eric in a nice way, but there was another person in the group. It wasn't just a problem with the volume of the bass guitar, it was the problem of being humiliated in front of 20,000 people. Jack used to get a bit tearful with the apologies and say, "I love you, man." But I just cannot play with other people playing too loud on stage. It's too painful.

Clapton accepted it was finally game over for three men now well into their sixties but still able at a minute's notice to pick over blisters that had never fully healed. "After that I was pretty convinced that we had gone as far as we could without someone getting killed. At this time in my life, I don't want blood on my hands," he declared while looking back on the Madison Square Garden shows. "I don't want to be part of some kind of tragic confrontation."

It really did still run that deep between Jack and Ginger, two old men who refused to give an inch in their own unyielding animus. Cream was a rock group but so far from being a band of brothers. In the end, sadly, only death provided the peaceful resolution neither man could find in life. Bruce died from liver disease in October 2014, his passing at the age of seventy-one drawing tributes from all of rock music's grandees, including, naturally, Clapton and Baker.

A lifetime of heavy smoking and drug abuse caught up with Ginger when he died in 2019 at the age of eighty in a hospital in Canterbury. It was the final curtain for rock's most pioneering drummer and the genre's most unapologetically irascible individual. One of his final sessions ironically took place with Malcolm Bruce, the son of the man with whom he had shared an unfathomable conflict while, at the same time, shaping some of rock music's most iconic songs.

They were making an album, with a number of other musicians, called *Acoustic Cream*, a homage to the lightning conductor that at one time bound Baker, Bruce, and Clapton together. And the experience took Malcolm back to the day of his father's funeral and the sight of Ginger milling alongside other mourners at Golders Green Crematorium in north London.

"I'm standing beside Eric Clapton and Ginger, and Eric's like very conversational, what you up to? That kind of thing. And that's not to pooh pooh Eric but, in contrast, Ginger was standing next to me just bawling his eyes out. And he just kept saying that he had lost Jack."

A poignant moment where guilt and regret came together for a valedictory farewell when there were no more earthly battles left to fight.

Oasis: lead singer Liam Gallagher and his brother Noel at the Cardiff International Arena
Pa Images/Alamy Stock

⑫

OASIS

They were the mono-browed brothers grim of nineties Britpop, two snarling pit bulls straining at the leash of their own unfiltered hatred for the Conservative-led establishment; the barrenness of their own delinquent, drug-addled adolescence on the tough side of the tracks in Burnage, Manchester; and, most blindingly obvious, for each other.

Noel and Liam Gallagher's mutual brotherly contempt was the combustible component that, ultimately, rocketed Oasis to megastardom. Reciprocal loathing and youthful rebellion were neatly parceled up inside a gauzy belief that their band was the sound of the Beatles reborn—until, of course, that same enmity brought the whole thing crashing down upon reentry to planet reality the day an exasperated Noel finally tore off his dog tags and walked out in 2009.

Looking back in anger since then has become the norm for two men—now both in their fifties, incidentally—locked in an omnipresent state of fuck-off gridlock. The notion of quibbling siblings is, of course, nothing new to rock music; but when it comes to trading poisonous barbs, Liam and Noel Gallagher are *artisans*.

The Gallagher brothers effortlessly elevated their animus to a new level by weaponizing social media and hijacking the internet as their own personal battlefield. In a *Q* magazine interview just weeks before he said his final sayonara, Noel revealed that the pair never played family guy.

"I don't like Liam," he said, citing his younger brother's drinking for bringing out the demon in him. "He's rude, arrogant, intimidating, and lazy. He's the angriest man you'll ever meet. He's like a man with a fork in a world of soup." Taking the bait, Liam was easily reeled in: "It takes more than blood to be my brother," he retorted in New Musical Express. "He doesn't like me, and I don't like him."

DNA apart, the only thing they had in common growing up was a Fab Four infatuation and a talent for seeking out trouble. Oasis was the muscle car that roared out of the pits of Manchester's grimy south side in 1991, spewing gravel in every direction. Five years later they were, arguably, the most exhilarating and most notorious band in the world. Supersonic doesn't do their chaotic rise to fame any justice whatsoever.

In 1996, 4 percent of the UK adult population jostled to get tickets for the band's two nights playing before an audience of 250,000 fans at Knebworth House. One of the lucky ones was Rob Fidderman, who had recently become an Oasis convert, and who, like any fan electrified by a band's music, plunged headlong into the chaotic days of their past, present, and future. Fidderman went on to become one of Britain's leading authorities on Oasis as well as being a huge champion of the entire Britpop movement. He told me,

At the time it was all boy bands sitting on stools with the suits. With the cuffs turned up over the jackets. Spikey hair. Lots of R&B. Mariah Carey, Luther Vandross. After Kurt Cobain died, there was a bit of a void. Oasis came along at the right time. I immersed myself in the band. They were just really cool guys playing these anthemic songs, the videos were great, and they looked cool, they had the attitude. It was a bit like the early days of rock 'n' roll when it was called the devil's music. Oasis were just so edgy. They had so much attitude.

They had played—and blown—a gig at LA's legendary Whisky a Go Go. But the stratospheric success of their first two albums, *Definitely Maybe*, and *What's the Story (Morning Glory)*, saw them standing on the shoulders of musical giants. It didn't matter a jot that every second song Noel wrote channeled the Beatles—or the Kinks, or the Jam. Or that the tunes often mined the Fab Four's catalog of snazzy chords and epic tunes. Nor did it matter if Liam believed he carried the spirit of John Lennon every time he leaned, legs bowed like Lennon, hands clasped behind his back, into a microphone.

The only thing that mattered was being "fooking mad fer it"—a postpunk manifesto that perfectly captured the boozy, nicotine-stained cocktail of laddish lethargy alongside a carpe diem recklessness. And at the center of the magic carpet ride sat Noel and Liam, two brothers fated to live the rock 'n' roll life they had always dreamed of only to see it turn them into music's Cain and Abel.

Their squabbles may not have ended in fratricide, but there were plenty occasions when it came close. Simultaneously, they were the band's greatest strength—and the weakest links in the chain.

"Oasis was like a Ferrari," declared Liam. "Great to look at, great to drive, and it'll spin out of control every now and then." Oasis, nevertheless, offered Noel and Liam Gallagher a road out of yesterday into a new tomorrow. Once, however, they had more in common than just genetics. The teenage dream they both nurtured was simple: to become rock 'n' roll stars like Lennon and McCartney; to hold society in contempt like Johnny Rotten; to play guitar like Johnny Marr; to adopt the seditious swagger and attitude of local heroes, the Stone Roses; and to escape the laddish post-punk desolation that had scarred Britain's apocalyptic post-Thatcher landscape.

And for those living with the economic deprivations of Thatcher's Britain, they symbolized ballsy rebellion to people like Fidderman. "Britain was just coming out of recession and people were very disillusioned," he said.

> It was retaliation not so much against society but people just needed something, young people just needed something. Oasis were like the working-class heroes. . . . They came from a council estate. They were just lads who had a dream, they had the attitude and the swagger. They just said fuck this. This is who we are and what we're going to do. And they had the balls to do it.

Born to an immigrant Irish family and brought up in the tough-as-nails suburb of Burnage, their early lives were pockmarked by the kind of family dysfunction that made Matt Groening's Simpsons look normal. Noel and Liam followed older brother Paul into a world where violent abuse from their thuggish father Tommy became run of the mill. Both blamed their later misanthropic traits on the unresolved emotional scars they carried from their father's brutality.

Eventually, mum Peggy, a matriarch at the end of her rope, hit the road in a midnight flit. "I left him with a knife, a fork, and a spoon and I still think I left him too much," she once declared. She then folded each of her children into a working-class unit that became the school of hard knocks. By their teens, Noel and Liam were cast adrift upon a sea of troubles.

Liam, the junior partner by five years, already had an appetite for greasy fast food, drugs, and self-destruction. A volcano trapped in ice, he could spark a fight in an empty room. Noel, more savvy and with an aspirational gift for the guitar and songwriting, was a loner who tempered a similar fondness for weed with an iron-clad belief that there must be something—anything—better than this.

Escape for Noel eventually came when he blagged his way into becoming a roadie for local indie band, the Inspiral Carpets, a "dream" job that took him as far afield as the United States and Japan. Liam first started chasing rock 'n' roll rainbows when he joined a band formed by school chums Paul "Guigsy" McGuigan and Paul "Bonehead" Arthurs called Rain, which right away he retooled as Oasis. The stars finally aligned one night when Noel saw his young brother's band play the Manchester Boardwalk and agreed to join.

Overnight, Noel's gift for songwriting and fluent lead guitar work took the band to a new level. Arthurs recalled being stunned when Noel arrived for his first proper band rehearsal. He said, "He came along to meet us armed with songs—the whole of *Definitely Maybe* and more—and played them to us. We were witnessing our own private Oasis gig before anyone—it was amazing."

In 1993, Oasis played a four-song set list at Glasgow's famous King Tut's Wah Wah Hut, despite not actually being on the bill. As a bitter standoff took hold with no-nonsense Glaswegian bouncers, they were eventually allowed onstage. They played "Bring It Down," "Supersonic," and a pulsating version of the Beatles "Helter Skelter." Transfixed in the audience was Alan McGee of Creation Records, one of only twelve people in the venue. Meeting them for the first time, he was convinced Liam was actually the band's drug dealer.

"I couldn't believe he was the singer," McGee recalled. Bowled over by their sound, however, McGee left with a demo tape and six months later signed them to Creation for an astonishing six-record deal. In late 1993 the band recorded *Definitely Maybe*, which was released on August 28, 1994, and went on to become the fastest-selling British debut album ever.

Their second album, *What's the Story (Morning Glory)*, only cemented Noel Gallagher's position as the best British rock 'n' roll tunemeister since John and Paul ruled the airwaves. Songs like "Wonderwall," "Acquiesce," "Don't Look Back in Anger," "She's Electric," and "Live Forever"—a song about the invincibility of youth—certified Oasis as the kingpins of Britpop and Cool Britannia.

It was, by any measure you care to make, an extraordinary ascent in the face of an extremely rickety alliance between two brothers constantly at odds with each other and the world. Fidderman, who also wrote a book on the group, is convinced the seeds of antagonism had been sown in early childhood and only properly took root when the group became more than just a hobby.

He told me, "There were issues very early on. Even in 1996 there was big trouble in the camp. Things had to be done in the background—and I've seen the paperwork—to keep them together very early on. There was always trouble in the camp with Noel and Liam. I used to think later it was a PR stunt but it was very true and very real." Even in those formative months, Oasis were already defined and demonized by the lore they had been happy to construct. Except the mythology that was easy tabloid fodder of two brothers constantly at war was anchored in reality. Touring regularly resulted in brotherly bedlam.

McGee was forced to turn to an ex–Special Air Service (SAS) paratrooper to try and bring some order from chaos on the road. As head of security, Iain Robertson was handed the mission impossible task of trying to check the Gallagher brothers' worst impulses. But even a man who had tasted sorties in foreign battle zones could still be shocked by the testosterone and lager-fueled fights that erupted between the two diametrically opposed siblings.

This was no charade to generate notoriety for its own sake. "The great-est difficulty on the road was the Liam-Noel thing," said Robertson. "It was genuinely dangerous to be around for anybody who was very, very close to it. And notably for the other members of the band. There was no pretense about it. They didn't wait for the cameras to be there when they fell out. They fell out wherever the hell they fell out. It was genuinely a violent thing to be around. There were occasions where my role was to protect one from the other. But the most important part of the job was to keep the band together."

Robertson faced his biggest test during Oasis's much-hyped first American dates in 1994 to support the newly released *Definitely Maybe*. Over-the-top advance promotion billed them as an amalgam of new wave Beatles/Stones and the Who. And in Liam they possessed a sneering proto-punk front man with all the couldn't-give-a-toss swagger of the Pistols and the Clash.

Untethered by any form of discipline, they were feral louts off the leash and on the lash in the world's biggest rock 'n' roll playground. Factor in the intoxicating know-it-all-ism of youth, the energy of a Duracell bunny, the backing of a nation smitten by their new rock and roll sound, a newfound bounty of cash and cocaine, and you are suddenly dealing with a septic stew.

Their show at the Whisky was only the second on a small U.S. tour that included dates in New York. But the wheels soon came off. The day before, a live interview on the KROQ radio station was quickly cut short when, true to form, they started swearing on air. Hours later, juiced up and high, they were thrown out of the famous Viper Room by bouncers who needed little invitation to organize hospital dinners for English yobs on tour.

The city's LAPD then visited Bonehead's hotel room at dawn with guns drawn after he began blasting out "Supersonic" from his hotel room. The portents for that night's show at the Whisky were indeed dark. Backstage, they gleefully—and naively—gorged themselves on copious lines of white powder believing it was cocaine. No one bothered to mention the lines were, in fact, crystal meth—which was an altogether different deal.

Chaos quickly ensued. A frazzled looking Liam staggered on to the stage to tell the audience "the fookin' band aren't coming. You've just got me tonight" only for the other four to eventually troop confusingly out of the darkness. The gig quickly descended into utter turmoil. Noel had a different set list to the rest and played the wrong songs at the wrong time; the rest were all hopelessly out of tune. They played "Rock 'n' Roll Star" back to back, the bass amp exploded, and Liam threatened to rearrange the face of one overly refreshed crowd surfer who knocked over his mic. Noel began singing in a camp tone.

Then, true to form, it all kicked off between the two brothers. Liam, prowling the stage like an angry tiger, got right up into Noel's face and told him to go "fuck himself" before bopping him on the head with a tambourine. Liam then abruptly walked offstage and straight out on to Sunset Boulevard with a towel draped around his neck while Noel later that night fled to San Francisco.

This was Oasis in full toxic bloom. McGee was forced to scrap the rest of the tour, write off the massive costs, while being left to ponder if he still had a band. It was a pattern that was to be repeated during future U.S. tours. Truth be told, Oasis never cracked America. And, true to form, Noel more often than not laid the blame at his brother's feet.

He declared, "Unfortunately for us, we got off on the wrong foot with America. Four tours in a row were either never started or never finished." Noel and Liam might have been living the dissolute life of rock 'n' roll dilettantes, but there was a stark schism between them over what that actually meant.

For Liam, rock 'n' roll was only an excuse to live a life of unbridled hedonism while raising some hell; Noel saw rock 'n' roll as an art form and a contract between the band and its audience. The rewards for keeping your end of the bargain were then justified. "He was getting a reputation as the bad boy of rock 'n' roll," said Noel. "But can we talk about the music first?" These differences were laid out in a now notorious joint interview they gave to the NME's John Harris in 1994, which is worth repeating here if only for the sheer comedy value of its profanity-laden insight into the state of brotherly relations. It came just after the band, with the exception of Noel, were arrested and deported from Holland after a mass brawl broke out on a ferry between Team Liam, high on drugs and Jack Daniel's, and a group of West Ham football fans. Asked about the incident, tempers between them both flared easily as faces turned puce with self-indignation.

Noel: The thing about getting thrown off ferries and getting deported is summat that I'm not proud about because . . .

Liam: Well, I am, la.

Noel: Yeah, alright. Well if you're, right, well if you're, right, well if, if you're proud about getting thrown off ferries, then why don't you go and support West Ham and get the fuck out of my band and go and be a football hooligan, right? Coz we're musicians, right? We're not football hooligans.

Liam: You're only gutted coz you was in bed fuckin' reading your fuckin' books . . .

Noel: No, not at all. Listen. No, listen. He says, right . . . Here's a quote for you from my manager, Marcus Russell, right . . .

Liam: He's a fuckin' . . . 'nother fuckin'. . .

Noel: Shut up, you dick. Right, he gets off the ferry after getting fuckin' deported. I'm left in Amsterdam with me dick out like a fuckin' spare prick at a fuckin' wedding . . .

Liam: It was a bad move, you know. . .

Noel: Shut up! Shut up! Right, he gets off the ferry and Marcus says, "What are you fuckin' doing?" . . . you know: "What the fuck is going . . ."

Liam: (mocking Noel) What the fuh, wha' the fuh, wha' fuh . . . . (?unintelligible?)

Noel: "What are you doing . . . ," and all that, and he says, right: "These lot think it's rock 'n' roll to get thrown off a ferry . . . to get . . ."

Liam: No I don't.

Noel: Shut up. These lot think it's rock 'n' roll to get thrown off . . .

Liam: I don't.

Noel: Shut the fuck up, man! These lot think . . . (laughing in background) . . . I'm gonna have to say this part, are you gonna shut up? (laughing) These lot think it's rock 'n' roll to get thrown off a ferry, right, to come into hotel foyers to get everybody at it and to go—shut up!—to start thinking: "Hey, it's rock 'n' roll." Do you know what my manager said to him? He said, "Nah. Rock 'n' roll is going to Amsterdam, doing your gig, playing your music, that's rock 'n' roll, right . . . and coming back and saying you blew 'em away. Not getting thrown off the ferry like some fuckin' Scouse schlepper with your fuckin' . . . with . . . being handcuffed. That's football hooliganism . . .

Liam: No it isn't . . .

Noel: . . . and I won't stand for it, Liam: No it isn't . . .

Noel: And listen, they all got fined a thousand pounds each.

Liam: We didn't at all.

Noel: Yes, you fuckin' did.

Liam: You can stick your thousand pounds right up yer fuckin' arse 'till it comes out your fuckin' big toe.

Noel: You think it's rock 'n' roll to get thrown off a ferry, and it's not.

Liam: I don't think it's rock 'n' roll.

Noel: You fucking . . . that was your quote, you prick! That was your quote.

It was incendiary stuff, especially coming hours after a gig at Glasgow's Barrowlands, where the audience mood turned sour when Liam, his voice cracking due to the effects of a cold, quit minutes into the gig. Noel, fearing the stage was about to be stormed by hundreds of angry Scotsmen, was for once gripped by fear.

> That was scary. We'd been up all night, as you tend to do and midway through the third song his voice was going. To be honest, he couldn't be arsed singing because he was knackered. He walked off and I finished the song and grabbed him and he said, "Fuck it, I'm getting off." So I said listen man, if there's one gig in the world you've got to do once you've started, it's Barrowlands. There's 200 screaming Jocks out there who'll fucking kill us. So I went back out and did an hour with an acoustic guitar.

The fault lines only widened with the money-is-no-object days that followed the success, especially of *What's the Story*. Noel married designer

Meg Matthews and bought a mansion in London's bohemian Primrose Hill that he christened Supernova Heights.

It quickly became the chic milieu for London's A-listers, such as actor Jude Law, his then wife Sadie Frost, supermodel Kate Moss, and actress Patsy Kensit, the future Mrs. Liam Gallagher. Noel's celebrity house parties were an excuse for Bacchanalian excess where guests were often shrouded in a permanent fog of drugs. These were heady days encapsulated by the rise of Tony Blair's New Labour government and a feverish belief that Britain was experiencing another watershed generational shift. Within weeks, Noel was being feted at No. 10, quaffing champagne beside a beaming Blair while Meg was given a tour of the premises, complete with an Oasis disc hanging on a wall, by his wife Cherie.

Cool Britannia ruled the airwaves while Oasis waived the rules. Noel's political compass was lost at sea. He later regretted being used as a pawn by New Labour's spin machine. "I just thought, if the prime minister of England wanted to see me, then, fuck me, I must be a fucking geezer," he declared. "I was convinced that I was going to get a knighthood that night. You live and learn, don't you?"

Liam's invite got lost in the post, Blair savvy enough to know that two Gallaghers downing Downing Street booze was a nuclear accident waiting to happen. There was, of course, no way a cynic like Liam would have been seen dead in such company. When he saw the images of pop star and politician schmoozing each other to death, he could taste the bile in his throat. Rather, Liam became the darling of the magazine set, posing lasciviously with Kensit underneath a Union Jack duvet on the cover of *Vanity Fair* and talked himself up as a social-realist—in stark contrast to his "sellout" brother. That stance only endeared him to fellow pop culture mavericks, such as the author Irvine Welsh who made clear where his preferences lay. He said, "There's no pretension about Liam, and that's always going to be appealing to working-class people, who act more by instinct than artifice. Liam retains this completely direct mentality. One of the things I hear people saying is that, in Liam's position, they'd do exactly as he does."

Seen through the mirror at that juncture, Liam was Oasis's Keith Richards while Noel was Mick Jagger, fawning before the establishment that normally held them in such utter contempt no matter how rich they had become.

But the whole risible period yet again exposed the personality fissures that ran deep between Noel and Liam. And success had only served to further widen the gulf that already existed. Lost amid the schmoozing, however, was a nagging certainty.

Oasis as a British pop culture phenomenon was already running dry.

Their everyman sensibilities simply couldn't survive the sudden flood of money and fame that came their way. Their era-defining appearance at Knebworth—two hours of the best band on the planet at the time performing to the best of their abilities and searing their name into British music history—marked the start of what was, in fact, a very long goodbye for the band as well as providing a requiem for Britpop. "Knebworth was the real end of it," said Alan McGee. "The gig was too big, The VIP section alone held 3,000 people. I don't know what it was, but it wasn't Oasis."

Hubris and hype had created the perfect storm, driven mainly by a blizzard of drugs. Weeks after playing before thousands at Knebworth, the band went to the other end of the scale by taping an unplugged show at London's Festival Hall. MTV executives were stunned, however, when Liam, after a two-day pub crawl, refused to appear only minutes before the curtain was due to go up for their twelve-song set.

Noel duly took over vocal duties, diplomatically blaming his brother's absence on a sore throat, only for Liam to suddenly appear on one of the upper balconies self-medicating his "sore throat" with cigarettes and alcohol and hurling abuse at the band. Furious, Noel repeatedly tells him to "shurrup" before realizing the best policy is to ignore him. "He sits in the stalls heckling. He does it one time and gets a giggle from the crowd, so he thinks it's cool to do that."

It was another foreshadowing of things to come. Turmoil erupted at the start of their 1996 American tour when Liam turned back just as he prepared to board the plane at Heathrow, throwing the whole thing into a state of flux while leaving promoters in a state of near cardiac arrest. Newspaper reports said he had abandoned the tour to buy a new house, but it only stoked the fires raging inside Noel, who insisted the show must still go on despite the absence of their mercurial front man.

"As I'm getting on the plane he's getting off because his wife called, saying, 'We need to buy a house.' What they were doing for the previous three months is anybody's guess," said Noel. "Probably picking gnats out of each other's hair like monkeys. . . . I didn't want to pull the gigs because that would be giving in to him, making him think he is more important than the band, which he isn't. I don't want it to look like that with a wave of his hand he gets to pick and choose what he wants to do."

Liam eventually joined midway through the tour, but it was already a car crash. At the MTV awards, he gobbed at a fan, an unforgivable act of self-sabotage. Fed up with yet more internal disarray, Noel again upped sticks and headed home early. He recalled, "The first gig was a 16,000-seat arena, and the singer's not turned up. That killed us stone dead in America. This is rock 'n' roll. Would Johnny Rotten have got a house on the eve of an American tour? Keith Richards? John Lennon? You either want it or you don't, and I blame him for us never becoming as big in America as we were in England."

Disorientated by the fame and the elephantine amounts of money now funneling into their bank accounts—inside a week Noel went from cadging cash from a friend to buy a round to seeing a £1 million royalty check landing in his account—both men were now caught up in the madness inherent in having everything they had ever dreamed of coming true.

Be Here Now, the album follow-up to *What's the Story*, was bloated and overheated, much like the band themselves at the time. The music media, having twice failed to catch the wind generated by the first two albums, this time fell for it hook, line, and sinker. Its path was paved with five-star reviews, like laurel leaves strewn at the feet of a Roman emperor.

The album, however, simply mined the same sixties rock template as their first two albums but without the youthful musical vim that made them sound so rebellious. No more could Noel, now living the life he wanted as a dissolute and debauched millionaire rock star, rely on the songs as a touchstone for escaping the shackles of his disaffected youth. It fell way short of the massive sales generated by the behemoth that was *What's the Story*. The champagne supernova was now just a black hole.

"It's the sound of a bunch of guys in the studio on coke not giving a fuck. All the songs are really long, and all the lyrics are shit," Noel would state, while reserving the right to revise his opinion at a later date, which he did.

Against all odds, however, Oasis would continue as a working band—releasing four more albums between 2000 and 2009 before the whole thing finally imploded in a massive rupture. Time had been unable to bridge the huge divide that kept Liam and Noel on a permanent war footing. Noel once threatened legal action when his brother drunkenly questioned the parentage of his daughter Anais after a gig was canceled in Barcelona. Noel leaped onto his brother, hit him repeatedly, and split his lip open in the process. Noel left the tour, but ultimately returned to the band yet again.

"I've never forgiven him because he's never apologized," Noel said five years after the incident. Psychological mind games were often deployed in the ongoing battle for the moral high ground. In one interview Noel claimed, "He's actually frightened to death of me. I can fucking play him like a disused arcade game. I can make him make decisions that he thinks are his but really they're mine." Regular media updates of backstage bust-ups and furious fisticuffs continued to puzzle and perplex.

Unanswered amid the maelstrom, however, was the question of how did it all begin? Eschewing all attempts at Gestalt therapy, Liam once claimed the roots of rancor lay in him coming home drunk one night as a teenager and "accidentally on purpose" urinating all over his brother's stereo. Iain Robertson is one of the few who perhaps got closer to the truth. "I stayed up talking into the night with him on a number of occasions," says Robertson. "One of the things Liam offered up, by his own admission, was that he had been spoilt, in a way that hadn't happened for Paul, and Noel probably didn't need. He kind of went from one bubble to another: from the bubble of his mother to the bubble of being in a band."

The bubble for Oasis officially burst in August 2009 ahead of an appearance at a festival in Paris days after another Liam no-show had forced them to scrap a headline slot at the UK's V Festival. Simmering tensions preshow between the two brothers in Paris reached boiling point again. Liam stormed out only to return wielding a guitar, which he promptly used to try and decapitate his older sibling. "He nearly took my face off with it," said Noel.

It was the final act in a drama that had beguiled and, in equal measure, bored the record-buying public for the best part of sixteen years. Fans became aware of a backstage incident after a message flashed up onstage, while social media was alerted by Scottish singer Amy McDonald, who took to Twitter to reveal rumors of a monumental bust up.

She claimed, "Oasis cancelled again with one minute to stage time!!! Liam smashed Noel's guitar, huuuge fight!"

Within an hour Noel also used social media to announce his exit. "It's with some sadness and great relief to tell you that I quit Oasis tonight," he posted on Oasisnet.com. "People will write and say what they like, but I simply could not go on working with Liam a day longer. The details are not important and of too great a number to list. But I feel you have the right to know the level of verbal and violent intimidation towards me, my family and friends and comrades has become intolerable."

Initially, Noel stuck to a kind of Oasis omertà over the breakup, refusing to go into the nitty- gritty over what actually transpired that night. Months later, however, he peeled back the curtain at a press conference:

Liam was quite violent. At that point there hadn't been any physical violence, but it was a bit like WWE wrestling, and he was like the Macho Man Randy Savage—he was like oooh yeah and all that going on—and it's like, "Fucking hell." . . . Liam does the "Fuck you and fuck you and fuck you" and he kind of storms out of the dressing room. And—I'm glad it never ended like this—on the way out he picked up a plum, and he threw it across the dressing room and it smashed against the wall.

Part of me wishes it did end like that, that would have been a great headline: "Plum Throws Plum and Finishes Fuckin' Oasis." Then he kind of leaves, he goes out the dressing room. For whatever reason he went to his own dressing room, and he came back with a guitar and he started wielding it like an axe. I'm not fucking kidding. And I'm making light of it because it's kind of what I do, but it's a real unnecessary violent act, and he's swinging this guitar around, and he nearly took my face off with it. It ended up on the floor and I put it out of its misery.

There were people who were in the band, not saying anything, kind of looking the other way. It wasn't even a big dressing room. And I was like, you know what? I'm fucking out of here. And at that point the tour manager came in and said, "Five minutes!" . . . I kind of got in the car and I sat there for five minutes, and I just said fuck it, I can't do it anymore.

The minute he heard his brother's comments, Liam pressed the legal button. He sued Noel for libel, although the matter was quietly dropped months later. The paroxysm in Paris was it seems, at the time of writing, the last time the two men were together in the same room. By the time of this fatal implosion, Oasis had long passed the point of cultural and commercial credibility. And Noel knew it.

In the 2021 documentary *Out of the Now*, he maintained, "It was not a decision I took lightly. I had written every meaningful song that was ever recorded by Oasis and creatively it was my thing. But with the benefit of hindsight, it was the best thing for me and for the band because by 2009 Oasis were not lauded as one of the greats of all time. I think people had stopped listening to the records."

Today, Oasis is remembered for two course-changing albums and the thinning vapor trails of their own musical legacy. Nevertheless, the ongoing feud between the Gallaghers has remained a point of obsession for Britain's tabloids, who gleefully devoured the sex, drugs, and rock 'n' roll downfall of the biggest British band of their generation. Perversely, it also meant both men were immutably guaranteed to be quizzed almost daily about a reunion in a mirror-universe way their heroes Lennon and McCartney were hounded exactly four decades earlier.

In rock 'n' roll, money is always the investment that pays the highest interest; and an Oasis reunion would still mean a bounty measured in millions for all concerned. Unlike the two Beatles, however, the Gallagher siblings have so far not enjoyed any kind of rapprochement—personal or otherwise. Distance has done nothing to slacken the ill-disguised contempt for each other that still seems to dominate both their lives. Rob Fidderman is among those longtime fans who are not unhappy at the prospect of Oasis resisting the lure to forlornly rekindle old glories.

> I think the antics between Liam and Noel has slightly put a dent in their musical legacy as a band and overshadowed slightly their past. But no band in my lifetime made such an impact on pop culture. I love them more than anything, but I don't think it would be right. Would it work? Who knows? In truth, I just don't know whether they would be that good. How would it work? Liam does a few solo songs, Noel does a few solo songs, and they end up with a couple of Oasis's greatest hits. And all the time you're waiting for an explosion.
>
> Everyone is on eggshells. If there were a reunion, I would want Bonehead there, I would want Guigsy there. Everyone would want to see the original lineup back.

That conflict subsequently turned the internet into a public playground for tit-for-tat taunts that can seem childish and funny in equal turn. Insults are traded on an almost daily basis. If anything, their mutual loathing seems to have intensified. Especially since new wives and an odd number of Gallagher offspring have now added their voices to a pernicious mix, ensuring the feud will be handed down to future generations like some malignant inheritance. In 2020, Noel refused to allow Liam to sing any Oasis songs for a new film documentary charting his solo career. Rationalizing the decision, he said in typically profane terms, "If some fucking moron is going to make a film slagging me off, calling my wife a cunt, after trolling my kids on the internet, after being a filthy little misogynist sexist prick who cannot keep his fucking mouth off Twitter, and then call *me* to ask me a favor, I'm like, 'Wow. You *are* as dumb as you fucking look.'"

Not surprisingly, Liam did not take the news well. "Him and his little people saw it and took the Oasis music out of it because that's all he's got left. Let him get on with it. It doesn't make me sad, it makes me fucking mad. I want to break his fucking jaw and his daft fucking manager. I didn't go home and cry, I just wanted to go and fucking put their windows through."

Seen through the distorted prism of almost thirty years, Oasis remains a British music curiosity, on the top ladder of nineties bands but unable to match the popular longevity attached to the Beatles, the Stones, the Who, Zeppelin, Pink Floyd, and a string of others. But you are still left to look back in wonder at the history of attrition, insult, argument, and abuse that has characterized the relationship between Noel and Liam Gallagher.

Paulo Hewitt, the music journalist whose book on the band even now comes closest to the truth, is clear. "The trouble with Oasis is you had two people vying for the job as prime minister. That tension and that antagonism drove the band and it killed the band."

The murders of Tupac and Notorious B.I.G., Season 1
USA Network/Photofest © USA Network

13

TUPAC SHAKUR
AND BIGGIE SMALLS

Bang. Bang. Bang. Bang. The acrid smell of gunfire from the 40-caliber Glock clung to the dark chill of a neon-lit autumnal Las Vegas night. In the distance, Sin City police sirens could already be heard. People, some fleeing, others rooted to the spot, were screaming in panic. And in the BMW, Tupac Shakur, to many the world's greatest rapper, was bleeding out, gunned down in a volley of bullets following a craven drive-by shooting.

Eyes glazed, he was already drifting into unconsciousness. Scrambling beside him was Suge Knight, the hulking and menacing CEO of West Coast–based Death Row Records, himself reeling from a head wound and trying desperately to keep Tupac in the land of the living. Amid the chaos of that time-frozen moment, a rented white Cadillac, its tires screaming, was making its frantic getaway, speed being the essence for the assassin and three other occupants, each of them African American. The date was September 7, 1996. Less than a week later, Tupac, having been placed in an induced coma, died without ever reopening his eyes. He was twenty-five and at the very top of his game. Knight said later of his friend and VIP client, "I would have taken those bullets for him."

Bang. Bang. Bang. Bang. Precisely 182 days later—March 9, 1997—a car carrying Christopher "Biggie" Smalls, to many the world's greatest rapper, pulled up at a red light in downtown LA. A white Toyota Land Cruiser was spotted making a quick U-turn, placing itself between Biggie's car and the security caravan behind him that included Sean "Puffy" Combs, the smooth-talking but combative CEO of East Coast–based Bad Boy Records. In the same instant, a dark Chevrolet Impala drew up alongside, the driver's window noticeably open. The man behind the wheel, an African American, was wearing a dark suit and a bow tie and for a fleeting moment made eye contact with the famous emcee. In the twilight, however, no one saw the blue, steel pistol emerge slowly from inside the car, but it was impossible to mistake the deadly sound of bullets being emptied from its chamber. Biggie, six foot two and weighing more than 280 pounds, was a hit man's gift, an impossible-to-miss target even in the darkness of a blacked-out car.

"They shot Biggie," screamed someone in Combs's car. He was struck at least four times. As the Impala accelerated away, Combs and other members of the Bad Boy crew raced to the car to try to keep Biggie in the land of the living. But his life was already draining away. By the time an ambulance ferried him to Cedars-Sinai Hospital, he was dead. He was twenty-four and at the very top of his game. His second album, bearing the prescient title *Life after Death*, was released just a week later and would go on to shift 700,000 copies in forty-eight hours and hit the *Billboard* summit within a week. Proof once again that, in the world of music, death trumps every marketing campaign—just ask Nirvana.

Combs said, "He didn't deserve to die like that. No one does." But at the end of days, the guessing game—and the blame game—began. It became music's biggest whodunit. They died months apart, but who killed Tupac Shakur and Biggie Smalls, the biggest hip-hop stars in the world? Two men whose once-firm brotherhood had been broken by petty jealousies, perceived slights, and personality conflicts. Were their deaths linked? Was Shakur the victim of an East-Coast, West-Coast "beef," the fires of which were deliberately stoked by Knight and Combs? Was it an FBI black op to silence two youth culture kingpins? Was Smalls's death an act of tit-for-tat revenge for Tupac's cold-blooded murder? Were both men simply collateral damage in a brutal gang war between the Southside Crips and the Bloods for control of the lawless streets of Compton, a sprawling city in southern LA? Was it a hit on Knight that went badly wrong? Or, bizarrely, did Knight order the assassination of his most famous client in a row over monies due?

Who knows what plots were hatched in the bitter watches of the night. Almost a quarter of a century later, both cases are officially still stone cold. Quite literally, no one has taken the rap for crimes that remain enmeshed in a dense undergrowth of wild conspiracy theories, red herrings, blind alleys, dirty cops, dirty corpses, uncorroborated confessions, prime suspects, and a refusal by those who know to break the gangsta code of the streets and give up the names of the men whose fingers were on the triggers.

Better to die with street cred than to be remembered as a rat. Grievances and grudges are as much a part of the music industry as gold records and Grammys. Friendships are sometimes necessarily sacrificed on the twin pillars of self-absorption and ruthless ambition. And money really is a poisonous, low-hanging fruit. But the slayings of Tupac Shakur and Biggie Smalls raised the stakes on a duel that, for the first time, was fought to the death.

This wasn't a mere falling out between friends a la Jagger and Richards or Lennon and McCartney. This was a blood feud between two ghetto gladiators, two homies from the hip-hop hood, and the Hugo Boss–suited handlers who pulled the strings from behind weed-perfumed rooms, closed doors, and shuttered windows. Rewind the clock three years, however, and a different tapestry can be glimpsed.

The benign winds of fate once brought Tupac Shakur and Biggie Smalls together in friendship. In 1993 Tupac emerged as the voice for millions of young black Americans in the immediate wake of the LA race riots that had again reignited the flame of civil rights in George Bush's divided America. A bright student and an aspiring dancer and actor, rebellion was nevertheless an intrinsic part of Tupac's personal and cultural DNA. His mother Afeni was a prominent Black Panther activist and an immersive voice in the movement during the late sixties and seventies. Inevitably, radical politics would shape the upbringing and rebellious tone of her son and much of his music.

Born in New York City in 1971, he eventually moved to Baltimore, where as a teenager he immersed himself in musical theater. Drawn to the emerging hip-hop scene, he quickly established a strong musical following. In 1992, he released his first album—*2Pacalypse Now*, a clear pun on Francis Ford Coppola's movie *Apocalypse Now*—and a hip-hop star was born.

Rap lyrics touched on the corrosive racial divide blighting America while narrowing the focus on police brutality of young black men and women. Then vice president Dan Quayle said the rapper's music "has no place in our society." Over the next three years, two more critically acclaimed albums established Tupac, by then based on the West Coast, as the world's foremost rapper.

Hailed as a kind of black messiah, he was anointed among young people of color—and rap-loving Caucasian counterparts—as someone who could give voice to the oppression and brutality of their lives. In many ways, Shakur blazed a trail for the Black Lives Matter movement that took hold across the world twenty-five years after his death.

Among the millions following this new redeemer was Christopher Wallace, who had himself established a reputation as a crude rapper of note on the streets of his native Brooklyn. Brought up by his mother Voletta after his father fled when his son was just two, he showed early academic promise.

By his teens, however, Wallace had drifted into petty crime and drug dealing. At seventeen, he dropped out of school and became more involved in the city's grim underbelly. In 1989, he was arrested on weapons charges in Brooklyn and sentenced to five years' probation.

In 1990, he was again arrested on a violation of his probation. A year later, Wallace was seized in North Carolina for hustling crack cocaine. He spent nine months in jail before making bail. Escape lay in his burgeoning hip-hop talent and a charismatic presence as a live performer. Recalibrating his identity as Biggie Smalls—the name was a self-mocking nod to his huge girth—a series of impressive demo tapes eventually caught the attention of Sean Combs, at that point an employee of Uptown Records.

Sensing an opportunity to make Smalls a major star—and himself major bucks—Combs set up Bad Boy Records and made Smalls his first signing. Within eighteen months, his first album, *Ready to Die*, had stormed the *Billboard* charts and quickly established Smalls—who also went by the moniker the Notorious B.I.G.—as a major hip-hop player in New York and its surrounding environs. Watching this new star rise in the East was Tupac.

Eventually, their paths crossed, and Tupac was eager to assume the role of master to Biggie's apprentice, a friendship cemented in LA by strong dope and a gift from Tupac of a bottle of Hennessey whisky. It was a rap rapport founded on appreciation and fashioned in hip-hop heaven.

In those early, breezy days, respect was mutual. Tupac, eager to give a homie a helping hand up the ladder, was happy to dish out seasoned advice on how to traverse the occasionally perilous hip-hop highway. He allowed Biggie to freestyle with him at Madison Square Garden in 1993. They even recorded several joint tracks. Despite the Garden cameo, Biggie still wasn't much known outside of Brooklyn.

Tupac, by then a platinum-selling rapper and movie star, was happy to keep playing the part of mentor. Biggie and other young rappers assembled in recording studios or hotel rooms to hear Tupac lecture about how to make it in the game. "Pac could get up and get to teaching," said E.D.I. Mean, a future member of the Shakur side project, the Outlawz. "Everyone was transfixed on this dynamic individual, and soaking up all the information we could soak up."

Another New York acolyte was Lil' Cease, a young rapper who would become a part of Junior M.A.F.I.A., a group that had close ties to Biggie.

"He was one rapper we looked up to. What we saw was a real person, like us, you know. He would come on the block and just sit with us. This was the time before Biggie even blew up. Tupac was shooting above the rim. We're like fourteen years old, and he was like a god to us."

Tupac devoted special attention to Biggie, grooming him in the way of the business and letting him perform at his concerts. Tupac even told him he'd like to be a part of another of his affiliated groups called Thug Life. "I trained him; he used to be under me like my lieutenant," said Tupac, who once gifted his friend a Rolex watch. Biggie wanted a piece of what Tupac had—and even hinted at ditching Combs to fast-track his career.

But Tupac insisted his young neophyte stick with Bad Boy. He told him, with no small amount of foreshadowing, "Puffy will make you a star." But it wasn't long before the first cracks in Biggie's pact with Tupac emerged. When Tupac shot a film in New York, he fell into the company of some gangsters from Queens. Aware of the notoriety of those in his own hood, Biggie warned Tupac he was swimming with sharks—and was way out of his depth. Tupac brusquely brushed him aside.

Weeks later, Tupac and several members of the Queen's crew were arrested on charges of gang raping a nineteen-year-old woman in a hotel. It added to a growing list of court cases closing in on Tupac, which would prove to be a major financial drain. He was burning through thousands of dollars a week.

He said, "Everybody knew I was short of money. All my shows were getting canceled. All my money from records was going to lawyers, and all the movie money was going to my family." On November 30, 1994, Tupac arrived slightly stoned at Quad Recording Studios in Times Square to freestyle on a track by L'il Shawn, for which he was to be paid a pretty meager $7,000.

The deal had been agreed with a business associate of Biggie and Combs named with no little irony James Henchman, a formidable figure in the Big Apple's rotten underworld. Just hours earlier Henchman had called Tupac to renege on the deal. Tupac angrily hung up before Henchmen then called back to say he would get his money at the studio. But there was a sense of swords having been crossed. Tupac arrived at Quad with three associates, none of whom were bodyguards. His sense of anxiety faded when he saw Lil' Cease hanging from an upstairs window shouting a friendly greeting. Walking into the lobby, Tupac then glimpsed three men in army fatigues and made a serious—almost fatal—miscalculation.

He recalled, "I'm thinking these dudes must be security for Biggie because I could tell they were from Brooklyn from their army fatigues. But then I wondered why they didn't look up. Even Biggie's homeboys love me." Not tonight. Before Tupac's crew could get in the elevator, the men in army fatigues drew 9mm guns and ordered them to the floor.

Instead, Tupac reached for his own gun. He was shot, beaten, and robbed of his bling. Bleeding profusely, he played dead to stay alive, and the assailants fled, at which point he staggered into the elevator and rode it upstairs. When the doors opened, he saw a group including Combs, Biggie, Lil' Cease, and Henchman. Recalling the scene, he declared, "Nobody approached me. I noticed that nobody would look at me. Puffy was standing back, too. I know Puffy, he knew how much stuff I had done for Biggie." By the time an ambulance arrived, it was chaos. Cops swarmed all over the studios as Tupac, wrapped in bandages, was placed on a stretcher and rushed to nearby Bellevue hospital. But there would be one one last act of defiance. On his way out, Tupac stared at Biggie and raised his middle finger. It was the moment that changed hip-hop history.

Suspicion and anger quickly seeped into Tupac's inner circle. His stepbrother Mopreme Shakur said, "We all knew what had gone down, and we knew who was behind it. The insult was that this person Pac had shown a lot of love to could be part of something like this. That's what Pac thought." Offering up a mea culpa contrast, Combs later claimed they showed him "nothing but love and concern." But Lil' Cease knew how it would play out, especially with Tupac. "That was the moment that changed a lot of shit," he declared. The eyewitness recollections could not have been more polarized. Tupac believed the incident was more than a random heist. "It was like they were mad at me," he said. "Until that moment, I never believed no black person would shoot me. I was like . . . I represent them. I'm their ambassador to the world. But everybody that was there knows what happened. There might be different accounts but I'm the one with the bullet holes."

He claimed to have taken five bullets, including shots to the head and through his scrotum, though forensic evidence incredibly suggested it was more likely he shot himself. Years later, it was claimed the attack was a punishment for Tupac's public criticism of black New York mobsters, including a guy called Haitian Jack, who was his codefendant on the hotel rape rap. One of those allegedly involved later told a magazine, "Nobody came to rob him; they came to discipline him."

An FBI investigation ultimately ran into a not unexpected wall of silence. Years later, however, Henchman broke ranks and told prosecutors he had hired a stick-up man. He was adamant that Combs and Biggie knew about the attack in advance. By the time he fessed up, though, the statute of limitations for pursuing the crime had run out. In any case, there was no way of proving his claims. Combs, meanwhile, has always remained steadfast in his denials about having anything to do with it.

Inside a few days, Biggie himself denounced the allegations. "I've heard the rumors that we set him up and that's crazy." Amazingly, the day after being shot, having checked himself out against doctors' orders—"I didn't feel safe there"—Tupac appeared in a wheelchair flanked by members of the Nation of Islam at a court in New York, where he was convicted of first-degree sexual abuse for his part in the hotel attack. In February 1995, he was sentenced to between eighteen months and four years in Rikers Island jail by a judge who brought down the hammer over "an act of brutal violence against a helpless woman."

The sentence outraged Tupac's fans, many of whom insisted the case had failed to meet the credibility threshold. One figure, however, remained conspicuously silent. By keeping schtum, Biggie Smalls was putting clear blue water between himself and his ersatz mentor. Meanwhile, prison only allowed paranoia to burrow further inside Tupac's mind. He released a third album—*Me Against the World*—which had been completed just before he began his incarceration. But long days in prison only served to convince him of one cast-iron certainty.

Biggie and Puffy had betrayed him and thrown his carcass to the black establishment wolves. "He owed me more than to turn his head and act like he didn't know niggas was about to blow my fucking head off," he said later. Biggie's denials that he knew nothing of the ambush at Quad—right in the heart of his own hood—simply didn't stack up. And then came the most incriminating evidence of all—Biggie's diss track "Who Shot Ya?" Appearing on the B-side to his third single "Big Poppa," the track has become one of the most contested and controversial in rap.

While arguments still rage over the intentions, it was instrumental in lighting up the East-West feud. Despite—or maybe even because of—this, the track made hip-hop history. It was imitated countless times, bettered never, a cipher classic and a boom bap high-watermark. Menacing lyrics like, "Didn't I tell you don't fuck with me? Huh? Didn't I tell you not to fuck with me? Huh? Look at you now, Huh? Can't talk with a gun in your mouth huh?" sounded like an unambiguous provocation, despite Biggie and Combs's protests of innocence.

Added for good measure were the following lines: "Everything around me two Glock 9s, Any motherfucker whispering about mines," and "I'm Brooklyn's finest. You rewind this, Bad Boy's behind this."

From his cell, Tupac seethed and ensured his fury became public knowledge on the streets. "Even if that song ain't about me, you should be, like, 'I'm not putting it out, 'cause he might think it's about him,'" he said. Elsewhere, he declared,

I'm just mad at my little brother for not respecting me, and when you don't respect me I am going to spank you. I don't give a fuck how rich you go on a block, I will break your big ass there. I feel he got out of hand, and he wronged me. He got seduced by the power, not because he's an evil person but because money is evil if it's not handled right. If you lose your composure, you could do anything. But they know the prodigal son has returned. . . . I'm alive. The ghost is rubbing away.

Imprisoned and impoverished, and with his mother about to lose her house, Tupac desperately sought a way out. As the mercury rose between the world's two most famous rappers, Biggie and Combs demanded Tupac apologize over the allegations that they had set him up for the attack at Quad Studios. As the back and forth continued to escalate, Suge Knight entered stage left. As the head of Death Row Records, Knight was the hip-hop equivalent of Led Zeppelin's fearsome manager Peter Grant.

Like Grant, he mixed personal intimidation with an undercurrent of criminal violence to ring-fence his artists from rip-off merchants. And, like Grant, he walked on the wild side and trampled over legal niceties. Allies included notorious kingpins in the Bloods gang from Compton, the West Coast city that had become the epicenter of gang wars between themselves and the Crips. For Knight, Tupac became an obsession; the chosen one, the hip-hop king who could reign supreme as a mainstay of the Death Row family.

For months Knight made his pitch from behind the glass enclosure that separated him from Tupac during dozens of prison visits. And he was happy to stoke his new homie's paranoia over Puffy, Biggie, and the rest of the Bad Boy crew who, he insisted, had likely sanctioned the hit at Quad Studios. His overtures became more and more provocative. Attending an awards ceremony in New York in August directly from having visited Tupac in jail, Knight strode into the lions' den and delivered a no-holds barred takedown of Puffy and Big Boy Records.

He told the audience, "To all you artists out there, who don't wanna be on a record label where the executive producer's all up in the videos, all on the records, dancing . . . then come to Death Row!" It was a pointed reference to Combs's habit of getting in on the act of his most high-profile clients. Equally, there was a less-than-subtle overture to the homie languishing in jail on the other side of town. "I'd like to tell Tupac to keep his guards up. We ride with him," he said, ignoring the derision that could be heard rising up all round the auditorium.

Knight knew his message would reach the ears of inmate #95A1140. Tupac's enemies, he said in a declaration of war, were his enemies. Within weeks a deal was thrashed out. In October, Knight put up the $1.4 million bail required to spring Tupac from his cell. In return, Tupac joined Knight's Death Row roster, signing the deal on little more than a scrap of paper, agreeing to a three-album deal, and beginning work on the first one—*All Eyez on Me*—within hours of his first taste of freedom.

The album quickly outsold contemporary U.S. releases by Madonna and Michael Jackson. Driven by rage, he immediately set out on a path of revenge against perceived enemies. Retribution was fast and furious and embroidered in the kind of incendiary and explicit language no one could miss. "Hit 'Em Up" was the Tupac diss track that took his beef with Biggie and Puffy to new and rabid heights—and drew Small's estranged wife, fellow rapper Faith Evans, into the battle zone.

The vicious lyrics put Biggie—and his by then buckling marriage—firmly in his former friend's crosshairs from the first line. "That's why I fucked your bitch, you fat motherfucker." In case anyone missed the point, the song's video showed him screaming the words at a Biggie look-a-like. Lewd and personal, the message could not have been clearer. Bragging rights were all too evident a couple of verses later: "You claim to be a player, but I fucked your wife . . . fuck Biggie and fuck Bad Boy."

Evans later insisted Tupac had indeed hit on her, but she had repeatedly rebuffed his advances. "That ain't how I do business," she said. However, the pin had been pulled. The track also delivered a venomous takedown of several other East Coast rappers signed to Bad Boy, including Combs, Lil' Cease, Junior M.A.F.I.A., and Lil' Kim, with whom Biggie was having an affair. Listening to the track today, it still stands as the most savage and violent diss track in music history. John Lennon's notorious "How Do You Sleep?" dismantling of Paul McCartney is not in the same league.

There was now no turning back. Battle had been joined between the East Coast and the West Coast. Tupac's former manager, Leila Steinberg, was among those in his inner circle left shocked by the brutality of the song's lyrics. She said, "I knew that another turning point was coming after he did 'Hit 'Em Up.' You can't have battle calls and not know that the battle's coming. I started crying when I heard that song. I didn't want that to come out.

I was horrified. There were lines that Tupac crossed. Once you publicly go at certain people, you can't pull it back. Too much pain has been caused."

Cynics could justifiably claim the beef was all about selling records and making a mint. For all their mutual antagonism, Combs and Knight had no complaints about the dollar notes pouring into their company bank accounts or about two empires being propped up by the vendetta waged by the genre's biggest stars.

Jake Brown, author of *Ready to Die: The Story of Biggie Smalls*, nailed it:

> A personal misunderstanding between Smalls and Shakur became a business opportunity for many who had nothing privately vested in the dispute and whose only true motive was the pursuit of money and power over any real interest in peace. The media played a prominent role as a catalyst for blowing the conflict so out of control that it would ultimately cost both Shakur and Smalls their lives. I am not sure that their loss to the hip-hop nation can ever be compensated and certainly not out of the billions of dollars the press and corporate record labels made at the expense of these young men's lives. That money is truly blood money.

The tone of "Hit 'Em Up" reflected the anger toward Biggie and Bad Boy that was now hotwired to Tupac's brain. Friends noticed a discernible change in his moods as the mere mention of his rivals brought about an uncontrollable rage. One said, "I don't know him. He's a monster now. It was crazy."

Reflecting his newfound hostility, Tupac formed a group called the Outlawz and gave each member names that were deliberately provocative. These included Yaki Kadafi, after Libyan leader Muammar Gaddafi; Hussein Fatal, after Iraqi leader Saddam Hussein; Mussolini (formerly Big Syke), after Italian dictator Benito Mussolini; and E.D.I. Mean, after Ugandan despot Idi Amin. For himself he chose the handle Makaveli, from Renaissance Italian philosopher and strategist Niccolò Machiavelli, whose writings inspired Shakur in prison but who also preached that a leader could eliminate his enemies by all means necessary.

Under this pseudonym, he released the album *The Don Killuminati: The 7 Day Theory*. The record presented a stark contrast to previous works. Throughout the album, Shakur continued to focus on the themes of pain and aggression, making this album one of the emotionally darker works of his career. He wrote and recorded all the lyrics in only three days and the production took another four days, ensuring the album was completed in just a week.

Meanwhile, 3,000 miles away, Biggie Smalls privately fretted as the beef accelerated. He made it clear to Combs that he was worried about his own security. Combs, while trying to reassure his most famous client, confessed to friends he was concerned that they could be the target for a hit if they stepped out on the West Coast. Tensions were, indeed, that high. Especially since Knight was flexing to expand Death Row into New York with the avowed intention of wiping out Bad Boy.

Greg Kading, the LA detective who would lead a special task force into Biggie's murder, related the following:

> Puffy was in fear for his life. He was really scared. Suge was openly recruiting people from Bad Boy to come to Death Row. So that's an affront to Puffy obviously. So Puffy looked to do the same. By now they are trying to encroach on each other's business territory. So you can see how it becomes a threat to both of them. Suge Knight and his guys were definitely coming after him. Puffy knew that if he came to California, he was a marked man and, out of that desperation and fear, he associated himself with the Crips gang members because he knew that they could provide a level of protection that nobody else could.
>
> They're from those streets, they recognized that threat before anybody else did. So he associated with those guys and realized he was a dead man walking if he didn't do something about it. Out of desperation, Puffy was just like, "Whatever it takes to handle this problem, I'll give you whatever, I want to live." And so it's that nuance that needs to be understood in relation to Puffy's involvement. I don't think he truly wanted to see anybody hurt, but he didn't want to get hurt.

Unseen forces were now also in play. A number of individuals, some clandestine, others less so, were moving onto the board, nearly all of them affiliated to the Bloods and the Crips, the two gangs who had for years waged a deadly turf war for control of Compton's crack dens and heroin hideaways. Suge Knight's links to the Bloods had been forged in early adolescence, an alliance that made him an enemy of the Crips.

Now the name of Tupac Shakur would be added to the blacklist, with, eventually, a bounty placed on his head by killers for hire. Straight out of gangsta central casting came several Crips members, including Duane "Keefe D" Davis, and his nephew Orlando Anderson. And it is at this point that the story takes a fatal turn. According to Kading, Combs made tentative contact with Crips commanders over providing a ring of steel to protect them from Death Row subordinates whenever they visited the West Coast.

He said, "Puffy at that point reached out to secure the Southside Crips as a security force. He wanted them to make him feel safe on the streets out here." In the course of discussions, according to police affidavits, Davis was allegedly tapped by Sean Combs and offered a million bucks to permanently remove Shakur from the play, an allegation Combs has emphatically denied.

"Puffy tells Keefe D he wants to take care of the situation with Suge and Tupac. It had become a serious conflict. According to Kading, Keefe D told him, 'No problem. That's what we do.'" In early September, Tupac attended the MTV awards in New York and used the occasion to again taunt Combs and Biggie and repeat his incendiary claim about Faith Evans.

There is a compelling argument that, from that moment on, the die was cast. On the night of September 7, 1996, Tupac, Knight, and their Bloods crew attended a Mike Tyson fight at the MGM Grand in Vegas. After congratulating Tyson on his quick-fire victory over Bruce Sheldon, Shakur, Knight, and a handful of bodyguards in silk suits headed for the exit. In the MGM Grand lobby, one of Shakur's Bloods spotted Anderson and recognized him as a Crips member who days earlier had robbed a Bloods affiliate of his cherished Death Row medallion—an affront to Knight's honor and a slight to the Bloods.

A fight broke out and Tupac—still out of jail on bail—was caught on CCTV attacking Anderson. His bodyguards jumped in, pounding and kicking Anderson to the ground. Knight joined in too just before security guards broke up the thirty-second melee, leaving the Death Row crew to run out triumphantly. News of the beating swiftly swept through the Compton gang underground.

Before he reached his room, Anderson's pager was beeping with calls from his Crips cohorts. Later that night, according to police evidence compiled over several years, Anderson and Keefe D tracked Tupac down in his white Cadillac, eventually seeing him at a stop sign between East Flamingo Road and Koval Lane.

The dead giveaway was the gangsta rap parade that had Tupac standing through the sunroof, waving at female fans. Music blared from the car's speakers. No one paid any heed to the car pulling up alongside. Police accounts later claimed Davis then handed the gun to Anderson who allegedly fired the fatal shots that ultimately shattered the windows and snuffed out the life of Tupac Shakur. "It all happened so quick. It took three or four seconds at most," said E.D.I. Mean, who was in one of the cars following behind. The shockwaves were profound. In New York, according to Evans, Biggie Smalls broke down in tears. Other accounts, however, spoke of indifference.

"Even though we were going through our drama, I would never wish death on nobody because there ain't no coming back from that," Biggie declared shortly after Tupac's death. "It kind of turned me down a little bit, but at the same time, you have to move on. I feel for his mom and for his family, but things got to move on." There were, though, moments of poignant reflection. He undertook a goodwill mission of detente to West Coast radio stations in a bid to tamp down the flames.

In his last interview, Biggie said,

> I kind of realized how powerful Tupac and I were. We waged a coastal beef. One man against one man made a whole west coast hate a whole east coast and vice versa. And that really bugged me out. This whole coast don't like me, so I don't like him. It just kind of lets me know how much strength I have, so now I gotta be the one to flip it because he can't do that. He can't be the one that's gonna squash it 'cos he's gone. So I gotta take the weight for both sides, and that's why I'm out here. That man had a beef for me, and I had a beef with him. That don't mean you can't like me.

The plea, aimed at his record-buying public, was more specifically a message for Suge Knight and his allies in the Bloods by a man who now feared for his life anytime he ventured to the likes of California or Nevada. Screwing his courage to the sticking point, on March 9, 1997, Biggie and his crew attended the *Soul Train* awards in LA—the very heart of Bloods territory—before heading to an after-party at the Peterson Automotive Museum. But the party was forced to break up early due to overcrowding, and they headed back to his hotel. It was a decision that cost him his life.

A week after his death, Bad Boy released Biggie's second album, a double CD carrying the portentous title *Life after Death*. As one writer put it, the only thing more powerful than a premature death is a death foretold. The album's cover art showed the rapper leaning nonchalantly against a hearse that bore the license plate "B.I.G." There were no sunglasses to hide his lazy eye. He wasn't smiling but neither was he mad. He was just stating the facts from the other side. It seemed like a prophecy.

Photographer Michael Lavine said, "That's one of the things that's so powerful about the photo. You have a photograph of a man in a graveyard who died violently weeks later—it makes the image more emotionally laden. It's not just a photo. What's the name of the album? *Life after Death*? That's crazy. Flirting with disaster." In an ominous parallel, Tupac had also seemed to foretell of a premature end to his life. In an early hit, the lyrics to "Soulja's Story" included the lines "The fast life ain't everything they told ya, never get much older following the tracks of a soulja."

The coastal beef between Bad Boy and Death Row also died with Biggie. Death Row eventually went bust and Knight ended up doing jail time for a hit-and-run incident involving a former business associate. In contrast, the career of Sean "Puff Daddy" Combs went from strength to strength in a post-Biggie world, a rise that saw him become the most important figure in rap before the likes of JayZ and Kanye West began their ascent to the hip-hop thrones in the new millennium. No one has ever been brought to justice for either man's death.

Keefe D "confessed" to being involved during a fake drugs sting set up by Kading, whose police task force appeared to have solved the crime before it was mysteriously shut down by the force's top brass who may have been fearful over evidence exposing the role of those within their own ranks who were on Knight's payroll at the time of Biggie's murder. But he was never brought to book—neither was Anderson, who was interviewed by police just once over the killing. Anderson insisted he had nothing to do with Shakur's death. "If they have all this evidence against me, then why haven't they arrested me?" he said a year after the shooting. "It's obvious that I'm innocent."

Like Tupac, there would be no old age for the gang member known among his homies as Baby Lane. Anderson's own life came to a premature end when he was gunned down in May 1998, in California, following an unrelated gangland shoot-out. In the case of Biggie's murder, the police trail ultimately led to Darnell "Poochie" Bolton, a Bloods member also on Death Row wages, who allegedly agreed to carry out a $13,000 hit on the New York rapper. Bolton died in July 2003, after being shot several times in the back while riding a motorbike in Compton.

Violence was a thread that, undeniably, ran through the later chapters of the story of Tupac Shakur and Biggie Smalls, two emcees who died at the top of their game. "The only justice in this case is the street justice," said Kading. "No one will ever be held accountable. Both shooters have died in the same violent ways they killed their victims. The streets have kind of taken care of their own."

Biggie biographer Jake Brown laments the early deaths of two men in their twenties who could have been serious spokesmen for their communities had they been prepared to put aside mutual enmity. He offered,

A comparison of the two is inevitable, given their friendship, rivalry, and the eerie similarities in their tragic murders, both in terms of the gangland style of the homicides and the fact that they both remain unsolved. The nature of their status as icons mirrors one another only in that they both were icons of the time, and as a result, of their deaths.

The chief distinction within an analysis of their status as idols is the fact that most hip-hop historians agree that Tupac's death was a bit more anticipated and ultimately accepted than Biggie's. Tupac's fans were more desensitized to the prospect of his demise through volumes of raps in which he prepared his fans for his passing, prophesizing it, and proclaiming himself an Outlaw Immortal. Tupac was an antagonist, even in his feud with Biggie, where Smalls played more of a defensive, diplomatic position.

Tupac expected to die, whereas shortly before Biggie's death, in interviews and to friends, he was clearly thinking ahead toward his future—retiring in a short matter of years, watching his children grow up, becoming a label head himself. In other words, he had no idea what was coming round the corner. Nor did his fans, which made it that much more difficult to understand or make peace with.

Lennon and McCartney
Everett Collection/Alamy Stock

14

JOHN LENNON AND
PAUL McCARTNEY

John Lennon took a deep breath, rolled up his sleeves, bent his legs forward, and gingerly placed both his hands around the ears of an oversized pig chomping on some feed on the ground. It was an incongruous setting. Neither the generously fed porker nor the former Beatle, it has to be said, looked entirely at ease in each other's company.

But for Lennon, this was a moment of priggish revenge, retaliation for those subtle barbs he and his wife Yoko had endured from the man who was once his musical partner and closest friend. So a moment's awkwardness was a small price to pay if it meant holding Paul McCartney up to worldwide mockery and embarrassment. And here was Lennon telling everyone what he really thought of McCartney in the nuclear winter of the Beatles' meltdown.

Held up to the light, Lennon's satirizing of the cover of McCartney's 1971 album *Ram*, which captured a welly-booted Paul holding on to a sheep at his Scottish farm, was more an attempt at infantile humor, the kind of mawkish, in-house whimsy that once offered shelter from the immense pressures that came with the baggage of being Lennon or McCartney. *Ram* was McCartney's second album after he walked away from the Beatles in April 1970, a record that at the time was wrongly dismissed by critics—*Rolling Stone* denounced it as "the nadir in the decomposition of sixties rock thus far"—as lightweight froth bubbling with cloying domesticity. The songs were considered melodically trifling, and the lyrics especially trite.

But Lennon found himself poring over every word after picking up on what he considered to be pointed arrows from one ex-Beatle to another. Hiding in plain sight between the grooves of tracks like "Too Many People" and "Back Seat of My Car" were coded "fuck-you" missives. And just in case John missed the point—he didn't, incidentally—the back cover included a picture of two beetles copulating. In "Too Many People," McCartney hit out at a mystery person who had taken his lucky break "and broke it in two."

The intro contained what sounded like someone saying piece of cake. Closer listening, however, revealed it to be a cheeky "piss off." And the refrain for "Back Seat of My Car" was "We believe that we can't be wrong," sung repeatedly into the fadeout, a party political broadcast on behalf of the McCartney party. The lyrics seemed pretty opaque to everyone except the one person they appeared to be aimed at.

In an interview with *Crawdaddy*, Lennon declared, "I heard Paul's messages in *Ram*—yes, there are, dear reader! Too many people going where? Missed our lucky what? What was our first mistake? Can't be wrong? Huh, I mean Yoko, me and other friends can't all be hearing things." It was a grievous mistake for McCartney to believe he could slug it out lyrically with a master wordsmith like Lennon, a point even he agreed with years later.

He said, "It's tough when you have someone like John slagging you off, cos he's a tough slagger-offer." That point is shared by respected Beatles scholar Martin Lewis who knew both men and had a neutral foot in both camps during and after the band's demise.

He told me,

> Paul was on a losing wicket there because nobody could be bitchier than John and he was at his most bitchy and most vitriolic with people he loved, and he loved Paul, but he had a wicked acid tongue. Paul could throw the ball back across the net pretty hard, but John was on a determined mission over the diss on "Too Many People" and a couple of other things. If John wanted to be acid, he very quickly could. He went with all guns blazing.

Picking up the gauntlet with considerable relish, Lennon quickly sought out the field advantage when he released *Imagine* seven months after *Ram* hit the shelves. Tucked within every album sleeve was the postcard of Lennon fondling the pig. And one of the standout tracks from his most commercially successful solo album was "How Do You Sleep?," a withering, five-minute evisceration of McCartney that took their feud to embittered new depths.

Paul, he sang, lived "with straits who tell you you was king" while his new material was denounced as "muzak." And those "freaks" who said he was dead—a pointed reference to the Paul-is-dead farrago—were, by the way, right all along. But, even though they were no longer in each other's wheelhouse, Lennon knew precisely where to hit McCartney in his most sensitive spot.

Calling out Paul's most famous song and, separately, linking it to his first post-Beatles single, he raged, "The only thing you done [*sic*] was yesterday, and now you're gone you're just Another Day." It was a vicious coupling, made all the more wounding by the inclusion on the track of a jagged-edge slide guitar played by George Harrison, making clear where his loyalties stood in the post-split battle of the Beatles.

And it further polarized Beatle fans who felt the need to take sides in the battle of the band in the same way the Beatles and the Stones once competed for public affection. Lewis, whose association with the Beatles goes back to 1967, compared the breakup of the Beatles—and the subsequent estrangement of Lennon and McCartney—to the cultural equivalent of watching your parents divorce.

> The Beatles were the ultimate parents. And kids don't want their parents to break up. The Beatles led us through the 1960s and from being entertainers all the way through to the far frontiers of artistic exploration that was never remotely on the cards when they started out. John was Alpha Male and Paul was Alpha Female, not attributing gender there. How could they be squabbling?
>
> Our fight, such as it was, was with the old guard, the establishment. Our fight was with those who did not have enlightened eyes. Our fight was not among ourselves. So for our parents to be squabbling was horrifying. But by 1969–1970 they are going in different directions and one of the directions that makes a difference is that John is in the fierce urgency of the political situation. Paul is going in a much sweeter, rural direction.
>
> The difference was this. In 1970, there was a cultural divide and it mattered what side of the barriers you were on. John planted himself very much on the side of the left, both politically and culturally, and was prepared to take that stand.
>
> Paul, while he had sympathies in those areas, was not prepared to take that stand. He was very attracted to domesticity and in a sense it was not much different than Dylan doing *New Morning* and *Self Portrait* and going rustic and inwards. That's not to say either was bad, but in the climate of 1970, you were being forced to pick sides.
>
> Everything became artificially polarized. You were black or white. You could not be both. Paul's homogenized domesticity rubbed up against John's agit prop side and we were being asked to choose sides. It was pathetic that we were being asked to choose sides but we were.

To that end, "How Do You Sleep?" was a new low, one that even Ringo Starr felt crossed the line. The drummer, always the most sensitive member of the Beatles, was reportedly taken aback when he heard the song for the first time as it was being recorded at Lennon's home studio in Ascot. More so since Lennon toyed with the idea of suggesting that McCartney had, in fact plagiarized "Yesterday," a baseless accusation that surely would have ended up in the civil courts.

Every line was written to inflict maximum pain. "How do ya sleep, ya cunt?" Lennon snarled during one outtake. "That's enough, John," said Ringo, distraught over the blame game that was now spiraling poisonously out of control.

Writer Felix Dennis was among those who watched the song take shape in the studio and often winced at the lyrics that didn't actually make the final cut. "Some of it was absolutely puerile," he recalled.

"Thank God a lot of it was never actually recorded because it was highly, highly personal, like a bunch of schoolboys standing in the lavatory making scatalogical jokes and then falling about with laughter at their own wit. Some of the lyrics were a lot ruder than you will find on the finished version."

Lennon later admitted a degree of guilt over the song's lyrics and even argued that it was really about him. An unconvincing plea for mitigation that generated more heat than light. He told *Playboy* magazine shortly before he died,

> You know, I wasn't really feeling that vicious at the time. But I was using my resentment toward Paul to create a song, let's put it that way. He saw that it pointedly refers to him, and people kept hounding him about it.
>
> But, you know, there were a few digs on his album before mine. He's so obscure other people didn't notice them, but I heard them. I thought, well, I'm not obscure, I just get right down to the nitty-gritty. So he'd done it his way and I did it mine.

The feud often spilled over into the music press, a delicious banquet for journalists eager to feed off the scraps. McCartney told *Melody Maker* after "How Do You Sleep?" hit the airwaves, "So what if I live with straights? I like straights. I have straight babies. It doesn't affect him. He says the only thing I did was 'Yesterday.' He knows that's wrong."

How had it come to this? Between them, Lennon and McCartney had written almost 300 songs as the Beatles became the greatest musical phenomenon of all time. They had been each other's closest intimate, mushroom-grown in the hothouse of celebrity, sharing moments only they could understand.

They had navigated the treacherous currents of confusing adolescence and sat opposite each other, eyeball to eyeball, almost telepathically crafting all those love letters to the world. They had striven to outdo each other in a sibling rivalry to write the best songs, crying over the cherished mothers they had both lost as teenagers. Together they dreamed of fame and fortune, the risk and reward for becoming stars, remembering the craziness of a "Beatle sandwich," lying on top of each other in the back of a tiny touring van. Laughing at the absurdity of Beatlemania from countless hotel bedrooms, they had wondered what path their lives would, eventually, take. Lewis maintains that it's extraordinary that their creative partnership—and friendship—lasted so long. And he's convinced the group could have survived had they agreed to take a Beatle sabbatical at the end of the decade.

They went through this cataclysmic, unbelievable escalation. They developed in ways that had never been envisioned in popular music. And they stayed together and stayed friendly for all that period. In hindsight, it's bizarre that they maintained their friendship under all those strains and without a wrong foot.

When the end came, as disappointed as I was as a fan and admirer, I can look back 50 years later and say how strange it was that their friendship endured through this warp-speed journey, especially from 1963 onwards. And that they didn't break up sooner. The other aspect is that what became the norm in the 1970s and beyond was that groups could go on hiatus. That you could put out a solo album, that you didn't have to have a release every six months.

All those things became the norm in the seventies. But that was not the norm in the sixties. . . . You had to put records out. In hindsight, what a mercy it was that the Beatles broke up at the height of their creativity. Leaving an astonishingly beautiful body of work. They exited at the right time. As messy as the split was, it was well timed and we were the better for it.

When it eventually all came crashing down in April 1970, recriminations were inevitable. By the end of the decade they had done so much to define, the Lennon-McCartney professional partnership was terminally malignant, and their friendship stretched to breaking point.

In February 1969, Lennon was lobbying hard for Allen Klein, a streetwise New York hustler who also happened to be manager of the Rolling Stones, to be brought on board at Apple to save the Beatles from bankruptcy as their finances tumbled into a fiscal black hole. For McCartney, Klein represented a toxic mix of fear and loathing. Hating him from their first meeting, Paul fought instead to install Lee and John Eastman, esteemed New York showbiz lawyers, who also happened to be his new in-laws.

The standoff pitted the two musicians in diametrically opposed corners and the gloves soon came off in the battle for the soul of the Beatles. By September 1969, Lennon had secretly left the band, having agreed a vow of omertà to preserve the myth. To the outside world, it was business as usual.

Then, after months of radio silence between them, Lennon unexpectedly got a phone call from McCartney to tell him that he, too, was quitting the Beatles.

"I was pleased," said Lennon, "because it meant that he had accepted the situation as well as me." Two days later, however, the front page of the *Daily Mirror* caused Lennon's mood to darken. Early press copies of Paul's debut solo album, the eponymously titled *McCartney*, included a Q&A insert that made clear to anyone reading between the needle-pointed lines that the Beatles were no more. Lennon was furious; he had started the Beatles, yet here was Paul pulling off "The Big Con" and using the worldwide publicity for the most self-serving of purposes—to sell a record. Lennon's innate sense of betrayal—and McCartney's later decision to go to court to dissolve the group's business partnership—left a wound that would arguably truly never heal.

Lennon had a recurring dread of "ending up like Mickey Rooney"—in hock to the taxman and being forced to write TV jingles "just to make some bread." When the Beatles' byzantine finances were exposed in court as a result of McCartney's actions, John feared his fiscal nightmare could become a ruinous reality. Paul's solution was naively simple—find a way out of the financial maze, split the money four ways, shake hands, and part as friends.

In a lengthy 1971 interview with *Melody Maker*, just after Lennon's release of *Imagine*, McCartney defended his overtures and insisted it was the best solution for all. "I just want the four of us to get together somewhere and sign a piece of paper saying it's all over and we want to divide the money four ways. No one else would be there, not even Linda or Yoko or Allen Klein," he said.

"We'd just sign the paper and hand it to the business people and let them sort it out. That's all I want now, but John won't do it. Everybody thinks I am the aggressor but I'm not, you know. I just want out."

When he read the comments, Lennon was apoplectic and demanded an instant right of reply in the next issue. He wrote,

> Maybe there's an answer there somewhere, but for the millionth time in these past few years I repeat, "What about the tax?" It's all very well, playing "simple honest ole Paul" in *Melody Maker* but you know damn well we can't just sign a bit of paper. You say, "John won't do it." I will if you indemnify us against the taxman!
>
> Anyway, you know that after we have our meeting, the fucking lawyers will have to implement whatever we agree on, right? If they have some form of agreement between them before we meet, it might make it even easier. It's up to you, as we've said many times, we'll meet whenever you like. Just make up your mind! Two weeks ago I asked you on the phone, "Please let's meet

without advisors, etc. and decide what we want," and I emphasized especially Maclen [Lennon and McCartney's songwriting company] which is mainly our concern, but you refused, right?

You said under no condition would you sell to us if we didn't do what you wanted, you'd sue us again and that Ringo and George are going to break you John, etc., etc. Now I was quite straight with you that day, and you tried to shoot me down with your emotional "logic." If you're not the aggressor [as you claim] who the hell took us to court and shat all over us in public?

Almost as an incidental poke in the eye, he scorned his former partner's complimentary verdict on *Imagine*, "How Do You Sleep?" notwithstanding. "So you think *Imagine* ain't political? It's Working Class Hero with sugar on it for conservatives like yourself!"

The acrimony was unnecessarily personal and unnecessarily public. Part of the problem was they remained prisoners of their own storied legacies. Every day brought some kind of inexorable reminder of their past. And every interview provided an opportunity to come out swinging for one reason or another, turning those inquests into a bizarre form of long-distance couples therapy. Lennon, of course, had already staked out his position in his excoriating sit-down with *Rolling Stone* editor Jann Wenner.

Tearing down every sacred Beatle myth he could think of while still mind deep in painful, ego-shredding primal scream therapy, he lambasted McCartney, denouncing him as an overbearing autocrat who had reduced himself, George, and Ringo to the roles of "sidemen" by the time the Beatles were on life support.

"Paul thought he was the fuckin' Beatles, and he never fucking was, never," raged Lennon to Wenner. For McCartney, it was the ultimate calumny from the man whose approval in all things he craved most. Honest enough later to withdraw many of the vicious things he'd said about McCartney, Lennon remained too self-absorbed to admit that his post-Beatles music was missing a vital spark, perhaps that necessary, creative tug-of-war with his old mate. Friends of both men were appalled by the constant sniping.

Lewis said, "I love John and Paul equally."

I've had the privilege of working with Paul on several occasions, and he has always been incredibly generous. So I will say this with all the love and affection of a Beatles' fan. They, like all human beings, were quite capable of behaving like a couple of squabbling schoolgirls. And no one squabbles more than people who love each other. That's what the squabbles are about. They love each other.

The Beatles are Gods to us, quite rightly for what they created, but that does not mean their personal behavior is always beyond reproach. They are human. When I look at John and Paul, I don't deify them beyond the ability to act like a couple of schoolgirls.

At its height, genuine distress could sometimes be detected in Mc-Cartney's responses. And perhaps this is what has always distinguished the Lennon-McCartney estrangement from rock music's other notorious post-split vendettas. Beneath the waspish comments and blame-game mentality lay the suspicion that a deep bond still existed between them, one that simply defied casual explanation. In private, neither could believe things had got this bad.

McCartney later confessed to writer and broadcaster Paul Gambaccini that he pored over every one of Lennon's comments. "He'd been hurt by it. He had known John for years, so he's thinking, 'John is saying this,' not primal scream John," recalled Gambaccini. "You can never stop caring about your boyhood friends. . . . Lennon and McCartney were teenagers together. So for Paul to think, 'Oh my God, John doesn't think I'm good,' that would be the most damaging, negative opinion there could be."

Occasionally, musical olive branches were proffered in an attempt to tone down the silly rhetoric of big boys bickering. None more so than Mc-Cartney's touching song "Dear Friend," which appeared on *Ram*'s follow-up *Wild Life*.

The song showed Paul reaching out to someone and asking if their friendship had finally crossed the Rubicon of no-return?

> That's sort of me talking to John after we'd had all the sort of disputes about the Beatles' breakup. I find it very emotional when I listen to it now. I have to sort of choke it back.
>
> But, for me, it is a bit like that. I remember when I heard the song recently. And I thought, "Oh God." That lyric: "Really truly, young and newly wed." Listening to that was like, "Oh my God, it's true!" I'm trying. This was me reaching out. So, I think it's very powerful in some very simple way. But it was certainly heartfelt.

Eventually, a truce was agreed upon amid an accord to no longer weaponize their songs against each other. The two men, along with their wives, came face to face in New York for the first time in two years before the sun had set on a rancorous 1971. Forced bonhomie, however, slowly gave way to awkward silences amid a realization that they were now more like old school friends instead of two men who had survived the maelstrom of "the greatest show on earth."

Outside of the ring, of course, they both still had careers to nurture and legends to live up to. Post-Beatles, Lennon had come flying out the traps with the searingly honest Plastic Ono Band, which included the track "God" with its line "I don't believe in Beatles," and the more commercial "Imagine." But McCartney's first three solo albums, *McCartney*, *Ram*, and *Wild Life*, had largely stalled on the runway after receiving critical maulings; trite throwaways like "Bip Bop" and "Oo You" were perhaps intentionally light years away from "Hey Jude" and "Let It Be."

Within eighteen months, however, their career trajectories would be reversed. McCartney, having formed Wings, planted the first shoots of recovery with *Red Rose Speedway* and then fully blossomed with the peerless *Band on the Run*, both albums being released within the space of twelve months in 1973. Lennon, meanwhile, hit a career nadir with *Sometime in New York City*, a slab of political radicalism that fans found easy to shun.

By the time *Mind Games* arrived in the summer of 1973, his personal life was in chaos. He was embroiled in a long-running battle with the American immigration authorities. It was later revealed he was being spied on by the deeply paranoid Nixon administration, who viewed him as a subversive whose avowed mission was—incredibly—to overthrow the U.S. government.

And he had separated from Yoko, five years of claustrophobic togetherness having proved too much for both of them. But while Lennon's marriage to Yoko foundered, he was still bound in legal and corporate wedlock to the Beatles—and McCartney. They remained contractually tethered to each other, to that bond, even as they worked hard to establish new identities for themselves as solo artists while trying impossibly to escape the long shadow of their old group.

Never a day passed without either of them being quizzed about a reunion. Lennon would veer from sentiment to scorn in the space of minutes; McCartney equally would keep the door open before slamming it shut in response to some caustic remark Lennon had made. One phone call to Lennon ended with Paul hanging up, frustrated by Lennon's suspicion and irritated by the faux Americanisms that had replaced broad Scouse in his vernacular.

McCartney told *Rolling Stone*,

We were submerged in business troubles at the time. There was incredible bitterness. At one point, to get some peace in the camp, I told my lawyers I wanted to give John an indemnity he had been seeking against a certain clause in one of the Apple contracts.

I said, "Someone's gotta make the first move. I'd love to be the voice of reason here." I happened to be on my way to the Caribbean, so, passing through New York, I rang John up. But there was so much suspicion, even though I came bearing the olive branch. I said, "Hey, I'd like to see you." He said, "What for? What do you *really* want?" It was very difficult. Finally . . . he had a great line for me. He said, "You're all pizza and fairy tales."

He'd become sort of Americanized by then, so the best insult I could think of was to say, "Oh, fuck off, Kojak," and slam the phone down. That was about the strength of our relationship then—very, very bitter—and we didn't get over that for a long, long time.

McCartney elaborated on these confrontations in *Many Years from Now*, the closest he has ever come to an autobiography. "I actually used to have some very frightening phone calls. I went through a period when I could be so nervous to ring him and so insecure in myself that I actually felt like I was in the wrong. It was all very acrimonious and bitter." Throughout it all, Linda McCartney quickly sussed out that northern English machismo was partly to blame for this intransigence. As an American, she had no such verbal hang-ups about face-to-face communication. She told *Playboy*, "The sad thing is that John and Paul both had problems and they loved each other and, boy, could they have helped each other! If they had only communicated! It frustrates me no end, because I was just some chick from New York when I walked into all of that. All I could do was sit there watching them play these games."

Standing in the way of any proper reconciliation, however, was Klein, Lennon's homunculus and the goblin king of the Beatles' story. Wariness over his nefarious business dealings had, however, seeped into Klein's relationships with Lennon, Harrison, and Starr.

Allegations repeatedly broke that Klein was instinctively creaming off the top. By early 1973 he had been removed from the circle of trust after the three ex-Beatles served notice that they would not be renewing Klein's management contract when it expired in March. Overnight, the biggest impediment to a reunion had seemingly been removed. More so after Lennon, asked to explain Klein's dismissal, grudgingly admitted, "Let's say possibly Paul's suspicions were right . . . and the timing was right."

McCartney resisted the natural temptation to gloat over Klein's predicament except when the inevitable lawsuits between both parties began to fly. "My God I hope they win that one," he declared. Then, on March 28, the moment Beatles fans had been hyping for so long happened accidentally on purpose. Lennon was acting as ersatz conductor in chief for a sprawling all-night jam session at Burbank Studios in Los Angeles.

It happened during the height of his so-called Lost Weekend separation from Yoko, during which he had decamped to America's West Coast to live a life of bachelor-style hedonism with his assistant May Pang, who also became his lover. Among those taking part were Harry Nilsson, Bobby Keys, Steve Wonder, and Jesse Ed Davis. Suddenly, the doors opened and in walked Paul and Linda—a jaw-dropping moment for everyone except, it seemed, to Lennon who hardly batted an eyelid. "Oh, hello," he said nonchalantly.

McCartney then slipped almost imperceptibly behind one of two drum kits—the other belonged to Ringo—almost, it seemed, trying to stay invisible. There was no mad charge to take what used to be a default position—sharing a microphone with John Lennon. "Right, McCartney's doing the harmony on the drums," said Lennon, who had already indulged in more than a little Colombian marching powder.

Besides, most of the participants were also off their faces as they ran through a number of fifties rock 'n' roll standards.

And then it happened. As Lennon screeched out the lyrics to "Lucille," he was joined by McCartney, and their voices blended together the way they used to, the way destiny had once decreed. It could have been the start to an incredible session—the twentieth century's most iconic songwriting duo getting back to where they once belonged, singing the songs that first brought them together in Liverpool in 1957—but things quickly went south.

"It is a little better if we think of a song," Lennon noted as the band started to drift. "Where's all that drink they always have at this place?" Then cocaine began to make its way round the room. "Someone give me an E [chord] or a snort," Lennon said, before launching into a series of complaints about the microphones and earphones. For all of its warts, this reunion was a genuine bit of history in Lennon and McCartney's manifold relationship—the only time that they made any kind of music together after the Beatles broke up. Yet the jam session has never been widely publicized or discussed, even among people who were close to both men during that time. Lennon said, "There were about fifty people in that room, and they were all just watching Paul and me."

Equally vague was McCartney, who has rarely spoken about it. "We were stoned," he told *Rolling Stone* in 2012. "I don't think there was anyone in that room who wasn't stoned. For some ungodly reason, I decided to get on drums. It was just a party, you know."

But the real purpose for McCartney "just being in the neighborhood" would become clear the next day. Lennon was renting a beach house full of drunken crazies that included Nilsson, Ringo, and the Who's Keith Moon. When Lennon duly emerged from his coke-induced slumber, he was apparently happy to see Paul and Linda in more lucid circumstances.

But this was not just a social call; McCartney was keen to talk about a reunion—just not the one the world expected. He was, in fact, acting as an emissary from none other than Yoko—and he had turned amateur marriage guidance counselor in an attempt to get them back together. It was, by any measure, an incredible turn of events. Paul McCartney trying to reunite his estranged songwriting partner with the woman who, at that time, was vilified the world over for breaking up the Beatles—the same woman, who had usurped him as Lennon's artistic partner and closest intimate. The wheels for this amazing volte-face had been set in motion several weeks earlier when Ono had visited the McCartneys in London and given them the lowdown on the state of their separation.

Like everyone else, Paul had been horrified by exaggerated reports of Lennon, off the leash and on the lash, acting with a devil-may-care abandonment in the City of Angels. Tentatively, he delicately broached the idea of him acting as an intermediary if Yoko wanted him back. But it does lead to one overarching question: why did McCartney see the need to become matchmaker? His solo career was now soaring. *Band on the Run* had become a stellar success. But he must surely have known that his heart's desire of one day rekindling that long lost magic with Lennon—and potentially bringing the Beatles out of mothballs—would be gone forever if he reconciled with Yoko.

Lennon's reaction to Paul's petition has never been disclosed. In fact, he never mentioned the encounter, and it was the last time the two men were ever publicly photographed together. Yoko, however, was more open when the matter later became public knowledge. She told *The Times*, "I want the world to know that it was a very touching thing that he did for John. He was genuinely concerned about his old partner. Even though John was not even asking for help—John, Paul, all of them were too proud to ask anything—he helped." She added, "John often said he didn't understand why Paul did this for us, but he did."

McCartney, later, felt his crucial intervention in the latest ballad of John and Yoko had been underappreciated by a public who by then really didn't give much of a damn.

> Nobody knows how much I helped John. Yoko came by our house in St. John's Wood and we started talking. She confided in us that they had broken up. She was strong about it and she said, "He's got to work his way back to me." And I said, "Would you think it is an intrusion if I said to him, 'Look man, she loves you, and there's a way to get back. I might see him around, and I'd like to be a mediator in this because the two of you have got something really strong.'" So Linda and I went to California.

May Pang, his new lover, however, had an alternative take on the conversation that ultimately took place in a back room at the beach house. According to one friend, she said, "Paul never told John that Yoko had sent him. Afterward, John told me, 'Paul doesn't get it. I'm with you now.'"

Whatever the truth, May was, however, a key witness to Lennon finally freeing himself of those old Fab Four demons and relaxing his contrariness toward McCartney. He began to openly chat about getting back together with Paul. Besides, he had already recorded "I'm the Greatest" for Ringo in a session that also included Harrison, the first time all three had been in a studio together since August 1969.

May said, "He wanted to write with Paul again. He asked me if I thought it was a good idea. I told him I thought it was a great idea 'because you two want to do it.' There are no contracts, no pressure. Just the most amazing songwriting team ever getting together to create some musical magic. Solo they were great but together they were unbeatable."

Lennon even ran the idea past, bizarrely, Art Garfunkel, amused as he was that they had both split up from collaborators called Paul. "I told him he should do it for the music," said Garfunkel. The men met backstage at the 1975 Grammys when Lennon and McCartney were in the same place at the same time—but never crossed paths or spoke. John handed out a gong for song of the year alongside Garfunkel and made smarmy references to "Paul."

McCartney had the last laugh, though, picking up the album of the year Grammy for the runaway success of *Band on the Run*, an award that must have stung Lennon just a tad. Of course, the dream of an official Lennon-McCartney musical reunion died the day Lennon walked back to Yoko, who soon became pregnant with their son Sean. And that was the signal for him to pull up the drawbridge on his career and turn his back on music for the first five years of his second-born son's life. It was yet another example of how the stars were never aligned for a full-fledged reconciliation—except for one night.

According to the well-spun tale, on April 26, 1976, the McCartneys arrived unexpectedly at the Dakota ostensibly to see the new baby—Sean was then six months old.

That night, they all tuned into the popular satirical comedy show *Saturday Night Live* only to watch in amazement as host Lorne Michaels made a tongue-in-cheek pitch to reunite the Beatles. The camera zoomed in on the piece of paper in Michaels's hand. "All you have to do is sing three Beatles songs," he declared. "'She Loves You,' yeah, yeah, yeah—that's $1,000 right there. You know the words. It'll be easy. Like I said, this is made out to 'The Beatles.' You divide it anyway you want. If you want to give Ringo less, that's up to you. I'd rather not get involved."

Unknown to Michaels and the rest of the world, of course, the Beatles' two principal songwriters were about only one-and-a-half miles away, watching the show along with 22 million other people. As Lennon said in 1980, "Paul was visiting us at our place in the Dakota. We were watching it and almost went down to the studio, just as a gag. We nearly got into a cab, but we were actually too tired. . . . He and I were just sitting there watching the show, and we went, 'Ha ha, wouldn't it be funny if we went down?' But we didn't."

McCartney subsequently confirmed that this took place. "John said, 'We should go down, just you and me. There's only two of us so we'll take half the money.' And for a second we thought about it. But it would have been work, and we were having a night off, so we elected not to go. It was a nice idea—we nearly did it."

It was, nevertheless, a mildly convivial evening. But, like so many old friends whose lives have veered in different directions, the easy kinship they once shared had gone. One Christmastime both families went out for dinner with the Lennons' friend Elliot Mintz, who saw for himself how their chats now drifted into an aimless void.

He told Philip Norman, author of weighty biographies of both Lennon and McCartney, "The conversation became less rhythmic, the words more sparse. It was obvious to me the two of them had run out of things to say to each other."

Paul, nevertheless, felt emboldened enough to return to the Dakota the day after one such visit carrying a guitar. But he was unprepared for the frosty welcome that followed as Lennon harangued him for simply turning up unannounced at the door. "It's not 1956 anymore," he said witheringly, tempering McCartney's hopes and dreams as he stood in the entrance lobby. It was the last time they met. "That was a period when Paul just kept turning up at our door with a guitar. I would let him in, but finally I said to him, 'Please call before you come over. It's not 1956, and turning up at the door isn't the same anymore. You know, just give me a ring.' He was upset by that, but I didn't mean it badly. I just meant that I was taking care of a baby all day, and some guy turns up at the door."

To Paul's sensitive ears, however, it sounded like a typical Lennon putdown without any filter applied. In the months and years Lennon had left, there were intermittent but cordial phone calls. These mainly centered on family, Lennon's emergence as a (rich) renaissance man who spent his lazy hours watching the wheels while looking after the baby—albeit with the help of a nanny—while Yoko curated the family business.

In the end, cruel fate ultimately turned any prospect of a reunion into a broken dream. The shots that rang out at the Dakota on December 8, 1980, were heard all over the world. McCartney, repressing his grief, decided work was his best therapy on that day but later broke down. "When I got home I wept buckets," he said in *Many Years from Now*. "I felt so robbed and so emotional." Four decades have now passed since Lennon's senseless murder, time enough for measured objectivity to be applied. In print, caustic comments often retain their own vibrations, reactionary words spoken in the heat of the moment. Paul, however, has often gone out of his way to insist the familiar narrative of their lost decade has been skewed by history.

The final conversations he had with John have become a sort of balm for McCartney, an analgesic that has helped to numb a "heartache" that will understandably never properly go away. In his mind's eye, the good times always hold sway. Lennon's shocking murder also killed off all hopes of a full-fledged Beatles' reunion, one that Martin Lewis believes would actually have taken place.

I have no doubt that it would have done. I offer the following evidence for those who doubt it. First of all, we are all aware of the massive contradictions between perception and reality where John and Paul are concerned. John is the acerbic and aggressive rocker. Excuse me, but who wrote "Goodnight" for his young son? Who's the one who wrote "Julia" for his mother and "Woman," which includes the most impressive line of all—"please understand the little child inside the man"?

And Paul is this sweet, butter-wouldn't-melt-person who wrote "Helter Skelter" and some of the most aggressive things and who has been extremely adventurous with some of his records as the Fireman and so forth.

So we have all been used to those oversimplifications, which were calcified by the likes of the film *A Hard Day's Night* and the Beatle cartoons. John always had a stock answer to the question of whether the Beatles would ever reunite and say it's like a high school reunion and I don't believe in those. But this is the same John Lennon, let the record show, who in 1979 asked his aunt Mimi to find his old school tie and is then pictured walking around New York wearing a Quarrybank Grammar School tie. John was as sentimental as anybody, but he was not going to show it except when he did show it.

The only obstacles to a reunion would have been the external expectations, the pressure game of will they reunite either for economic reasons or for the fans' yearning? And I think, wisely, they tried to avoid that, but I believe that the natural bonds of friendship would have caused them to get back together. If they had been smart, it would have been for themselves. And only something public if they had wanted it to be. But I believe John and Paul were reconciled to each other personally, and there would have been a natural curiosity like we all have to explore our past. And that would have happened.

The Band: Rick Danko, Levon Helm, Richard Manuel, Garth Hudson, and Robbie Robertson. Once Were Broth
Shed/Bell Media Studios/Imagine Documentaries/Polygram Ent/Landy, Elliot/Alamy Stock Photo

(15)

THE BAND

Sweat glistened on Levon Helm's forehead and trickled down his neck onto his lilac shirt. Panning in, the camera lit on every nuance, every emotion and the sheer overarching wistfulness of "The Night They Drove Old Dixie Down."

Standing just a few feet away, Robbie Robertson and Rick Danko chimed in on the harmonies as they had done countless times in the past, their guitars jerking to the song's locomotive chug.

To their right at his piano sat Richard Manuel, possessing the voice of an angel but desperately trying to fight off the craving for a drink or some blow, just enough to take the edge off his nerves.

And at the back, hunched over his Lowrey organ, was Garth Hudson—enigmatic, professorial, focused—his fingers dancing over the chords as the mighty chorus kicked in. This was "The Band" in its purest form, a company of craftsmen where, for once, the definite article really did represent the sum of the parts. The venue was San Francisco's Winterland Ballroom and the date was November 25, 1976—Thanksgiving Day. And if ever there was a day to give thanks to The Band, this was it. *The Last Waltz* was the end of the road, the final performance of a group that once were brothers. Never again, would we hear Levon sing "The Night They Drove Old Dixie Down" as part of that unique quintet in that mournful but wonderful southern drawl.

Never again would these five men break bread on stage again, sharing in that joyous communion of belonging to a church without borders. Deep down, perhaps Levon knew it himself, which is why he poured every ounce of himself into a performance that, decades later, still has the power to make the hairs stand up on the back of your neck. It was awesome and aching and framed by a beautiful yearning that carried with it an almost hereditary weight.

"I never heard Levon sing it better than he did that night," declared Robbie Robertson, the author of the Civil War epic that seemed to have been handed down like some mystical, long-lost oral family secret. Within months, though, the symbiotic fraternity that once bound both men so tightly had turned to tumbleweed. Long-suppressed animosities, built up over years of being holed up in dark studios and claustrophobic dressing rooms, broke the surface.

Unspoken grievances suddenly found a voice. Trust became a festering sore. And solidarity between Helm and Robertson gave way to spite over the division of the mighty dollar. In the dock over claims he was guilty of self-enrichment and had chivvied his bandmates out of a small fortune in songwriting royalties stood Robertson, an act of grand larceny considered the ultimate betrayal in any band. This fallout over money, over time, became a fissure not even death could remedy. The sweet had begun to turn sour with the release of The Band's eponymously titled second album in 1969 when Helm first glanced at the record sleeve. And immediately something jarred. His response was scathing.

> When *The Band* came out we were surprised by some of the song-writing credits. In those days we didn't realize that song publishing—more than touring or selling records—was the secret source of the real money in the music business. We're talking long term. We didn't know enough to ask or demand song credits or anything like that. Back then we'd get a copy of the album when it came out and that's when we'd learn who'd got the credit for which song. When the album [*The Band*] came out, I discovered I was credited with writing half of "Jemima Surrender" and that was it. Richard was a cowriter on three songs. Rick and Garth went uncredited. Robbie Robertson was credited on all twelve songs. That's not the way I recall things. Someone had pencil-whipped us. It was an old tactic: divide and conquer.

Helm waited until the sun had set on The Band before allowing his feelings to burst forth. True or not, the accusations would pitch Helm and Robertson headlong into a rest-of-life vendetta that cast a long shadow over their once cast-iron friendship and musical achievements. One that

Helm ultimately took to the grave, having been unable to set aside in life the level of vitriol he felt toward Robertson and his anger toward the music industry in general.

It wasn't meant to be like this. Once they were brothers, not by helix-linked DNA but hotwired through a connection that was almost telepathic in its closeness. They met as teenagers, Levon the ornery redneck from Turkey Scratch, Arkansas, and Robbie, the son of a Mohawk mother who grew up on an Indian reserve outside of Toronto. Three years his senior, Levon took the younger boy under his wing, tutoring him in the ways of the South, driving him along rock 'n' roll's super information highway, and soldering the ties that would manacle them closely for sixteen years.

Ties forged by more than a thousand nights on the road, playing cheap dives, earning their stripes. Appearing as the Hawks behind rockabilly king "Romping" Ronnie Hawkins, uncouth, untamed but a master mentor for kids on a dreamy quest for the big ticket. Co-opting Rick, Richard, and Garth along the way. Headhunted eventually by Bob Dylan to become his human shields when he traded in his folk lineage for a full-blown electric group to the disdain of grassroots fans. Going it alone in Woodstock and recording two tour de force albums—*Music from Big Pink* and *The Band*—that gave birth to Americana music and plowed the path for the likes of the Eagles; Crosby, Stills, Nash and Young; and the Grateful Dead. Paths crossed and signposts fixed on the way to becoming the best band in the world. Before it all went horribly wrong.

"Levon had been my dearest friend in the world," recalled Robertson in his 2016 memoir *Testimony*. "My teacher. The closest thing I had to a brother. We had seen it all together and survived the world's madness, but not our own." Not long after the final note of *The Last Waltz* had sounded, there was blood on the dance floor. Cast in the role of anti-hero was Robertson, the man who had, by necessity, become the putative leader of The Band, the workhorse who combined his songwriting roles with that of a CEO who kept one eye on the transformative fortunes of business and the man whose perceived villainy was exacerbated by the sad aftermath of The Band itself.

It was his decision to turn the concert into the group's live swan song. The reason was plain and simple; he firmly believed that unless they stepped off the touring carousel, some of them would soon be dead. The smart money was on Richard Manuel, a man who had long been in rock star freefall.

By 1976, Helm, the group's drummer as well as vocalist, Danko, whose soulful voice also infused many songs, and Manuel were schmoozing with Satan. The first two were mired in a serious heroin habit, a drug Robertson admitted "scared me to death." Manuel was a chronic alcoholic and had been for years. And all three possessed a self-destructive chromosome that Robertson was convinced would eventually kill one or all of them if they stayed together as a touring band. Barney Hoskyns, author of the seminal Band tome *Across the Great Divide*, said, "They could not have gone on the road again with Richard. He was in really bad shape. If they toured again, Richard might die. I really think that is how Robbie saw it. They couldn't exactly tell Richard he wasn't welcome to come on tour."

Manuel did indeed appear to have a death wish. Once, he wrecked a Mustang while under the influence, with Robertson's then wife Dominique fearing for her life in the passenger seat. Some time later, he drove a speedboat at full tilt into a rising wave causing an accident that almost left him with a broken neck and forced them to scrap several gigs.

Robertson had already seen the pressures of fame and rock 'n' roll excess snuff out the lives of Janis Joplin, Jim Morrison, and Jimi Hendrix. Within the next two years after *The Last Waltz*, the Who's Keith Moon would be added to that grave litany followed not long after by Led Zeppelin drummer John Bonham.

"The road was our school, it gave us a sense of survival and taught us all we know," a maudlin-sounding Robertson told Martin Scorsese during the filming for *The Last Waltz*. "You can't press your luck, the road has taken a lot of the great ones. . . . It's a goddamn impossible way of life."

In time, his portents for The Band would prove grimly accurate. In March 1986—a decade after *The Last Waltz*—Manuel, depressed and wrecked by years of booze and drug addiction, hanged himself in a Florida hotel room after having rejoined a reconstituted version of The Band along with Helm, Danko, and Hudson but notably minus Robertson. In December 1999, twenty-one days before the turn of the millennium, Danko, impoverished and bloated by decades of heroin and alcohol abuse, died in his sleep from heart failure three weeks short of his fifty-sixth birthday. He had long ago seen danger hurtling toward him but remained powerless to stop its ruinous trajectory. "Ever make a million dollars fast?" he once enquired rhetorically. "Well, I have. I've seen it ruin people. I've seen it kill people. It's a goddam crying shame what success can do to some people. . . . It came to us like a big, ugly beast. Try having the money and having all the drugs you want."

Their premature deaths cast a terrible pall over The Band but did nothing to heal the sceptic breach between Robertson and Helm. In fact, it only served to further widen the rift and deepen Helm's sense of bitterness toward the man who was once his musical neophyte. Suspicion over Robertson's involvement in the business side of The Band had long gnawed away at Helm, a chariness that went back to the days when the first six-figure checks rolled into their bank accounts. And the distribution of songwriting credits on their first two albums was, in Helm's mind, vindication that some kind of corporate carve-up had secretly been carried out.

Robertson had always nurtured close ties with their manager Albert Grossman, an imposing figure who also looked after Bob Dylan and had guided the career of Janis Joplin. From the moment The Band first hooked up with Grossman, the feeling persisted among some that he and Robertson were allowing self-interests to supersede band interests.

Helm declared,

> I complained that he [Robbie] and Albert had been making important business decisions without consulting the rest of us. And that far too much cash was coming down in his and Albert's corner. Our publishing split was far from fair, I told him, and had to be fixed. I told him that he and Albert ought to try and write some music without us because they couldn't possibly find the songs unless we were all searching together. I cautioned that most so-called business moves had fucked up a lot of great bands and killed off whatever music was left in them. I told Robbie that The Band was supposed to be partners.

Barney Hoskyns acknowledges the fact that disagreement over who wrote what opened up the great rift between the group's two alpha males. He recognizes the bigger dichotomy—Robbie sometimes shared writing credits with Rick and Richard—but still has some sympathy for the plight of the others, especially Levon. Hoskyns says,

> Robbie's song-writing credits remain a matter of some contention, and it is hard to believe that a similar "unit" working today would divide up the publishing royalties quite so unevenly.
>
> Even Robbie had admitted he was often obliged to turn to Garth for help in finding chords. I think it is a really tricky thing to say the credits should be split equally between these five members. But if you have a situation where, not to put too fine a point on it, people are pretty fucked up and only one of them [Robbie] is doing the heavy lifting, should the others get the credits?
>
> Levon's argument was that that songwriting really became three-dimensional when they worked on the material in rehearsal, and I think that is probably the point.
>
> The songs simply wouldn't be what we know them to be today without the work Levon did on his drum fills or Garth's keyboard fills. That is where the songs turn into something special. It's not that they suddenly learned a part Robbie had taught them. If Levon had been given a credit on "The Weight,"

it would have made a difference to him financially. But where there is a co-credit on "Jemima Surrender," there won't be that much of a difference. I think this is where you can really figure that injustice was done.

Running counter to that view, however, is the equally valid observation that Helm's gripes, however, were egregious and had little basis in fact. His comments were, at best, wholly inaccurate and, at worse, a grievous failure to recognize Robertson's monumental contribution to The Band as the group's principal songwriter and musical director. But it was far from a dictatorship. Robertson often worked in tandem with Manuel and Danko on some of their best-known pieces—and history has recorded the shared credits. Standing outside the circle, however, was Helm, who struggled to match his bandmates' work ethic when it came to writing songs.

Over the years, Robertson maintained an air of indifference over the charges lodged in the court of public opinion against him by Helm, mostly refusing to bite on the bait dangled in front of him by gossip-hungry journalists. Eventually, however, his tolerance spilled over during an interview with *Chicago Tribune* writer Greg Kot in 2002:

> To say that it was an issue [while they were together in the Band] is just utter nonsense after all these years. Who did the work? I tried, I begged Levon to write songs or help me write songs—all the guys. I always wanted everybody to write.
>
> You can't make somebody do what they don't want to do or can't do and he's not a songwriter. He didn't write one note, one word, nothing. What he's saying now is the result of somebody thinking about their financial problems. I wrote these songs and then 20 or 30 years later somebody comes back and says he wrote the songs?

In a 2019 interview to promote *Once Were Brothers*, the documentary about the history of The Band, Robertson hinted that Helm did, in fact, benefit financially from songs where his songwriting input was minimal at best.

> Levon didn't write songs. I gave him credit on some songs because he was around. Garth was a great musician, but he couldn't write. Ringo Starr doesn't write songs. Charlie Watts doesn't write songs, and they don't share publishing credit with the other guys in their groups.
>
> After sixteen years together, Levon never once mentioned song writing. When it came up, I was generous about it. I did stuff I didn't have to do, and I did it to be a good friend. It was ten or fifteen years after that when Levon was struggling financially, and he's blamed someone else for what happened with him.

Again, it wasn't meant to be like this. Levon and Robbie had met as callow teenagers sharing a passion for the early shoots of rock 'n' roll that carried like electricity on the radio airwaves. Soon, they became made men on the road. The Band consisted of four Canadians—Robertson, Danko, Hudson, and Manual—and one "bitter southerner"—Helm, mannered but raised dirt poor on his parents' farm in Turkey Scratch. They were five musicians thrown together by fate in the early 1960s.

Their lives became forever intertwined when, over time, unknown forces shuffled them round the board. Helm, already an accomplished drummer-singer was first to encounter Hawkins and joined his band in 1958. They played a rockabilly circuit that stretched from North America all the way to Toronto, carving out a reputation for no-holds-barred rock 'n' roll. In Toronto, they picked up Robertson, then just a fifteen-year-old idealist carrying a guitar who hung around their sound checks, eager to hitch a lift on Hawkins's bandwagon. Even at such a young age, no one could fail to be impressed by Robbie's precocious fretwork or the fact that he already possessed a gift for writing songs. Naturally, the two young musicians—Levon and Robbie—gravitated toward each other. "Levon and Robbie became Siamese twins," said Hawkins. "Levon could do all the shit that Robbie couldn't, and Robbie could come up with good ideas for songs. I thought they were gonna be another McCartney-Lennon." By 1965, they had established themselves among the North American underground as musical thoroughbreds. Word reached Bob Dylan, then undergoing a career mutation, that this was the band he needed to take his music to a new level. And the rest, as they say, is history.

The Band toured the world with Dylan, enduring the catcalls and jeers from audiences resistant to his new electric sound. They stayed with him at a sprawling property in Woodstock called Big Pink, where they would jam joyously and endlessly in the basement. And they stood sentinel behind him at his legendary comeback show at the Isle of Wight in September 1969 before an audience of thousands that included three Beatles.

Making their own albums was a natural, evolutionary step. Released in 1968, *Music from Big Pink* sent a fission-reaction through the music industry as did the follow-up, called simply *The Band*, both of them giving rise to a new genre of roots-driven music feted by such industry heavyweights as George Harrison and Eric Clapton, who disbanded Cream the minute he heard this game-changing new music seeping out from Upstate New York.

Part of their appeal also lay in the mystique that grew around them, incubating their songs in the town that had nestled in the foot of the Catskills. Interviews were kept to a minimum, and album sleeves showed them to look more like a group of Amish than the influential rock 'n' roll band they would become. By the time the sixties morphed into 1970, The Band was America's best-known secret, appearing in caricature on the front of *Time Magazine* and lauded for pioneering a new path for rock music.

Unknown to everyone, however, the group's comet, like their collective spirit, was already burning out. Manuel's songwriting muse deserted him as he sought to numb the pressures of fame with Grand Marnier and cocaine; Danko and Helm were also mired in drugs, having graduated from grass to smack as part of an openly narcotized life. Robertson, by now married with a child, was no stranger to the likes of marijuana but bristled at the thought of heroin—and was swift to recognize its destructive impact on his bandmates and their work in the studio and on stage. More and more, he saw himself as the only adult in the room.

"On some nights we could hit our stride, but more and more it was becoming a painful chore," he recalled. "The best painkiller is opiates, and heroin had been creeping back under the door. I worried that Garth and I had three junkies in our group."

Fearful that the group was spiraling out of control, Robertson felt compelled to confront the issue head on with Helm as he drove him home one night from a studio session. The discussion, well meant, quickly descended into a bitter shouting match between two men for whom the bonds of friendship were already splintering. Robertson recalled the conversation in his book *Testimony*.

"On the way, I said how horrible it was watching Rich, Rick, and him on this drug binge. I confessed how helpless I felt in the midst of this monster. 'It's destroying us. It's tearing our band apart. You are my brother, my best friend and I can't stand watching this happen.'"

In Robertson's account, Helm, stung by the claims, went ballistic and launched into a ten-minute rant. "What do you think? I'm strung out? I wouldn't do that shit. I'd tell you if I was sick, you know that. I got it under control. You don't need to worry about me. You wanna see my arms? You wanna check for needle marks? Here, let me show you? Look, clean. I did a little skin popping a while back, but I'm cool now."

To Robertson's ears, it was classic junkie denial. Echoing the words of his fellow Canadian Neil Young, he had indeed seen the needle and the damage done. More importantly, however, he viewed this heated exchange as the real moment their friendship took a major downturn.

"We had never lied to each other," he wrote. "Things changed in that moment. A distance grew between Levon and me that I don't know we were able to mend. It wasn't about the drugs; whatever he wanted to do, that was his business. It was about the betrayal. About disrespecting the brotherhood and our partnership."

Robertson's premonitions proved achingly accurate. Over the next few years, the quality of The Band's output deteriorated and album sales dwindled. By the time the seventies had passed the halfway mark, punk rock was already on the rise on both sides of the Atlantic—a wind of change that would blow the old rock gods away. And Robertson, for one, had no intention of being caught in the downdraft. Weighing heavily on his mind was a quick-burning realization—that The Band's run was indeed over. And, in truth, he was fed up shouldering much of the musical burden not to mention keeping an eye on the bottom line.

Not even a reunion with Dylan in 1974 for an album and tour was enough to stifle his view, long formed, that they were running out of cards.

Enter stage left, then, Robbie's idea for *The Last Waltz*, a full stop to their days as a touring band, an appropriate moment to bring the curtain down. The whole thing quickly took on a life of its own. The Band would play their own set at Winterland before then acting as the backing group to a stellar lineup of musicians who had either influenced them or given them a helping hand on the road from clapped-out clubs to sold-out stadiums.

Martin Scorcese, then filming *New York* with Robert De Niro and Liza Minnelli, was hauled on board to turn it into a cinematic spectacular, the greatest concert of all time. And it would take place at the San Francisco hall that was the venue for their first live show as "The Band" back in 1969, a logical choice for a group that had come full circle. Robertson has always insisted the agreement was only to put The Band into temporary cold storage—not disband it for all time—only until such times as batteries were recharged or individuals cleaned up. And it was a group choice, not just one taken to satisfy the whims of one.

Robertson said,

> This was five men making a decision. It wasn't just my decision. Whatever happened happened because of every one of us. The idea of *The Last Waltz* was that everybody was going to take a break and gather themselves. We were going to refocus and then come back and do some great, creative work together. Everybody went off and did some individual projects, shuffled the deck and nobody came back. And at some point you just have to see the writing on the wall.

According to Robertson, even Helm agreed to a timeout. But when the cold water of reality splashed across his face, it was a sobering prospect. Seething, Helm suddenly saw the flow of dollars from The Band's pipeline being choked off. A pipeline that had for seven years bought him the best cars, the best women, the best booze, and the best dope—not to mention the private Beecher jet, paid for by their record company that flew them to and from long-distance gigs. In a flash, he was now the drummer and main singer in a group without a record deal, a road band without a road, a group without its principal writer and seemingly without a future. Gripped by panic and fear of the unknown, he lashed out at Robertson, blaming him for the tap to the good life being suddenly turned off and leaving them to soldier on in the face of declining audiences.

And when he even suggested that the remaining four could continue as The Band and leave Robertson by the side of the road, he was allegedly met with an implied threat of legal action. The meeting, held in the buildup to *The Last Waltz*, broke up in bitter anger and division—and not for the first time. Helm recalled his own incendiary account of the discussion in his own memoir, *This Wheel's on Fire*.

> I didn't want to break up The Band, and I told this to Robbie one day at our lawyer's office. It was one of many acrimonious meetings. "You could stop it," I said. "I know big business is running this thing now, but if you think you have control over my life, I'll meet you back here in the morning with my lawyer and we'll see who has control. We'll go over the goddamn contracts and see who ends up running the show because I'll fight you tooth and nail just to feel better about it." He didn't say anything. I walked out.

Between Rick, Levon, Richard, and Garth, the overriding suspicion was that Robbie had been seduced by Tinseltown. His growing friendship with Scorcese, then part of Hollywood's new wave of hotshot young directors, had given him an entrée into the film capital of the world.

All of a sudden he was mingling with Minnelli and dining with De Niro. But all it did was to isolate him further from the group politic. The Band's endearing absence of showbiz glitz ensured they had always steered clear of the rock 'n' roll celebrity circus—until now. When the end credits rolled on *The Last Waltz*, Robbie's name was up in lights as the film's producer. An acknowledgment that guaranteed him more recognition, leaving Levon, Rick, Richard, and Garth accepting the per diem reward for simply playing the gig.

Barney Hoskyns recognizes the paradigm shift that had taken place.

> Robbie just arrived at the point where he'd had enough, and I have some sympathy with that. The problem is how Robbie used *The Last Waltz* in a Machiavellian way. I think it was a play for the big time. He was auditioning for the LA music business and Hollywood. It was a way to turn The Band's

farewell into a launch pad for the next stage of his life. He was ambitious and there is nothing wrong with that. The other thing is that Robbie wasn't a junkie. He was kind of the grown up in a way that the others weren't. Robbie was the guy who went to work while the others, Garth excepted, were sleeping off their hangovers.

This just wasn't his vision for what a group should be. But at this point Levon started to become pretty hostile. There is real acrimony there, real suspicion. *The Last Waltz* was a brilliant swan song. But what we don't see is that these guys had fallen out of love with each other.

Resentment toward Robertson—and Scorcese—was not slow in arriving. A renowned straight-talker, Helm led the charge, accusing the group's lead guitarist, with Scorcese's guiding hand, of shaping the film's narrative so the spotlight shone directly on him while reducing the rest of the band, each of them a critical contributor to the group, to mere bit-part players in their own farewell.

Richard Manuel was barely seen except for his star turn on "The Shape I'm In." It was, insisted Helm, nothing more than a vanity project for Robertson, who craved the kind of intellectual credibility on offer with Hollywood's elite.

He said, *"The Last Waltz* was the biggest fucking rip-off that ever happened to The Band. People always used to tell me how they loved *The Last Waltz*. I try to thank them politely and usually refrain from mentioning that for me it was a real scandal." Time did nothing to mellow his views. It wasn't until the gun smoke eventually cleared that the full extent of the discord within The Band became clear. Songs such as "Dixie," "The Weight," and "Up on Cripple Creek" remained staples on American AM radio. But every new listen only served to inflame Helm's smoldering sense of injustice over the publishing royalties he earnestly thought should have been split five ways. So it was no surprise that he hung out the dirty linen for all to see, and continually picked at an old scab. His rancor showed no sign of ever abating—and it didn't.

In later life, having endured three bankruptcies, nearly every sentence about his illustrious past was laced with venom. He frequently told interviewers, "If you got a lawyer that can sue the motherfuckers—I ain't got that money myself—and knows how to sue them, you tell him I'll split it with him." Again, it shouldn't have ended this way, in a slew of profanities. Hoskyns takes a more balanced view of the bad blood that hemorrhaged from the end of *The Last Waltz*. History, he reckons, could not fail to take account of the fact that Robbie's sheer musical ambition was the vital ingredient that had allowed The Band to make "The Big Step Forward."

In a sense Robbie was always up on another level. If he hadn't been, The Band would never have made the extraordinary music they did. Without Robbie's insatiable need for artistic credibility, they might have been content with exactly the kind of good-time, beer-drinking, country rhythm and blues they ended up purveying without him.

But without them, Robbie Robertson might have been nothing more than a pretentious, frustrated singer-songwriter. It was Levon and Rick who rooted him, Garth and Richard who gave his songs flesh and blood. This is what made The Band a band.

After *The Last Waltz*, each individual band member faded into the mist. Robertson began a lengthy musical sabbatical to patch up his marriage and reboot his life. Scorcese remained his patron, with Robertson providing memorable musical scores to "Marty" productions such as *Raging Bull*, *The King of Comedy*, and *The Color of Money*.

Otherwise, though, Robertson remained enigmatic and largely stayed under the radar. Incredibly, a decade would pass before he released his first proper solo album, ten years in which he kicked back and reconnected with real life. It was easy to shun the trappings of an old life in the knowledge that every year a shedload of dollars were flowing into his bank account—his reward for having written some of The Band's best-known tracks.

Garth Hudson, in many ways The Band's musical avatar, chose obscurity, joining in on sessions for the likes of Elton John, Leonard Cohen, the Gypsy Kings, and Tom Petty. Levon Helm discovered a hitherto undiscovered acting gene, turning in a highly acclaimed performance in the 1980 film *The Coalminer's Daughter*, Hollywood's take on the career of country star Loretta Lynn, while at the same time trying to keep alive the flickering embers of his musical career.

Rick Danko often teamed up for gigs with Helm in a bid to rekindle the old band spirit. Richard Manuel, unable to beat old, habitual demons, tragically continued his slow march toward an early grave. In 1983, they took the dollar bait and reformed as The Band, fleshing out their lineup with several other musicians.

Missing, of course, was the one man who bestowed on them that unmistakable sense of star power. Robbie Robertson gave them his blessing but by then had no intention of becoming part of an ageing heritage act, cranking out nostalgic versions of "The Weight" or "Chest Fever" night after night in small-town dives just a decade after they had played to festivals and toured with Dylan. It felt like such a comedown.

Yet it was the only life they had ever known. And for Levon, Rick, and Richard, especially, climbing back aboard the rock 'n' roll bandwagon was simply a matter of financial urgency. They did not have someone like Scorcese in their corner.

Sadly, for Richard and Rick, the song remained the same. Offstage, the cost of living became the cost of dying. On March 4, 1986, Manuel drank several bottles of brandy before hanging himself from a shower curtain rod after they had played the Cheek to Cheek Lounge in Florida, the venue's name itself a stark illustration of how far their star had fallen.

Rick Danko's death in 1999 was partly caused by years of personal debasement through cocaine and booze—another victim of self-abuse and self-neglect. As true as this was, Helm also saw two friends forced to eke out a meager existence as waning rock stars before dying young, having been, in his eyes, bilked out of millions by a former bandmate.

Years earlier, Rick and Richard had both sold out their publishing to Robbie to keep their decadent lifestyles afloat. While Levon raged over publishing royalties, however, Rick, humble and altruistic, took a different view. "I don't have a problem with any of it, you know? I'm a very thankful person. Whatever publishing I've shared with people, whatever songwriting credits I've shared, and whatever payments I've gotten, I'm thankful. I could have ended up having to get a real job. I'm thankful for what The Band has represented and what The Band has done. I'm not gonna sit here and tear The Band apart."

Their deaths, however, took Levon's sense of outrage to a new level. Placing Robbie and Albert Grossman, who died in 1986, two months before Manuel, directly in his crosshairs, he kept delivering verbal salvos at familiar targets: "If Rick's money wasn't in their pockets, I don't think he would have died because Rick worked himself to death. And the reason Rick had to work all the time was because he was fucked out of his money."

By the turn of the millennium, an increasingly embittered Helm was himself already far down the same impecunious path. He had been made bankrupt several times and was constantly having to fend off fresh demands from the U.S. taxman.

But rather than examine his own frailties, he repeatedly trained his ire on an old foe. In 1994, The Band were inducted into the Rock & Roll Hall of Fame, with superfan Eric Clapton doing the honors. Garth, Rick, and Robbie accepted the recognition while also paying tribute to the dearly departed Richard.

Helm refused to touch the event with the proverbial drumstick, unable to contemplate being in the room with Robertson for even a second. In the acceptance speeches, only Robbie name-checked the elephant in the room. He told the audience in Cleveland, "I'm convinced now, as I was then, that nobody could sing and play the songs that I wrote with as much belief and soulfulness as they did."

Later the same year, Helm got his revenge. He published *This Wheel's on Fire*, a vastly entertaining read that mapped his journey from Arkansas to Woodstock, from Ronnie Hawkins to Bob Dylan, and from rags to riches to rage. But it also provided him with a platform to settle old scores with Robbie, while opening a window into a tortured soul.

Hoskyns reckons the court of public opinion long delivered its verdict on the uncivil war that went on for decades. And he makes it clear which camp he's in.

> You see it in *The Last Waltz*. Robbie is so pretentious and self-regarding. Levon is so much more charismatic. There was something calculating about Robbie. It was as if he was taking their talent and shaping them into something that made sense to him.
>
> Was that exploitation? Possibly. Robbie just became Mr. Santa Monica and left behind all trace of his musical journey. I can't argue with the magic of the songs that he wrote or cowrote. I think they were uniquely poetic and soulful. But I don't know what happened to that guy.
>
> I think he is someone who believed his own hype. But the counterpoint is you take these guys away from Robbie, and they just regress to being bar band guys singing old Louis Jordan songs. You have to bring these five guys together for extraordinary things to happen and obviously you can't do that any more.

Pained by grievances undimmed by the passage of time, Robertson still couldn't believe one man could carry so much hate for so long. He was loath, however, to douse the flames with gas, preferring instead to believe his connection to Helm at a subatomic level was "untouchable." "He was my dearest friend. He was one of the most musical people I ever encountered. But there was an anger and bitterness growing inside him, like some strange demon. I did my best to try to say to him, 'Levon, this is eating you up, this is no good, man.'"

The time for overtures ended when Helm died from throat cancer in April 2012. Days before he passed, Robertson visited him at his bedside one final time, knowing his former friend's time was short. It was, however, a one-sided rapprochement as Helm lay unconscious the whole time. "I am so grateful I got to see him one last time," Robertson said, "and I will miss him and love him forever."

Helm was buried at Woodstock Cemetery within a stone's throw of Rick Danko. And then there were two, the reclusive Garth Hudson and Robbie Robertson, a man blessed with extraordinary powers of recall.

These were employed to the full in *Testimony*, which walked back the first act of his career, ending curiously when the curtain closed at *The Last Waltz*. In contrast to Helm, he offered a more measured account of their differences while celebrating their unique friendship in those early, rose-tinged days.

The book provided the template for the 2019 film called *Once Were Brothers*, a confessional, cautionary, and occasionally humorous stroll through the lives of one of the most critical groups in the history of music. Inevitably, revisionism mingled with reality and occasionally stood adjacent to another man's truth.

Still, though, the often-grainy footage served as a potent reminder of The Band at their imperious and collaborative best. In 1975, writer Greil Marcus described them in *Mystery Train: Images of America in Rock and Roll* as "committed to the very idea of America: complicated, dangerous, and alive. Their music gave us a sure sense that the country was richer than we had guessed; that it has possibilities we were only beginning to perceive."

Not even years of dissension between Robbie and Levon could alter that. A point made fully by the group's lead guitarist in the film: "All these spark plugs needed to be ignited . . . or it didn't work. We wanted to create something you had nothing to compare to."

The Kinks: Ray Davies, Dave Davies, Pete Quaife, and Mick Avory
Photofest

⑯

THE KINKS

Inside the Clissold Arms, a quaint, old English pub straddling the district boundary between London's Muswell Hill and East Finchley, the fiftieth birthday celebrations were in full swing. Nostalgia and memory were naturally the ties that bound so many of the lives among those present.

They were especially important to Dave, the man enjoying the landmark occasion, and his older brother Ray, who had put up the money for the bash. Growing up, this was their father's local. And it was the venue at which they had taken their first teenage steps together on rock 'n' roll's highway with a fledgling band in the early 1960s. The symbolism was inescapable.

Halfway through the evening, a cake was trundled out and Ray delivered a heartfelt speech. The fact that the monologue was mainly about himself surprised no one in the room. Then, without any fanfare, Ray adroitly planted his foot in the middle of his brother's cake, scattering pieces of icing-topped crumbs in every direction.

It was, without doubt, a jaw-dropping moment. But in many ways, it was just another day in the lives of Ray and Dave Davies, the creative gene pool behind the Kinks, siblings locked forever in a Romulus and Remus cycle of love-hate and mutual debasement, a tragi-comic soap opera peppered with tales of drunkenness and cruelty.

Only this time it was different. This time there would be no fraternal forgive and forget—and no reunion of the band whose influence has trickled down through six decades, pollinating through a form of musical photosynthesis the seeds of punk rock, Britpop, and primordial heavy metal, and creating a timeless musical diaspora. "I think he probably paid for the cake," recalled Dave, "but that was Ray all over. He'd want me to have something like that—but then he couldn't bear to see me with it."

The incident, however, just a few months after their final gig as the Kinks in 1996, was in many ways the ultimate fork in the road for this most infuriating of bands. Dave said, "You've heard of vampires. Well, Ray sucks me dry of ideas, emotions, and creativity. It's toxic for me to be with him. He's a control freak. . . . I think the music is so beautiful it shouldn't be tainted. It would be a shame. You don't need to see silly old men in wheelchairs singing 'You Really Got Me.'"

The dichotomy of their sibling rivalry is not lost on Ray, the elder of the two by three years. A self-confessed loner, this is after all the man who admitted in his most famous song that "I don't need no friends . . . as long as I gaze on Waterloo sunset, I am in paradise."

More introverted but driven by an unbending competitive drive, Ray—the architect of their biggest hits—is painfully aware of the toll their career has taken on family ties. "Dave has his problems with me sometimes, but that's inevitable," admitted Ray. "I'm not an easy person to work with."

Internecine warfare is, of course, a routine by-product of rock 'n' roll. Cloistered inside a combustible bubble, conflicts inevitably erupt; the claustrophobia of touring, arguments over musical direction, petty jealousies over the limelight, the lead guitarist's solos are too self-indulgent, and the endless knockdowns over who's getting paid what.

But the brawling Davies brothers often took those familiar components to a poisonous level within the Kinks, a group that easily sits in the upper echelons of rock alongside the Beatles, the Stones, Led Zeppelin, and the Who. Their status runs counter to those early jibes that dismissed them as just another cheap coin in the Merseybeat-appropriated juke box.

Yet it is a relationship that has, nevertheless, endured in the face of onstage estrangement, bouts of alienation, drug overdoses, mental illness, a shooting in New Orleans, and in the case of Dave, a life-altering stroke.

And it wasn't above moments of self-mockery. Ray's tongue-in-cheek song "Hatred" effortlessly captured their malign relationship. In the case of the Kinks, traumas, tantrums, and tears before bedtime have underpinned Los Bros Davies during a lifetime of internecine volatility.

It's an enduring saga of defeat grimly snatched from the jaws of seemingly inevitable victory, two men unable to iron out the kinks of their own muddled pathology. Yet it was often countered by an innate sense of brotherly love that was posted missing from the schadenfreude that often enveloped the Everly Brothers or the Gallaghers.

One moment Dave would describe Ray as "a vain, egotistical arsehole," but just as quickly he could profess profound genuine respect and affection, saying, "How could I not love my own brother? I just can't stand to be with him." One writer summed up the differences in their personalities thus: "Dave has always played the kid brother, his joie de vivre and cheerily high speaking voice in stark contrast to Ray's brooding, penny-pinching cynicism."

When Dave, at fifty-seven, suffered a near-fatal stroke in 2004, Ray insisted he recover at his own house in London. An olive branch that lasted only a few weeks before they fell out, would you believe, over pasta, and Dave hit the road. Dave was cynical about the reasons for his brother's attentiveness in the first place. "I'm undecided whether he was pleased I was ill or jealous because I was getting all the attention. I stayed at his house afterwards. I was ill in bed and could barely move, but he started saying, 'I'm sick, I'm sick.' He was screaming in pain from his stomach. A doctor from Harley Street came around at 3 a.m. and said, 'There's nothing wrong with your stomach.' He just wanted attention."

Other members of the band were also left jumping through hoops to avoid being caught in the crossfire when the verbal bullets started flying.

Pete Quaife, the group's original bass player and a school friend of both brothers, often had a ringside seat when the bell rang to signal another round of infighting. "You could feel early on that there was a lot of animosity between them," he recalled. "Ray felt he had to be better than Dave, and Dave felt he had to be better than Ray. You could put them together for two minutes and then it would be a case of 'ring 911 . . . ambulance.' They could start a fight over absolutely nothing."

They couldn't even find common ground on the chainsaw guitar riff that defined their 1964 breakthrough hit "All Day and All of the Night." Dave insisted that the distorted intro happened by accident after he took a razor blade to his 10-watt Elpico amp in a bout of adolescent frustration; Ray later attempted to take ownership of the iconic moment by claiming he stuck a knitting needle in the amp to achieve that unique sound.

> That came about because at home, we had a record player the family played records on. Dave and I played records so loud, it made the speakers distort. And we thought it would be a nice idea to make the guitar sound that distorted. And we cranked up the amplifier. And I stuck a knitting needle in it. And I think legend has it that Dave tried it with a razor blade, although I wasn't present.

Of course, another person was present and insists his recollection is correct. "The only person who was there when I did it was me, so who would know better?" said Dave. "I just wanted to torture my amplifier. It kept giving me the same sound."

Barely out of their teens—Ray was twenty—neither man was arguably mature enough to be considered an adult in the room. John Gosling, who joined the Kinks in 1970 to add keyboard textures, quickly learned the danger of favoring one brother over the other. He said, "You had to be careful not to take sides. Anything could set Ray and Dave against each other. And you had to be careful about what you said a lot of the time."

Studio staff also learned to pick up on the signals for when it was time for a less-than-subtle exit. Shel Talmy, the pioneering record producer who was a key figure in the early Kinks sound, was another who discovered neutrality was essential to keeping the band on track. "There was always tension between Ray and Dave," he says, "and Pete would be the arbiter from time to time. In fact, if things got too heavy-duty when we were recording—which did happen very occasionally—I would just call a fifteen-minute coffee break and let them fight it out."

Yet it was this abrasive edge that made the Kinks, the decade's great underdog band, rebels with a cause. Sanitized by their manager Brian Epstein, Lennon and McCartney, wanted to hold your hand. And the Stones, still in suits, were happy to buy into rebellion as a media invention. But for the Davies brothers, nonconformity wasn't an act; it was a pushback rooted in the gritty reality of their family's proud working-class roots.

The lineage of the Kinks can be found in Muswell Hill, just a stone's throw away from the Clissold Arms. Ray was the seventh child of Fred and Annie Davies—and their first boy. Pampered by all his sisters, Ray was the golden child—until the arrival three years later of the brother with whom he was destined to chafe for large chunks of his life.

"I think Ray was only happy for the first three years of his life," mocked Dave. "Then he realized there was another boy in the house." With the family living in a cramped house, Ray was shipped off to live with his sister Rosie in the country, and for several years he thought she was his mum.

Dave, meantime, was folded inside his true mother's tender embrace. By the time the brothers were reunited under the same family roof, blood ties mingled with confusion, suspicion, mistrust, and a shared love neither of them could ever quite fathom out. This was borne out by a childhood incident where a playful fight turned into something more combative.

Picking up a pair of boxing gloves left round the house by an uncle, the pair were soon pounding lumps out of each other until things got out of hand. Swinging wildly, Dave hit Ray, knocking him off balance. As Ray stumbled to the floor, he grazed his head against the family piano and lay still, seemingly unconscious. Hovering close to his face, Dave whispered, "Are you OK?" Ray bolted upright and punched his brother hard in the face.

"It's symbolic of our whole relationship, really," Dave maintains. "I felt the pleasure that I'd knocked him over, then concern that I'd hurt him.

But all he really wanted was to get back at me." Arguably, that formative episode created the template for their future, mercurial selves. Enmity may have been lurking at the family gate, but the two boys did find common ground in the vanguard of rock 'n' roll as they entered their teenage years.

Ray, especially, was transfixed by the music of American bluesmen like Big Bill Broonzy and Muddy Waters. By the early 1960s, both boys were already channeling their occasional antipathy toward each other by pooling their developing musical smarts in a band. Despite his youth, Dave was already displaying a precocious talent on the guitar.

And Ray was discovering a way to marry his Byron-like passion for words with his family's love for British vaudeville. The first proper iteration of the Kinks saw drummer Mick Avory join the Davies brothers and Quaife to create the band's quintessential lineup. With record companies clamoring to discover the next Fab Four, they were signed by Grenville Collins and Robert Wace, who quickly secured the group a deal with Pye records.

Within months, the success of "You Really Got Me" and "All Day and All of the Night" saw the Kinks ride the surf of the new wave of British bands taking the world by storm. Among the millions joining in this new communion was fourteen-year-old Bill Morton, himself an aspirational musician who instantly recognized the sea change taking place within the music industry. It was the start of a lifetime's affiliation with the Kinks that later saw him becoming president of their UK fan club.

He told me,

> Despite my young age, I could recognize a great melody, and a great band performance on the record, I was also a budding songwriter and was really impressed that the same person had written both sides of the record, as opposed to other discs of the day by such as the Monkees, Manfred Mann, Tremeloes, etc.
>
> I knew nothing of the band's history up to that point, and was mainly aware of the Beatles, Stones, Dave Clark Five, etc. I must admit to being initially confused when "Death of a Clown" by Dave Davies came out but gradually picked up on the *Well Respected Kinks*, and later in the year *Something Else by the Kinks* LPs and then learned something of the band's chart history from a Life Lines article in the *NME*.
>
> It seems unreal now but back in the day, you could only buy a limited back catalog as most discs were deleted after a few months, so it really was the whole package, song writing, band performance, and diversity of material.

British filmmaker Julien Temple also recalled the visceral impact the Kinks had on a mainly male audience looking for an identity. He wrote in the *Guardian*,

> I first heard the Kinks at the age of eleven—listening to Radio Caroline on a crystal radio set beneath my bedclothes. It was August 1964, and the rabid-dog

riffs of 'You Really Got Me' came crackling through my tiny earpiece, blowing my world apart like a dirty bomb.

Those distorted guitar chords went on to rearrange the sonic architecture of the 1960s—but Ray Davies' lyrics also heralded something new and profound. In contrast to the saccharine Mersey sound, Davies sang of obsessive teenage love, teetering on madness. It seemed a more honest, rebellious way of understanding the world: you didn't have to unquestioningly accept what your school and parents were teaching—or omitting to teach—you.

You could read between the lines of those great, raucous singles and discover your own way of looking at things. Prefiguring punk, the songs seemed to belong as much to the listener as to the band. Unlike the other groups who emerged from the R&B boom, like the Rolling Stones, the Kinks had in one stroke made U.S. music their own, reinventing it as north London blues.

Indeed, London was the swinging capital of the world and the Kinks had tapped perfectly into the zeitgeist. Onstage, the band cultivated a Victorian look, wearing ruffled shirts and dandy-esque jackets, images that railed against those dedicated followers of fashions who opted to mimic the Beatles' collarless jackets or Nehru suits.

But it was in their own evolving sound that the Kinks would triumph. Quaife and Avory were more than just subsidiary players, but the real lifeblood of the Kinks came from Ray's songs and Dave's guttural lead guitar. By the halfway point in the decade, their contemporaries were swapping pop for psychedelia and heavy rock. Swimming against the tide, Ray Davies went into full-blown Byron mode with songs of charm, mannerliness, and satire such as "Well Respected Man"; "Dedicated Follower of Fashion"—a cynical thrust at Carnaby Street couture; "Dead End Street," and the peerless "Waterloo Sunset."

Each song seen through the viewfinder of a working-class man mocking the bowler-hatted orthodoxy of the era's old guard with genteel but poison-tipped barbs. Nearly all Ray's songs during this period—a deliberate move away from the riff-heavy sound of their first two hits—revealed an eccentric yearning for the loss of the green and pleasant land that was postwar England.

They were harbingers of the groundbreaking concept albums that saw the Kinks continue to willfully go against the grain of popular trends as the swinging sixties mutated into the cynical seventies. *The Kinks Are the Village Preservation Society*, a remarkable record that extolled the countryside of William Blake, was released in the same week—November 1968—as *The Beatles*, the eponymous double album which ran the full gamut of Western music from pop, folk, and heavy blues.

Known forever as the White album, it shifted 2 million copies worldwide in its first week; *Village Preservation Society* sold 25,000. Undaunted, however, Ray Davies continued to adhere to his vision for the Kinks—and damn the torpedoes for the rest of the world. One of the few times he allowed people to see beyond the characters he created was in the biographical "I'm Not Like Everybody Else," the B side to "Waterloo Sunset" and a coupling that easily rivaled the Fabs' double A side of "Penny Lane" and "Strawberry Fields Forever" as one of the best singles ever made. Fame and success are, however, capricious companions.

In 1964, Ray had married a Lithuanian immigrant called Rasa Didzpetris, and they already had a daughter. But he found it hard to balance his obligations to the band with his responsibilities as a husband and father. By 1966 he was on the brink of a breakdown brought on by sheer exhaustion, touring fatigue, the burden of being the band's principal songwriter and front man, and an as-yet-undiagnosed bipolar disorder. Running parallel with these was a tragic childhood scar, which would never heal.

On the eve of his thirteenth birthday, his sister Rene presented him with his first guitar. Hours later she died from a heart attack in the arms of a stranger in a local dance hall. It was a ghastly twist of fate, one referred to in the band's 1980s surprise hit "Come Dancing." Contrast that with his teenage brother's headlong pursuit of sex, drugs, and rock 'n' roll.

In 1967, his third year of Kinks hits and hedonism, Dave was still only twenty years old and already suffering the early pangs of inner conflict, unable to find a work-life balance. To general surprise, not least his own, he would turn his disillusionment into his debut solo single, "Death of a Clown," and watch it follow "Waterloo Sunset" into the upper reaches of the UK singles chart.

Feted for his instrumental ingenuity, it was his first real moment in the spotlight as the band's singer. But when sibling relations entered Ice Station Zebra, the song became a blunt instrument to be wielded like a stiletto by Ray. Employing a gift for sarcasm, he often introduced Ray onstage as Mr. Dave "Death of a Clown" Davies, mocking him like some sad, one-hit wonder.

"That used to be really upsetting," Dave complained. "Something that was a big event for me, and a shedding of a lot of things in my life, had become an instrument of ridicule. It got to the point where I didn't want to play it." Other times, he would introduce Dave as "the little twerp."

Reckless and unpredictable, Dave was, nevertheless, the epitome of excess in all areas. And his unbridled behavior inflamed tensions, not just with Ray but also other members of the band, most notably Mick Avory. Bad blood flowed easily between the two men. A trickle at first and then a torrent. Mick could put up with Ray's mood swings, but Dave's constant sniping about his drumming was an entirely different matter.

Matters came to a tempestuous head during an incident that has become part of Kinks folklore. Just two numbers into their set at the Capital Theatre in Cardiff in 1965, Dave reputedly goaded the good-natured Avory to the precipice of fury by saying, "Why don't you get your cock out and play the snare with it? It'll probably sound better." Incensed, Avory hurled a drum pedal at Dave—some witnesses wrongly claimed it was a cymbal—an act that laid his bandmate out cold, causing chaos on the stage and in the theater.

Panic stricken, Ray was first to react, cradling his brother's bleeding head in his hands while fearing he was actually dead. Avory said, "We had a row the night before, and they kept us apart. When Dave counted the second number in, he proceeded to kick my drum kit stage right, and there was only the hi-hat left.

"I picked the hi-hat up and whacked him with the pedal end, but it was a rubber pedal, an old Premier thing. But it hurt him and that was the end of the show, and the tour actually. It was all over stupid stuff 'cause Dave would go over the top about everything. He was an extremist and had a healthy temper on him." In the chaos that followed, an unconscious Dave was rushed to Cardiff Royal Infirmary to receive sixteen stitches, while Avory fled the venue and into the night—convinced that he had, indeed, killed his bandmate.

One of their first managers, Larry Page, learned about the incident in a 3 a.m. phone call. "I was told that basically the police were hunting Mick Avory down for attempted murder," he said.

Looking back at these events years later, Ray said, "We were just kids, don't forget—Dave and Mick were just seventeen and nineteen back then and forever having a go. I just guess that on that evening Mick decided to do something about it, and that meant cutting my brother's head off. That could have been the end of the Kinks right there. It had a tremendous emotional effect on me.

"The police wanted to do Mick for attempted murder. Britain's *News at Ten* even interviewed him later on that night from a secret location," added Ray, who admitted to carrying on playing "for a few beats" oblivious to what was going on behind him. "When they finally caught up with and arrested him, Mick tried to deny it all. But the cops turned round and said, 'Mr. Avory, we've got five thousand witnesses!'"

Dave did eventually drop all charges in the interest of keeping the band together. Down through the decades, however, plenty of similar incidents followed. While the tug-of-war between Ray and Dave was mainly personal, differences with Avory were mainly musical. And time did nothing to blunt their knife-edge hostility toward each other. More than a decade later, they were again embroiled in a highly publicized onstage fight that ensured newspapers could dust down stories of the Kinks in chaos. *Washington Post* reporter Larry Rohter was among those stunned at the city's Constitution Hall as the guitarist and the drummer came to blows amid shameful scenes.

The Kinks were hardly a verse into their third encore when the fight began. Dave Davies walked over to Mick Avory and began to poke at the cymbals. Avory glowered at Davies; Davies glowered back. Ray Davies came over and led his kid brother away from trouble, but a minute later Dave was at it again. At the end of his guitar solo, standing directly in front of the drummer, he launched a gob of spit that hit Avory right in the face.

Avory spat back, and Davies retreated to the other side of the stage, where with the sweep of his arm he knocked over the microphone stand at Avory's side. That did it. Avory stood up, threw his drumsticks at Dave Davies and stormed off the stage. The rest of the band hesitated, the beat lost, so Ray turned around noticing for the first time that Avory was gone.

"I've had it with these boys," he calmly told the crowd. Everyone left the stage—except for Dave Davies, who mounted the platform where Avory's drum kit was sitting and assumed the stance of a football punter. With one swing of his leg, he booted the entire drum kit off the platform; with another he devastated the remaining microphone stands.

The fracas continued offstage, with the two men trading insults in the dressing room. Tour manager Ken Jones blamed it on the band going stir crazy, a situation brought on by the pressures of being on the road. He said, "We've had a bad day, Dave had a little too much to drink. I wouldn't want you to think that this kind of thing happens all the time, because it doesn't."

History, however, frequently told a different story. The band's first tour of America in 1966 ended in chaos when the powerful musicians union banned them from the country for four years. The suspension followed numerous clashes between the Davies brothers and promoters at every hick town they played. The tour's low light occurred in Los Angeles on July 2. The Kinks were backstage for a taping of *Where the Action Is*, Dick Clark's afternoon TV show.

"Some guy who said he worked for the TV company walked up and accused us of being late," Ray Davies wrote in his autobiography *X-Ray*.

Then he started making anti-British comments. Things like "Just because the Beatles did it, every mop-topped, spotty-faced limey juvenile thinks he can come over here and make a career for himself. You're just a bunch of Commie wimps. When the Russians take over Britain, don't expect us to come over and save you this time. The Kinks, huh? Well, once I file my report on you guys, you'll never work in the U.S.A. again. You're gonna find out just how powerful America is, you limey bastard!" The rest is a blur. However, I do recall being pushed and swinging a punch and being punched back.

"The band was in disarray," Avory recalled. "Everything was going pear-shaped. We shouldn't have actually gone."

On the tour bus and on planes, it fell to Larry Page to keep the warring band members apart. "We had to have two up the front and two at the back. It was war out there. To be honest, Ray was manipulating Dave and trying to destroy him."

The suspension inflicted an almost fatal wound on the Kinks since it came at the peak of their commercial powers. By the time the group was allowed to return to the United States in 1969, the Woodstock generation had arrived and the Kinks were almost forgotten. It was only through lashing themselves even more to the album-tour-album treadmill that they enjoyed a second coming in America.

And it was stateside that they finally found their audience and, temporarily, a new frontier. The 1970 single release of "Lola," a Ray story about a transvestite that was full of risqué allusions, cemented the band's comeback and, for a while, offered a veneer of commercial success. Risk, however, failed to bring reward. Ray continued to steer the Kinks down the road of concept albums embroidered with thematic vignettes, mining a strain of Englishness like no other songwriter. But records such as *Arthur (Or the Decline and Fall of the British Empire)* and *Preservation Act 1* and *2* failed to reignite their midsixties appeal.

Waning popularity, high costs, dwindling finances, and the ongoing discord between Ray and Dave ensured a tipping point was inevitable. It came in July 1973 during a shambolic appearance at London's White City stadium. Before the gig even started, alarm bells over Ray's state of mind were ringing. He had been taking uppers mixed with copious amounts of alcohol.

Press secretary Marion Rainford recalled at the time, "Ray never drinks. When he does it's not a good sign." *Melody Maker* writer Ray Hollingsworth recalled Rainford muttering, "Christ, he's in a dreadful state."

Ray, drained and haggard with matted hair, and toked out on pills and booze, looked like he was on the edge of collapse. As the chords to "All Day and All of the Night" drifted across the slate-gray skies, Ray, balancing a can of beer on his head, walked up to Dave, planted a kiss on his cheek and announced to the crowd he was quitting. "I'm sick up to here with it." John Dalton could feel his jaw slacken. "We had no idea this was coming. It was a very depressing experience."

Hours later, still dressed in his sweat-stained and garish stage clothes, Ray walked into a hospital and delivered a melodramatic announcement to reception staff: "My name is Ray Davies. I'm the lead singer with the Kinks . . . and I'm dying."

Few people, however, were unaware of the personal drama that had taken him to the edge. Two weeks earlier his wife Raza had upped sticks and taken their children with her. That was the cue for Ray to counter his misery with copious amounts of amphetamines washed down by Dom Perignon.

First to react was, inevitably, the kid brother with whom Ray had been at odds for almost all their lives. "When I went to the hospital, Ray looked like a ghost, a scared little kid in pajamas," Dave later recalled. Recovery was spent in Denmark as the two men took time out from life on the road with the Kinks and tried to reconnect as brothers.

Recalling those days, Ray declared,

> The White City was not a happy place to say goodbye. The sun wasn't shining, my shirt was not clean, and anyway rock festivals have never held many happy memories for me personally, and I want these shows to be happy. I have just spent a couple of weeks with my brother Dave.
>
> At first we didn't talk about music, but then we started singing and playing guitars one day, and before we knew it we were like a couple of ordinary "punk rock punters" trying to play some Chuck Berry riffs.

Two decades later, Ray repaid the gesture when Dave suffered a serious stroke, insisting that he recover in his own home, less than a mile from where they grew up in Muswell Hill. It was, sadly, a short-lived reconciliation. There had been other occasions when they had put down the gloves, most notably when Ray in 2004 was shot and wounded in the leg after being mugged in New Orleans, five months before his brother's stroke. Just as quickly, however, a new ice age could form. Yet the Kinks amazingly soldiered on, playing to ever-decreasing crowds, a fading sun setting on the band's horizon but not their musical legacy. Unquestionably, their traceable influence and outline remained unbroken.

Renewed interest in the Kinks was fostered in the 1980s and 1990s by the likes of the Pretenders—a new-wave band fronted by Ray's future and former lover Chrissie Hynde—Paul Weller, and Britpop flag bearers Blur. And once again a light was shone on a catalog of songs bearing Ray Davies's unmistakable imprint.

In 1990, the original band reunited for the last time with a blistering mini set when they were inducted into the Rock & Roll Hall of Fame, an overdue recognition of the impact they had made on the musical landscape. Characteristically, Ray was a reluctant draftee.

He said, "I guess it's a privilege, but I don't know why I'm here to do it. It's everything I normally run away from. There's something about the

Kinks that should remain non-establishment and this is almost too establishment for me."

His antiestablishment views appeared, however, to have mellowed somewhat by 2017 when he bent the knee to Prince Charles in acceptance of a knighthood that moved him onto the same "national treasure" plateau occupied by his sixties contemporaries McCartney and Jagger.

At the turn of the millennium, a new generation peeled back the layers of the band's storied history when two songs—"Living on a Thin Line" and the majestic live version of "I'm Not Like Everybody Else" (with Ray on vocals, in contrast to the original)—were used in episodes of the groundbreaking TV drama *The Sopranos*.

Bill Morton, like all the band's hardcore base, has never wavered in either his loyalty to the Kinks or in his appreciation of the laconic beauty to be found in the songs. Understandably, he is saddened that much of the band's history remains more easily focused on the fractured kinship between the band's two principal partners than the musical heritage they created. Acknowledging the conflicts in play, he said,

> I rate Ray Davies up there with anyone, the fact that so many composers from all eras rate Ray as an influence tells you enough.
>
> I think Ray is a complex character, who knows what he wants and how to get it, he does not suffer fools and the music business is full of idiots and fools who are there to suck blood out of anyone with exceptional talent. Dave Davies has never had full credit for his contribution, and the fact that the Kinks moved away from being a "guitar god" rock band to a more "story line songs" band obviously worked against him, but once again the number of modern-day players who rate Dave's input tells you that he is so underrated.
>
> I do not think the Kinks as a group could have existed without the contrasting styles of Ray and Dave and the unique vocal harmony that made the sound. Obviously the group could not have carried on without the prolific song writing of Ray Davies. I don't think the relationship with Ray and Dave is any different to many ordinary families.
>
> The main difference is that they had to live and work together, and money got involved. They certainly do have a shared love/hate for each other which the press are quite happy to overplay, and I am sure at times Ray and Dave are happy to play up as well. I wouldn't blame one more than the other. If you look at the history of all groups most deep-rooted arguments come down to one thing—money. Some bands are more diplomatic, pretending to share song credits production, etc., but in the end usually someone ends up with more than the other. Usually because he has looked after it and the others have not. These arguments never heal.

Julien Temple also bore new witness to the intractability of the friction that still seeped through the cracks. In 2010 he announced plans to bring the Kinks' story to the big screen in a film tentatively titled *You Really Got Me*. The focus, he said, would be on the dynamic between the two brothers. Outlining the project, he told *ScreenDaily*, "At the heart of it is the extraordinary love-hate relationship between these two brothers: love/hate, sibling rivalry is at the core. I think it's a very rich social, cultural nexus around the Kinks. Their story is the untold story of all those big bands of the 1960s."

Actors were reportedly cast and principal photography schedules put in place. Later, the project was apparently quietly shelved. Perhaps Temple made the mistake of shining too bright a light on the siblings' notorious past, present, and future. More likely, the whole thing foundered over money, Ray's famous frugality a potential obstacle. But it failed to put a spoke in the rumor mill surrounding reunions—onstage or in the studio.

In 2015 Ray stunned fans attending a Dave solo concert at London's Islington Assembly Hall by strolling on stage to deliver a lusty rendition of "You Really Got Me." It was a homecoming of sorts. Dave, now largely recovered from his stroke, later tweeted after the show, "We had a great night. It was a fun show—had a blast with Ray."

The comments were enough to reopen the book on a full-fledged reconciliation. But the odds grew longer with each passing month during which the two men remained at contradictory odds over the prospect. When Ray talked it up, Dave set it on fire. When Dave warmed to the opportunity of rebuilding the house, Ray burned it down. Pete Quaife had died in 2010, but Mick Avory remained a vital part of the band's shared history—and allegedly an obstacle to Dave returning to the fold. Old wounds continued to weep. Then in June 2019 came the news—greeted with weary skepticism by many—that the Kinks were indeed recording new songs for their first potential album in more than a quarter of a century. The fact that the music was reportedly being recorded separately—thanks to new digital recording techniques— exposed an inconvenient truth that remained at the heart of the Kinks.

Yet, for all the strife, the Kinks are perhaps living proof that the band that fights together stays together. But only up to that singular point when the hourglass finally runs out. The band survived as a working group through various iterations until 1996 when it finally became clear that it was time for the Kinks to step off the page of history and into memory. It remains an irresolvable story.

"We were battlers," reflected Ray. "But the very thing that makes a band special is what ultimately causes it to break up. What made our music interesting ended up being the very thing that destroyed it."

Simon & Garfunkel: From left, Art Garfunkel and Paul Simon
Photofest

17

SIMON & GARFUNKEL

It was late in the evening in August 1983 when Art Garfunkel picked up the phone in his New England home. On the other end was the soft, slightly feathery voice of Paul Simon, the musical partner he had known since he was twelve years old. The two men had been working for the best part of two years on an anticipated reunion album, their first since 1970's acclaimed *Bridge over Troubled Water*.

Forthright to a fault, Simon felt no need to indulge in social niceties. Garfunkel recalled, "He said, 'Artie, I'm wiping all your tapes (from the album), all your harmonies.' But then just to show there should be no hard feelings, he tossed out a curve ball before hanging up: 'Oh, I'm marrying Carrie [Fisher] on Tuesday . . . wanna come to the wedding?' I guess I was supposed to conclude that Paul Simon is the cutest guy I know," said Garfunkel, sarcasm dripping resentfully from every word. Simon's rationale for jettisoning Garfunkel's contributions was brutally simple: the songs he had written for the album, now retitled *Hearts and Bones*, were searingly personal, an open book of his life, especially his turbulent relationship with *Star Wars* actress Fisher, who he would divorce within a year.

And he had reached the uncontestable conclusion that "Artie" had no part to play in such intensely autobiographical material. Simon told *Playboy*,

These new songs are too much about my life—about Carrie—to have anybody else sing them. He said, "Look, these aren't the events of my life, but

I understand the emotions you're dealing with. I understand what it is to be in love, to be in pain, to feel joy. I'm a singer. I'm able to interpret. That's what I do."

I said, "All right. Let's try. However, I have to produce this because it's not like it was in the sixties. I know what I want to say musically. So if that's all right with you, and I can have the decision on how to produce the tracks, then we can try." He said, "Well, you're dampening my enthusiasm because of your ambivalence."

It was yet another glimpse inside the Rubik's Cube of a relationship, one that had been twisted around time and time again for years in frustrated angst, both men trying desperately to solve the nature of their own personal paradoxes, but frequently coming up short.

Two years earlier, New York's most famous musical sons had parked their differences long enough to play a "neighborhood concert" in Central Park before a crowd of 500,000 fans teary-eyed with youthful nostalgia. It was a dreamy, magical event, its restorative powers a reminder of the times when Simon & Garfunkel were a touchstone for sun-dappled optimism in the mid- to late sixties. Everyone went home happy.

So, too, did record company fat cats and tour promoters rubbing their pudgy hands in expectation that the motherlode of deals was ripe for the taking. Millions of dollars were waiting to flow into a new S&G pipeline at a time when the careers of both men were whooshing down the toilet.

The fact that they barely looked at or spoke to each other during the concert was lost in the rush to hit pay dirt, but the dark portents for the future were clear for anyone willing to see what lay beneath.

Normally puffed up with self-importance, Simon had been left devastated by the critical and commercial mauling meted out to *One Trick Pony*, his first album in years, which came out some eighteen months before the reunion gig. It also shared its ill-fated destiny with a doomed vanity project film of the same name, which Simon starred in, causing him to rush headlong into therapy.

But neither man was able to resist the smell of filthy lucre wafting in the early autumn breeze along Fifth Avenue. They agreed to hit the road for a world tour while simultaneously laying down tracks for a new record notionally titled *Think Too Much*. As the tour wound its way through Australia, New Zealand, North America, and Europe, they even felt emboldened enough to play some of their new material live.

But it didn't take long for old insecurities and antagonisms to kick in, the same ones that had signaled the death knell of Simon & Garfunkel as the sixties turned the page into a new decade. In the studio, as they gingerly tried to find common ground, collaboration was swiftly replaced by combat.

Garfunkel insisted on writing his own harmonies to Simon's new material while on a walking tour of Switzerland with a Sony Walkman clamped to his ear and managed to eke out this tortuous process for months. Garfunkel finally said, "Look, the way I want to do this record is you sing the song, make the track, and then leave me alone and I'll go to the studio and overlay my voice."

Both men were control freaks, two silverbacks locked in an eternal battle for jungle supremacy, with neither prepared to cede ground. But with Simon writing the songs and dictating the play, there could only have been one logical outcome; airbrushing Garfunkel's vocals out of the mixes ensured the album would become a full-fledged Paul Simon solo project—end of discussion.

Simon said, "A year sailed by. So now, not only was the work process painful, in that the personality clash was constant, but the artistic differences were becoming more articulated. I was getting to feel that I didn't want him to paint on my painting. Finally, I said, 'This is not a good idea. I think what we have here is the partnership that wasn't.'"

The toxic story of *Hearts and Bones* perfectly captures the ever-changing currents of a friendship that had its roots in high school in the mid-1950s. Both hailed from Jewish New York backgrounds, living only a few blocks from each other in Queen's, a patchwork of dozens of unique neighborhoods, each with its own distinct cultural and ethnic identity.

Their paths first crossed in 1953 in the sixth grade when both were handed parts in their elementary school graduation play of *Alice in Wonderland*. A teacher cast Simon as the White Rabbit and Garfunkel as the Cheshire Cat, roles that in some respects—and with no little degree of irony—buttonholed them forever.

As well as bonding over baseball, the two teenagers quickly discovered a shared love for the drumbeat of rock 'n' roll and, especially, the bewitching harmonic blend of the Everly Brothers. Simon was also knocked out by Garfunkel's cantor-like tenor, which meshed perfectly with his own warmer, folkie tones.

Within weeks of meeting, Paul and Artie had formed their own group called Tom and Jerry, and even enjoyed a minor hit with a song called "Hey Schoolgirl"—the only song they cowrote—that effortlessly channeled the Everlys. Written in under an hour, the song became their party piece, performed at amateur stages across their home borough.

Convinced of the song's potential, the boys ventured into Manhattan to hawk 'Hey Schoolgirl' to the Tin Pan Alley publishers cloistered in the heart of midtown. Together, they banged on doors throughout the famous Brill Building, desperate to perform their tune for anyone who would listen. Unfortunately, no one would. So they decided to record a demo that they could hand out to executives, thus eliminating the need for awkward in-person recitals. In early October of 1957, they ponied up $25 and crammed into the photo-booth-sized live room at Sanders Record Studios on Seventh Avenue and West 48th Street. In a move straight out of Hollywood fantasy, a promoter named Sid Prosen happened to overhear the session and offered to sign the pair on the spot.

Contracts were drawn up, their parents consulted, and in days they were officially artists on Prosen's Big Records label. The song went on to sell over 10,000 copies, enough to bring it to a respectable #49 on the *Billboard* charts. More importantly to the high schoolers, it earned them major respect from their peers. "You can't imagine what it was like having a hit record at sixteen," said Simon later. "It made me a neighborhood hero."

But this early whiff of celebrity had also given Simon a glimpse into a future studded with fame and riches, the twin elixirs for any performer. Exhilarated, Simon saw their partnership in the starkest of terms; he would write the songs and they would both sing them. Unknown to Garfunkel, however, he also secretly penned his own solo deal with Prosen, a move that inflicted his first Judas kiss on Garfunkel, who said the betrayal left him shattered.

"Things were never the same after that," he declared. Outraged when he discovered the double-cross, Garfunkel unloaded on Simon, zeroing in on his most basic insecurity: his height. Paul Simon would go on to become a giant of the music industry, but even as a full-grown adolescent, his height—he only stood five foot four—was his Achilles' heel—and Garfunkel knew it.

Years later, Simon recalled that source of early friction:

I remember during a photo session, something happened and Artie said, "No matter what happens, I'll always be taller than you." Did that hurt? I guess it hurt enough for me to remember sixty years later. It came up all the time. There is a prejudice against small men and that has been a problem at times because I happen to be a sort of alpha-male-ish type guy. It becomes a competitive thing.

There's this attitude that I'm taller, so I could beat you up or I should be in charge. Eventually, somewhere in my thirties or forties probably, I told myself, "Listen, man, if you're going to make a big issue out of what you don't have, you're taking your actual gifts for granted." So I said, "That's the hand I've been dealt. That's the way I'm going to play it."

Over the next few years, intermittent reunions were followed by abrupt partings. Garfunkel focused on university while Simon was convinced his destiny still lay in songwriting. By 1963 Simon had caught the new wave of folk music sweeping America's youth and called Garfunkel to reforge the chains of their partnership. Having long buried Tom and Jerry, they resurrected their musical hopes with *Wednesday Morning, 3AM*, the first album released under the Simon & Garfunkel imprint.

The songs, including an acoustic version of "The Sound of Silence," a gorgeously haunting track, chimed with the mood of many young Americans but still failed to make a dent in the *Billboard* charts. Disillusioned, they again went in different directions, with Simon heading for England in the hope of finding a new musical muse and, for a while, embracing a freewheeling life as a busker.

Back home, meanwhile, a producer heard "The Sound of Silence" and decided to amplify its sparse production with electronic guitars and percussion. Suddenly, the newly retooled song was sprinting to the top of the charts, eventually selling an astonishing 100,000 copies.

Contacted by their record company, Simon was forced to rush back from the UK and put a call into Garfunkel to quickly revive their partnership, this time more permanently. Between 1966 and 1968, three hugely successful albums and a string of hit singles placed Simon & Garfunkel at the apex of Western pop culture, sharing that rarefied terrain with the likes of the Beatles, the Stones, and Bob Dylan. Songs like "The Boxer," "Mrs. Robinson," "Scarborough Fair," "Hazy Shade of Winter," "Bookends," and "America," to name but a few, saw them plant their flag on rock's Mount Olympus.

Theirs, though, remained a fragile alliance. On the road, Garfunkel indulged in all the usual trappings while remaining a reluctant live performer; Simon was born to play his songs to an audience but was a loner away from the spotlight.

Offstage, there was little rapport, only the silence that like a cancer grows. Simon envied Garfunkel's effortless vocal talent that helped bring his own songs to a rich bloom; Garfunkel, on the other hand, was acutely aware that without Simon's magnificent songs, his career could easily flatline.

By the time they came to record *Bridge Over Troubled Water* in 1969, their fifth studio album, the mirror had cracked. And nowhere were their differences more exposed than on the titular track, a lightning-in-a-bottle track sung wholly by Garfunkel.

Simon envisioned "Bridge" as a gospel song and thought it was perfect for Artie. Instead, according to Simon, he flatly rejected it. "He didn't want to sing it," Simon told *Rolling Stone* in 1973. "He couldn't hear it for himself. He felt I should have done it. And many times I'm sorry I didn't do it." Simon expanded on this issue during a 1975 interview with the BBC's Michael Parkinson. "When the partnership is in the ascendancy, things are going well and you are really united, there is a meshing of egos and you tend to think as one," he said.

> As the partnership reaches its zenith—and in our case that was around the time of *Bridge Over Troubled Water*—it starts to disintegrate in that each person has a clear self-image.
>
> At that time, Artie was going into movies. I wrote this tune, and he was in Rome at the time and I was in New York. I spoke to him on the phone and I said, "I really wrote a real good song for you. Come on back and we'll record cause it's a real goodie." So he came back and I played it for him and he didn't think so. So, awkward, you know.
>
> I insisted it was good. He felt I should sing it. Now why I wouldn't know. But why I didn't listen to him and sing it is something that is psychologically interesting, I think. I actually wrote the song in a key that was too high for me to sing in order for him to sing. And I don't regret it because he sang it very well.
>
> But when we used to perform it on stage, Artie would sing the song in his beautiful choirboy voice and the piano player would play and I would be standing off to the side. When he first finished the song, people leaped up and gave him a standing ovation.
>
> And my reaction was "I wrote that song." I'm standing here in the side and then Artie introduces the piano player and I shuffle back on and do the next tune. Anyway, that's how partnerships break up.

Garfunkel naturally remembers things differently:

> When Paul showed me *"Bridge Over Troubled Water,"* he did say it was for me. And I loved the song immediately. My way of saying thank you was "Are you sure? Because you sound lovely singing it, and it's almost like you could do it." Now, the famous story is that he took offence and that became a thorn between us, as if I was rejecting the song. That's nonsense. I don't remember him having a hard time with my grace. He said, "No, I wrote it for you." I said, "Thank you, man," and got into singing it.

In another interview, he revealed the depth of his dismay over Simon's comments. "How many songs did I sing upfront and have a real tour de force vocal?" he asked. "Does he resent that I had that one? I find that ungenerous."

Running in tandem with this minor obfuscation was a drama of a different kind. Mike Nicholls, who had directed *The Graduate*, the seminal sixties film that showcased several Simon & Garfunkel tracks, had cast both men in *Catch-22*, an adaptation of Joseph Heller's black war comedy novel. Simon's part, though, was dropped before a roll of film had been shot, giving Garfunkel Hollywood bragging rights.

It also saw him spend months on location under a baking hot Mexican sun with the film crew throughout 1969 while Simon was left to sweat it out alone in the studio writing the songs for what would be the *Bridge Over Troubled Water* album.

"He knew how I'd feel, but he did it anyway," Simon said. "Mike told Artie he was going to be a big movie star, and Artie couldn't say no. He later told me he didn't see why it was such a big deal to me—he would make the movie for six months, and I could write the songs for the next album. Then we could get together and record them. I thought, 'Fuck you, I'm not going to do that.'"

Angered by the film snub, resentment built up inside Simon's head like the sound of a steam train gathering speed. They were even forced to turn down an invite to Woodstock because Garfunkel refused to interrupt his film commitments.

By the time he returned to the studio, the breach had become a chasm. Like many songwriters, Simon funneled his anger inside a song. The lyrics to "The Only Living Boy in New York" were as subtle as an electric bath. In the studio, relations reached a new low. They couldn't even agree on the album's closing track.

Garfunkel vetoed Simon's political "Cuba-Sí, Nixon-No" while Simon point-blank refused to even contemplate his erstwhile friend's wimpy Bach chorale. As a result, the album, which, nevertheless, would go on to garner five Grammys, was released with only eleven songs. And when Artie casually announced he would be doing another Nichols film, *Carnal Knowledge*, the game was up. "Definitely I was hurt, though I'm not sure I realized then how much," said Simon. "I felt as if Artie had fucked me over."

It was as if he were saying, "Hey, I've always felt like a nobody. Now you're going to be the nobody." And he rammed that home. I realized then that I was certainly going to follow my own instinct and make my own albums. We did our last concert at Forest Hills tennis stadium, shook hands, and didn't see each other for years.

News of their unpublicized split sent shockwaves through the corridors of power inside Columbia records. When Simon told label president Clive

Davis the partnership was finished, he implored him to change his mind. The album had turned into a huge cash cow for Columbia, and now the teat had been squeezed dry by that age-old cliché cited as musical differences.

"Relations between Paul and Artie had become frayed beyond repair, unfortunately," wrote Davis in his autobiography, *The Soundtrack of My Life*.

As much as anything else, it was a case of two young artists whose ambitions and egos got in the way of the brilliance of their collaboration. Artie was seeking a film career in part because of feeling overshadowed by Paul's talents as a songwriter. Artie made about $75,000 for his role in *Catch-22*, while he made more than $1 million at the time from *Bridge Over Troubled Water*, so he clearly wasn't acting for the money. Paul, on the other hand, grew jealous of the attention that Artie got as the group's main vocalist and "front man." Paul called and said he wanted to meet with me at my office. When he arrived, he got straight to the point. "Before others find out, I want you to know that I've decided to split with Artie," he said. "I don't think we'll be recording together again." I was shocked. I understood Paul's frustrations, and his desire to have more control over his music. I simply believed there were ways to satisfy those concerns without breaking up the duo. I also knew how competitive Paul was and how much he valued success. I believed he was underestimating the challenge of what he was setting out to do. It was simple: I did not want Simon & Garfunkel to break up.

There was, though, no going back. The duo handed over their folk-rock crowns to the young pretenders spilling out from the West Coast's Laurel Canyon, the creative melting pot that spawned the likes of Joni Mitchell; Crosby, Stills, Nash and Young; Linda Ronstadt; Bonnie Raitt; and the fledgling Eagles.

But for Paul Simon, the split simply meant one thing: freedom and an end to the interminable internecine warfare that would sap anyone's creative energy. Over the next five years, he emerged as a serious artist in his own right. Three albums—the eponymously titled *Paul Simon, There Goes Rhymin' Simon*, and *Still Crazy After All These Years*—established him in the upper echelons of solo musicians.

Solo stardom naturally suited someone with an unchecked desire to control everything. In contrast, Garfunkel's desire to fly without wings as an actor looked like a serious misjudgment. *Carnal Knowledge* was panned and Hollywood sniffily turned its back. While Simon's solo career headed for the stratosphere, Garfunkel's stalled on the runway.

At one point, he even took a job teaching math at a school in Connecticut, although the kids were more interested in asking him questions about the Beatles than figuring out the Pythagorean theorem. During this period,

Simon and Garfunkel kept a respectful distance from each other, observing self-imposed rules of neutrality.

That policy of noninterference ended when Simon sat down with *Rolling Stone*'s Jon Landau in 1972 and opened the book on his own frustrations as the boy in the S&G bubble.

During the making of *Bridge Over Troubled Water* there were a lot of times when it just wasn't fun to work together. It was very hard work, and it was complex, and both of us thought—I think Artie said that he felt that he didn't want to record—and I know I said I felt that if I had to go through these kind of personality abrasions, I didn't want to continue to do it. Then when the album was finished, Artie was going to do *Carnal Knowledge* and I went to do an album by myself.

We didn't say that's the end. We didn't know if it was the end or not. But it became apparent by the time the movie was out and by the time my album was out that it was over. It left me free to do what I want. I wanted to sing other types of songs, that Simon & Garfunkel wouldn't do.

"Mother and Child Reunion," for example, is not a song that you would have normally thought that Simon & Garfunkel would have done. It's possible that they might have. But it wouldn't have been the same, and I don't know whether I would have been so inclined in that direction. So for me it was a chance to back out, and gamble a little bit; it's been so long since it was a gamble.

But he couldn't resist scratching his long-time itch over musical credibility and the nagging irritation that some people saw them as a partnership of musical equals. He said,

There was no great pressure to stay together, other than money, which exerted really very little influence upon us. We certainly weren't going to stay together to make a lot of money. We didn't need the money. And musically, it was not a creative team, too much, because Artie is a singer and I'm a writer and player and a singer.

We didn't work together on a creative level and prepare the songs. I did that. When we came into the studio, I became more and more me, in the studio, making the tracks and choosing the musicians, partly because a great deal of the time during *Bridge*, Artie wasn't there.

I was doing things by myself with Roy Halee, our engineer and co-producer. We were planning tracks out and to a great degree that responsibility fell to me. Artie and I shared responsibility but not creativity. For example, we always said Artie does the arranging. Anybody who knows anything would know that that was a fabrication—how can one guy write the songs and the other guy do the arranging? How does that happen? If a guy writes the song, he obviously has a concept. But when it came to making decisions, it had always been Roy, Artie, and me. And this later became difficult for me.

Simon's biographer Robert Hilburn is convinced Simon simply couldn't have flourished musically in the way that he did had he still been with Garfunkel. The inventive Latino textures of "Me and Julio Down by the Schoolyard" and the African pulse of the songs on *Graceland*, for example, would never have sat comfortably with Garfunkel.

Hilburn said, "Like so many of those 1960s guys, he would just have started recycling himself if he had stayed with Garfunkel. He was able to move in new directions without him. If they had stayed together, Garfunkel would have been a ball and chain round his leg. He couldn't have moved that way."

Détente broke out only occasionally. In 1975 they recorded Simon's song "My Little Town," an upbeat track with bleak lyrical overtones that eventually found its way on to both *Still Crazy After All These Years* and Garfunkel's debut solo offering *Breakaway*.

That same year, they mingled together backstage at the Grammys, Simon presenting an award alongside John Lennon. Artie removed the knife from his former school friend's back long enough to share a microphone for three songs on a special edition of *Saturday Night Live* cohosted by Simon. But, despite the clamor of fans, six years would pass before there was a further thaw.

The 1981 Concert in Central Park should have been the bridge over troubled water they once sang of. Initially, the plan was for Simon to play solo while holding out the hand of friendship to his old sparring partner to make a guest appearance, an idea that didn't sit well with Garfunkel.

"I didn't want to be an opening act for Simon & Garfunkel. So I figured: 'Well, let's try to do a whole Simon & Garfunkel show.'" From day one, however, the writing was writ large on the subway walls. Simon recalled,

> The rehearsals were just miserable. Artie and I fought all the time. He didn't want to do the show with my band; he just wanted me on acoustic guitar.
>
> I said, "I can't do that anymore. I can't just play the guitar for two hours." Afterward, our first reaction was, I think, one of disappointment. Arthur's more than mine. He thought he didn't sing well. I didn't get what had happened—how big it was—until I went home, turned on the television and saw it on all the news, the people being interviewed, and later that night on the front pages of all the newspapers. Then I got it.

Of course, what he really got was dollar signs. Millions of them stacked up at various points all over the world. But the price was the nuclear fallout that eventually enveloped *Hearts and Bones* and the tour that followed Central Park. Curiously, before he wiped Garfunkel's vocals, most of the album was in the can. And some of those who heard it rated it better than the one Simon eventually released under his own moniker. Dan Nash, one of the dozen or so engineers who worked on the album, is convinced that even the rough mixes sounded "a hundred times better" than the album that wound up in the shops. He said, "The entire thing was finished with Artie on it, without a doubt. I have a copy. When Paul made the decision [to make it a solo album], he had Roy Halee make rough mixes of the whole thing."

That view was shared by Arlen Roth, one of the all-star cast of musicians who made up the duo's touring band. "He was on almost every song, as I recall, and we were all so excited about this being a true S&G reunion album, as well as reunion tour. Live, we performed 'Cars Are Cars,' 'Allergies,' and 'Hearts and Bones.'"

As they headed into the future, though, neither could close the book on the past. Old hostilities reemerged during a joint interview on the set of ABC's *Good Morning America*, during which Simon delightfully revealed he buried a mocking message of "so long already, Artie!" on the fade of "So Long Frank Lloyd Wright," the last track on the first side of *Bridge Over Troubled Water*. Judging by the ashen look on his face, Garfunkel was completely unaware of the dart hidden between the fadeout grooves of their swansong album.

In 1990, they were inducted into the Rock & Roll Hall of Fame, an occasion that normally merits handshakes all round and a healthy dose of letting bygones be bygones. Stepping up to the microphone, Garfunkel thanked his partner, calling him "the person who most enriched my life by putting those songs through me," to which Simon responded in mocking tones, "Arthur and I agree about almost nothing. But it's true, I have enriched his life quite a bit."

After performing three songs, they left without speaking. A decade later Simon, having by now released classic albums like *Graceland* and *Rhythm of the Saints*, was deservedly inaugurated as a solo artist and used the occasion to pay tribute to Garfunkel for the contributions that were rightfully his during their joint musical odyssey.

Again, though, he couldn't resist plundering all the grace from the occasion and, inadvertently, handing Garfunkel the higher ground. "I regret the ending of our friendship," he told the audience. "I hope that someday before we die, we will make peace with each other," before adding after a pause, "No rush."

But that day arrived unexpectedly on February 23, 2003, at Madison Square Garden when both men were honored with lifetime achievement

Grammys. Bonhomie was once again in the air along with the lure of a multimillion-dollar retirement nest egg. The sold-out Old Friends tour that surprisingly followed over the next twelve months included forty dates in America before crossing the Atlantic for a European leg that was reported to have earned a staggering bounty of $123 million—serious money in any language.

However, it also included some shocking backstage flashpoints, one of which came close to serious violence between them. During one show, there had been a mix-up, with no little irony, for "The Boxer."

"I made a mistake over when to come in, and it threw Artie off for a second," said Simon.

> But it was an accident; it wasn't intentional. So later, we're singing "Feelin' Groovy," and suddenly Art just stops singing at the part that goes "Life, I love you," and I'm just left there by myself, trying to figure out what to do. I assumed it was another mistake—no big deal. But then at intermission, Art comes up to me and says, "You tried to make me look like a fool on 'The Boxer,'" and I said, "No, Artie, it was a mistake. Mistakes happen, just like you forgot to do "Life, I love you." That's when he looked me in the eye and said, "I didn't forget. I just wanted you to see what it feels like to be made a fool of."

The flare-up was witnessed by Simon's business manager Joseph Rascoff, who feared at least one of them would take a swing. "They never came to blows, but there was shoving, and I had to step between them," recalled Rascoff. "I genuinely believed that if there had been a knife on the table, one of them would have used it."

There then followed another long hiatus before they tentatively agreed to one last hurrah in 2010. By now both men were sixty-nine years old and weathered. Garfunkel's vocal gift had been badly corroded by a lifetime of nicotine addiction, a fact that became all too evident when they headlined the New Orleans Jazz and Heritage Festival and Garfunkel, by his own admission was way below par.

It would be the last time they stood side by side on the same stage. The tour was placed in an indefinite deep freeze after Garfunkel was diagnosed with vocal chord paresis while Simon seethed on the sidelines. He told Robert Hillman in *Paul Simon, The Life*, "He let us all down. I didn't feel I could trust him anymore."

It was indeed the end of the road for Simon & Garfunkel. Simon, now settled into his third marriage with singer Edie Brickell, maintained his own sound of silence and simply refused to countenance any more reunions. He didn't need the money or the unseemly drama of two old and bald men fighting over a comb. He wasn't even tempted to counterpunch when Artie lashed out with an incendiary salvo in the *Daily Telegraph* in 2016: "How can you walk away from this lucky place on top of the world, Paul? What's going on with you, you idiot? How could you let that go, jerk?"

It was an ill-advised entreaty that smacked more of desperation and money than music. Robert Hilburn got a sense of the ill-feeling between the two when he got in touch with Garfunkel as part of the forensic research for his book, which was published in 2018.

Artie rebuffed all overtures over a two-year period to offer a fresh perspective on the man who had been the biggest musical influence on his life. "The impression I got was that he didn't want to do anything that would help Paul," says Hilburn. "I said to him, 'Look, I will treat you with the equal respect that I give Paul. I'm not taking sides.'"

Garfunkel wouldn't relent despite the author's two-year attempt to try and change his mind. "Finally, he wrote me a letter," says the author. "It basically said, 'Please don't contact me anymore. I just don't want to do it.'"

Paul Simon finally brought the curtain down on his touring days in September 2018, closing with a euphoric show at Flushing Meadows Corona Park, two miles from the high school where he and Artie once played baseball. As thousands came to worship one last time, the benediction included "Bridge Over Troubled Water," the song that precipitated the first, serious dissolution of Simon & Garfunkel almost five decades earlier.

"I have a strange relationship to this next song," Simon told his local congregation from the comfort of a familiar pulpit. "I wrote it a long time ago, and when I finished it I said to myself, 'Hmm, that's better than I usually do.' Then I gave it away and I didn't sing it for a long time, though occasionally I'd try it on tours, though I never actually felt like it was mine since the original versions are so unique. But this being the final tour, I'm going to be playing my lost child."

There would be no park bench bookends for Simon & Garfunkel, no sight of two old men lost in their overcoats waiting for the sunset. How terribly strange, indeed, to be well past seventy, memory brushing those same years. Yet, Simon and Garfunkel's joint legacy in the Valhalla of rock 'n' roll is in no way diminished by the riptides that often broke the surfaces of the river that ran through them.

Perhaps Art Garfunkel captured their duality best: "We are indescribable. You'll never capture it. It's an ingrown, deep friendship. Yes, there is deep love in there. But there's also shit."

INDEX

Page numbers in *italics* reference photographs.